Top 10 Greatest Lies About Pregnancy

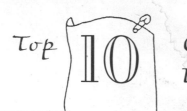

10

Lamaze Works.

9

Morning Sickness Is Gone by Lunchtime.

8

Maternity Clothes Are So Much Cuter Now.

7

You Will Have Your Pre-pregnancy Figure Back in
Three Months, Especially If You Nurse.

6

Oil Massages Prevent Stretch Marks.

5

Pregnant Women Have the Most Beautiful Skin
and Hair.

4

"I Swear, Your Face Hasn't Changed at All."

3

Pregnancy Brings a Man and Woman Closer
Together (Yeah, You and Your Obstetrician!).

2

"You Haven't Gotten Big Anywhere but Your Belly!"

1

Pregnancy Only Lasts Nine Months.

The
GIRLFRIENDS'
Guide to
PREGNANCY

Or Everything Your Doctor Won't Tell You

VICKI IOVINE

POCKET BOOKS

New York   London   Toronto   Sydney   Singapore

An *Original* Publication of POCKET BOOKS

POCKET BOOKS, a division of Simon & Schuster Inc.
1230 Avenue of the Americas, New York, NY 10020

Iovine, Vicki.
    The girlfriends' guide to pregnancy: or everything your doctor won't
tell you / Vicki Iovine.
        p.   cm.
    ISBN 0-671-52431-3
    1. Pregnancy.   I. Title.
RG525.I58   1995
618.2—dc20   95-21981
                                                           CIP

First Pocket Books trade paperback printing October 1995

20 19 18 17 16 15 14

POCKET and colophon are registered trademarks of
Simon & Schuster Inc.

Cover design by Lesley Ehlers
Cover art by Gary Johnson and Lesley Ehlers
Text design by Stanley S. Drate/Folio Graphics Co., Inc.

Printed in the U.S.A.

For Jamie, Jessica, Jeremy and Jade

Acknowledgments

Here I am, winner of the life lottery. I have a bunch of kids, a great husband, a new computer (that I sort of know how to use) and *I have written a book*, for heaven's sake! What's left for me now, except perhaps rejoining the other mothers in the car pool? I am grateful to so many people for helping me pull this off. My family, of course, tops any list. My kids will probably talk about this book with their therapists in adulthood, but so far they have been ardent supporters. Not only did they provide me with most of my material, but they cut me some slack to write when they really wanted me at karate practice or the school Christmas Pageant. Only a man with my husband Jimmy's confidence and sense of humor could take the beating I occasionally give his gender. Only a man who really had faith in me could believe that I could write a book, raise our kids and remodel the house with one hand tied behind my back. And only a man who really loved me could never once ask me to cook him dinner during the entire process. I love my family so much that, when I think of them, I can't quite catch my breath.

Before there was the Iovine family, there was the McCarty family, and they are as responsible for this book happening as anyone. First, there is my father, who, in his soul, is really the writer of the family, and my stepmother, Linda, who has been loving me and covering for me since I was twelve. Then there is my mother, who in her soul is really Lucille Ball and who showed me candor and humor in their most uncontrollable forms. And there is my beloved brother, Gregg, who is really my first baby. He always thought his big sister could accomplish anything, and he uncomplainingly allowed me to hone my mothering skills on him. It was he I fed cat food to during *Captain Kangaroo,* and it was he I *almost* convinced to drink water out of the toilet in my new plastic tea set. It was for him that I beat up a neighborhood kid who teased him for wearing saddle shoes. (See, I told you my mother had a good sense of humor.)

Then there were the people who stood behind me and pushed when my energy or self-confidence failed. They start with my friend of so many years and adventures, Bobby Shriver, who has always gotten a kick out of encouraging me to do ridiculous things. He introduced me to Bob Bookman, who was kind enough to laugh at my jokes and help me find the perfect agent. He was assisted in this task by Angela Janklow Harrington, who appropriately got pregnant with her first daughter during this process. Then there is that perfect agent Angela and Bob found for me, Cynthia Cannell, who with her calm and sweet manner (that belied her ability to be a tough advocate if the need arose) actually made me believe I could string more than five words together, and who became a Girlfriend in the process. She also introduced me to the funniest (but not funnier than I) and smartest editor in the world, Dona Chernoff. With that, the Matriarchy was formed. We three mothers were on a rampage, and this book reflects our combined point of view. No day seems complete without a nice long kvetch with each of them on the phone.

I deeply and lovingly thank all my Girlfriends for sharing their stories (and for letting me tell their stories to complete strangers) and for being part of every decision I make every day, from writing this book to cutting my hair to deciding whether it's time for plastic surgery. I cherish our alliance and interdependence. I also love our birthday parties.

I have no false pride that I completed this endeavor alone. It could not have happened without my assistant, Frances Tsow. When she wasn't busy proofreading or numbering the pages of a manuscript that changed several thousand times, she was making sure my kids didn't miss their dentist appointments and organizing their playdates. Best of all, she knew when I needed to take a break (or risk accidentally erasing my manuscript from the computer), when to run out and surprise me with an extra-large iced coffee or when to just stand back and laugh at the chaos.

I am eternally grateful and endlessly excited, and I look forward to the day when I can walk into a bookstore and see this book (with my name on it, no less) on the shelf.

Contents

Foreword

Welcome to the Sorority

Pregnant, huh? Well, come on in and sit here beside me, because there is nothing I like more than a woman who is about to have a baby. In fact, just about every mother I know feels the same way. Being pregnant is a time of such anticipation and optimism and dreaming . . . and fear and insecurity and self-doubt (but more about that later). The world loves a pregnant woman, because we all want to protect her and encourage her, and other women who have had babies are ecstatic to have a new member joining their ranks.

In any gathering of women there is a camaraderie that exists among those who have experienced childbirth. It's like a secret handshake or an ultraviolet mark that only they know distinguishes them as veterans of the same war. Complete strangers can bond in ten minutes in a ladies' room sharing the grisly details of their labors. A pregnant woman such as yourself is a probationary member of this sorority. You will be included in all bonding sessions, and you will be embraced and guided by all the other members. And after this forty-week (more or less) probationary period will come the magic time when you will become a charter member, when you have passed the ultimate hazing ritual: DELIVERY.

For the rest of your life you will feel a kinship with the other members of the world. You will learn to appreciate each other as only someone who has had a baby can. This sorority of women is full of all sorts of self-congratulation, because only another mother knows what each of us has gone through to qualify for member-ship. Like veterans of a war, we show our battle scars like medals:

cesarean sections, stretch marks, our inability to sneeze without wetting our pants! This is one of the few places where mothers can exhale and stop holding their tummies in. We may weep uncontrollably at kindergarten Christmas pageants, and we may not be able to stay awake past nine o'clock, even on a weekend. But secretly we know, we are Earth's real heroes.

Why I Wrote This Book

I have given birth to four children in six years, two boys and two girls with no twins in the lot, and the lesson I learned (aside from not to trust the rhythm method) is this: Ninety percent of the information I needed to get me through these pregnancies came from my Girlfriends who had already had children. Sure, there are a lot of books about pregnancy that you can read. Good student (and terrified person) that I was, I bought them all and read most of them. (By the way, you will probably do the same thing: buy every book on the shelf pertaining to pregnancy and then read the ones that don't confuse, frighten or depress you, leaving you with not much to read.) In fact, I now know so much about the technical aspects of this pregnancy business that I am certain that I could deliver *your* baby, even by cesarean section, with nothing but newspaper to wrap it in, on the floor of a speeding taxi. I know all the exotic terms like "Braxton Hicks contractions," "placenta previa" and "fundus."

But the experience of pregnancy is so much more than medical; it is emotional, physical and social, and I never found a book, in seven years of searching, that addressed those aspects of the experience in the way a good, experienced and, most important, *candid* Girlfriend could. None of these books ever really seemed to capture the essence of *my* pregnancies. They were too detached, too calm, too neat, too *moderate* for what I was experiencing. To me, pregnancy is an alarming, charming, sloppy and sentimental affair. Phrases like "momentary discomfort" and "tender to the touch" come nowhere near describing what a procedure like amniocentesis feels like or what newly pregnant breasts feel like. "Sensitive" or "moody" are really lame descriptions of a pregnant woman's emotional life, trust me! When a book told me that I would have a discharge for a few weeks after delivery, I was in no way prepared for the fact that I was unable to go the four feet from my hospital bed to the bathroom without leaving a grisly trail that looked like a murder had taken place. No, it was not my beloved doctor or the traditional pregnancy books that prepared me, but rather my Girlfriends. It was my Girlfriends who warned me not to courageously decline my doctor's offer of pain medication after delivery because after he was home and sleeping in his warm cushy bed, my epidural would wear off and I would be in my hard little hospital bed with nothing more than a Tylenol for comfort. It was also my Girlfriends who reassured me that my husband would still make a good father even if he fainted during ultrasounds and refused to cut the umbilical cord. It was my Girlfriends who told me which outfits made my behind look even fatter than it was or if I was acting unbearably premenstrual. This pregnancy business knocked me broadside at times, and it was usually my Girlfriends who propped me back up.

"But," you are saying to yourself, "I have a wonderful doctor to tell me everything I'll need to know about having a baby." What turnip truck did you just fall off of? Doctors are among my favorite people on earth—in fact, I pray that at least one of my children gets into medical school someday—but I rarely asked my doctor the questions that really mattered to me. Sometimes I was afraid of wasting his time; how could I bother him with endless questions about the earliest point at which I could get an epidural when there were women in his practice with *real* problems? Sometimes I was afraid to reveal how indelicate and, perhaps, unattractive I often felt I was becoming; for some reason I was completely unconcerned about this man touching my cervix, and yet I withered at the prospect of asking him why I had found a hair growing from my nipple one morning. Often my questions weren't really medical in nature, like, "Why is there no denim in maternity jeans?" and I was paralyzingly afraid of looking as stupid as I felt. After all, having babies is so natural and common that women must be *born* knowing what to do, right? You will be amazed at the things you do not know! If I were to have called my doctor every time I had a question about pregnancy, he would have been on the phone with me two to three hours a day, and at least half an hour in the middle of the night after I had gotten up to pee for the fifth time.

The Girlfriends' Guide to Pregnancy is the book I always hoped to find when I was pregnant. It is the compilation of the experiences, opinions, concerns, complaints and remedies that my Girlfriends and I had when we were pregnant. If any real medical information is passed along in this book, it is largely accidental, for I leave that domain to the doctors. Desperate as you may be at this point in your life for someone to tell you what to do, I would feel a whole lot better if you would run any of my suggestions by your doctor before adopting them. Think of this book as the jumping-off point for some very interesting and informative conversations with your obstetrician. In fact, if there is anything you are too embarrassed to ask him or her, just mark the page in *The Girlfriends' Guide* that discusses it and ask him or her to take a look. You should feel free to disregard or disagree with any part of this book. For example, if you are one of the blessed ones who never experience one single gag of nausea during the nine months of your pregnancy, go ahead and ignore the parts that deal with morning sickness. Just don't talk too much about your good fortune. A safe rule of thumb is: BE CAREFUL NOT TO GET SMUG BECAUSE THE GODS OF PREG-NANCY ARE USUALLY FAIR. In other words, if you don't get morning sickness, you will probably be cursed with uncontrollable gas.

We have all heard of women who do pregnancy perfectly. You know the type: a model or a soap opera star who is reverently portrayed in women's magazines with bouncing hair and maternity clothes that actually match. Or *worse*, she is the daughter of your mother's best friend so you have to hear about and be compared with her every single day. She gains the recommended twenty to twenty-five pounds, her skin stays clear and rosy, she prepares for birth by listening to meditation tapes, she plays singles tennis up until she is about six centimeters dilated and she swears she has never felt better in her life. She also has a husband who thinks his wife is at her most beautiful when swollen with his child, who actually *asks questions* at the childbirth preparedness classes, and who, after the baby is born, takes the placenta home and buries it beneath an old oak tree.

This Book Is Not for These Women

It is for the rest of us; those of us who put on twenty pounds between the home pregnancy test and the first doctor's visit. It is for those of us who get our first case of acne since the Homecoming Dance. It is for those of us who have hemorrhoids so bad that we have considered never eating solid food again in hopes of avoiding another bowel movement for the rest of our lives. It is for those of us who have considered murdering our husbands in their sleep because we thought we heard them say "moo" when we were getting dressed. It is for those of us who can no longer watch a Pampers commercial without being moved to tears and who feel it is our responsibility to memorize the faces of children on milk cartons so that we can reunite them with their bereft parents.

In other words, this book is for *every* pregnant woman, because I believe that any woman who tells you that her pregnancy is, without exception, the most pleasant and fulfilling time of her life is either lying or has a personality disorder. Besides, I'll bet good money that during their pregnancies, even some of those models and soap opera stars got hemorrhoids.

A Brief History of Girlfriends and Pregnancy

Simply put, having babies is women's work. Until about seventy years ago, men were there for conception and then for the congratulations and the passing out of cigars, but they had precious little to do with the what happened in the nine months in between. (Speaking of nine months, let's get one thing straight right now: Pregnancy lasts an average of forty weeks, and by my calculations that equals *ten* months of pregnancy. You may say, "But who's counting?" And I reply vehemently, "*You* will be!" And you will be confused the whole darn time. Are you six months pregnant because you have not seen your period for twenty-four weeks? But that means you have sixteen weeks left. See, there's that ten-month figure again. After you have been without periods for twenty-four weeks, are you "six months pregnant" or "in your seventh month"? God, the whole countdown gave me a headache. All I know for certain is, it didn't go as fast as I hoped it would.)

Anyway, when a woman found out she was pregnant, she naturally turned to the other women of her tribe—her mother, sisters, aunts and friends—for guidance because, as common as pregnancy is, no first-timer has any idea what the heck is going on when it happens to her. And women who have had children are always more than happy to share their wisdom with the uninitiated.

In those days, doctors were still busying themselves with trying to cure malaria and sewing up farmers who had fallen into their threshing machines, and there was precious little medical business related to pregnancy. The more experienced women of the social group assisted the dumbfounded novice by telling her what to expect, by advising her on how to stay as comfortable as possible during the pregnancy and, most important, by reassuring her that her experiences were normal. Since nothing about pregnancy feels in the least bit normal, this was cherished advice. Of course, there was also a lot of passing of what I call "hoodoo wisdom" (you know, those sixth-sense, intuitive, hocus-pocus "truths" that some believe in with all their hearts), such as dangling needles over the pregnant woman's stomach to determine if she was having a boy or a girl, but we have tried to sift through that kind of information in this *Guide*.

Now doctors usually run the show, except for those fringe people who are willing to face delivery without a neonatal unit next door and a full-time anesthesiologist in residence. Remember all those episodes on *Bonanza* when the poor women died in childbirth? You almost never hear about that happening anymore, thanks to God and the American Medical Association. In addition to protecting our babies' lives, and our own, doctors monitor our pregnancies and tell us whether there is too much protein in our urine, or if we are at risk for gestational diabetes or some other such tribulation. And let's not forget my personal favorite—doctors tell us how very fat we are getting.

It is never my intention to undermine the role of doctors in any way, and I would be forever relieved if you would think of this book as a "supplement" of sorts to the very serious advice and counsel of your obstetrician. With that burden of guilt and responsibility removed, I would like to say that I believe that women learn some of the most valuable things about pregnancy from other women. Not only were my Girlfriends endlessly giving of their experience and knowledge, but they constantly reassured me that I was normal, and that was surely the greatest gift of all. While every woman believes her pregnancy is unique and special (especially if it is her first), she also yearns to be told that she is no more confused, insecure or neurotic than the rest of us mothers.

The only problem is that we are a very mobile society and we no longer stay within our "tribes." Or as my Girlfriend Kelly's grandmother used to say, "We don't always grow in the garden where we were planted." That means that your mother, aunts, sisters and experienced Girlfriends may not be around to help you when you get pregnant because you live in San Diego and they live everywhere from Duluth to Staten Island to St. Petersburg. And, if you are like most women who have not yet had children, you have been spending your time at a job for the years preceding your pregnancy, instead of bonding with the other women in the neighborhood over potluck dinners and coffee klatches. Millions of us wouldn't know our next-door neighbors if we ran over them in our driveways. So that pretty much leaves you alone with your husband (which is the same as alone, in this particular situation) to navigate the choppy waters of pregnancy.

Even if your mother is nearby when you are pregnant, you will soon learn something critically important: EACH GENERATION HAS ITS OWN SET OF PREGNANCY RULES, AND OUR MOTHERS' RULES ARE NOT OURS. For example, our mothers were free to enjoy a cocktail when they felt like it. Nowadays a woman can't go into a restaurant without seeing a warning plaque on the wall connecting fetal alcohol syndrome to a nice cabernet with dinner. Smoking, too, was allowed, which was particularly helpful because our moms had something nonfattening to put in their mouths to help them avoid gaining more than the fifteen pounds that their doctors prescribed, unlike some of us who reached for jelly beans about once every six minutes.

You will also learn from talking to your mother that the experience of pregnancy, intense as it is while you are going through it, is gradually forgotten almost entirely as are entire episodes of your babyhood. It sounds absolutely impossible to you now, doesn't it? But you can test it for yourself. Show your mother a baby picture of you and one of your brother or sister and ask her to tell you who is who. Chances are she will really have to think about it or use unfair indicators like the model of the car in the background or the style of her hair. Even I, with my oldest child only seven years old, am often unable to tell my kids' baby pictures apart unless I can see if my hair is brown or blond, short or long. (Make a mental note to yourself now to mark every baby photo that comes into your house as soon as it arrives, because Mommy Alzheimer's is ferocious.)

I occasionally asked my mother things about how it was when she was pregnant with me, and she really only seemed to recall two things: She craved chocolate peanut clusters, and her water broke on the floor of Sears when she was shopping for my layette. Oh yes, and she told me she sneaked a cigarette in the hospital bathroom to help get her bowels going because she couldn't get discharged until she had had a "movement."

If you mention such concerns as whether or not to get an amnio-centesis or whether you should stop using the microwave for the duration of your pregnancy to avoid exposing the fetus to some sort of radiation, your mother will look at you as though you are the biggest chump in town, listening to all the New Age medical mumbo jumbo. Remember, you're talking to a person who was sound asleep when her baby was born and whose health insurance allowed her to recuperate in the hospital for *two weeks*. She will probably say some-thing like, "Honey, you have *got* to relax. When I was pregnant with you, I just went on with my life. You kids *think* too much about everything. Do what you like — the baby will be fine. But for God's sake, you've got to stop eating, because you're beginning to look like the side of a barn."

Needless, to say, this is not welcome advice in a generation of women raised to analyze and understand everything from their psy-ches to their g-spots. Add to that this very nineties desire to be per-fect at everything we do at home and at work, and you can have a substantial group of women in need of some real support. This book is just what the doctor ordered (or would have if we'd told them about it). *The Girlfriends' Guide to Pregnancy* provides the reassurance, advice and road signs that are invaluable to a pregnant woman. It will also come in handy for all the fathers-to-be who are convinced that their lovely mates have been taken over by the Body Snatchers. You will learn the fundamental rule of parenthood, which begins with pregnancy: You don't have to be a perfect mother, just good enough. We Girlfriends have absolutely no doubt that you will be more than good enough, and we are here to see to it that you are.

The

GIRLFRIENDS'
Guide to
PREGNANCY

I

So, What Makes You Think You're Pregnant?

Quite often nature provides us with physical clues that might make us suspect we are pregnant even before modern science confirms it. Usually, when you find out that you are, indeed, pregnant, you say to yourself with a sudden awakening, "Oh, so *that's* why my . . ." (Fill in the symptom "boobs hurt"; "bladder fails"; "husband drives me crazy.") Especially in retrospect, you will see that there are usually abundant physical changes to inform you in no uncertain terms that you are pregnant. That is why I am always cynical when I read those stories about unsuspecting women giving birth to babies in airplane bathrooms after nine months of not knowing they were pregnant. Come on now! Most eight-month-old fetuses kick and tumble so fiercely in your stomach that you can watch your abdomen go from round to nearly square. And what about that inevitable weight gain? Who are these women trying to kid? Either they are trying for the Immaculate Conception excuse or they just are not really paying enough attention to themselves. There are plenty of other changes that, when put together, might lead you to suspect that you are pregnant long before you confirm it with a pregnancy test. What follows is a list of the common early warning signs.

Breasts

One of the most common changes in the pregnant woman's body is in her breasts. The newly pregnant woman often gets the same puffy breasts that she gets premenstrually, but the consensus among the Girlfriends is that these breasts are a lot more *sensitive*. In fact, taking a shower can be agonizing if you face the stream of water, sleeping on your stomach becomes unbearable and if your husband should happen to touch your breasts you will feel completely justified in hitting him with the bedside lamp. Not only are they sensitive and sore, but they are getting bigger and bigger every day. The good news, especially for those of us who have always secretly longed to be big busty gals, is that they will continue to grow, and they will stop hurting eventually. In a month or so, you and your husband will have a nice new set of playthings.

Peeing

Another symptom that the Girlfriends found in early pregnancy was the need to urinate *a lot*. You may find yourself getting up two or three (or more) times a night to pee when you used to sleep all night long without even hearing a peep from your bladder. Since fatigue is often another early sign of pregnancy, you will probably learn to loathe all of these interruptions of your precious slumber. There is some old folk wisdom that says that all this geting up and down all night to pee is nature's way of preparing you for early motherhood, when the up-and-down drill is much the same. I happen to think that this folk wisdom is incorrect, because you will start being able to sleep again later in your pregnancy and everyone knows a pregnant woman cannot be expected to remember something that she learned six months earlier; heck, she probably can't remember what happened *yesterday.*

   All these nighttime trips can, indeed, be annoying, but it usually is not as bad as it sounds because almost all of us Girlfriends discovered that we could get out of bed, walk to the bathroom, pee, wipe, walk back to bed and crawl in, all without opening our eyes one single time. Some of us could even manage to take a drink of water without looking. I, however, was almost always hungry at night, and I frequently ended up in the kitchen after one of my nocturnal pees. If the trip downstairs hadn't awakened me, the refrigerator light was sure to.

Exhaustion

The tiredness of a newly pregnant woman is like a heaviness or being on nighttime cold medication permanently. One of my Girl-friends, Becky, who sells real estate, was so tired that she fell asleep in the car every single time she went to houses of prospective clients. Fortunately for Becky, she has a partner who did most of the driving. The newly pregnant woman may find herself at work, unable to think of anything but lying down. My Girlfriend Rosemary used to lock her office door and nap on her sofa for a few minutes every day. Those of us who are fortunate enough to actually take a nap sleep like the dead, waking up with blanket creases on our faces, red cheeks and bedhead hair — and usually little more refreshed than we were before. Forget about renting a video for a cozy night in with your husband. You will be snoring by the time the warning not to bootleg the tape and sell it for profit is over. This fatigue can also lead to an inability to stay awake long enough to have sex. Please hand this book to your husband right now.

**ATTENTION,
HUSBANDS OF
NEWLY PREGNANT WOMEN:**

DO NOT TAKE IT PERSONALLY WHEN YOUR
WIFE WOULD RATHER SLEEP THAN SLEEP
WITH YOU! SHE REALLY CANNOT HELP IT
AND IT IS ABSOLUTELY NO REFLECTION ON
YOUR MANHOOD OR HOW MUCH SHE LOVES
YOU. TRY AGAIN TOMORROW MORNING
AFTER SHE HAS HAD SOME REST. (UNLESS, OF
COURSE, SHE HAS MORNING SICKNESS, TOO,
IN WHICH CASE, TRY THE PLAYBOY
CHANNEL.)

Crampiness

Phantom menstrual cramps can be another sign of pregnancy. Many Girlfriends have never been more certain that their periods were going to start than when they were pregnant. Pregnancy and serious PMS (which is always serious) have several similarities, such as lower back pressure and that slightly crampy feeling you get right before your period starts. Since I was always paralyzed with the fear that I might miscarry (which, by the way, I never did), I really hated the feeling that my period might start at any minute. I can't count the number of times I felt a little trickle and dropped everything to fly to the bathroom to see if my period had begun. As you will soon learn, in pregnancy, there is a lot of trickling going on as your body goes into overdrive in the vaginal secretion department.

With all four of my children, I did experience some bleeding early in the pregnancies, and while this is not particularly common, it may happen to you. A general rule of thumb is that if the blood is brownish with no clots and doesn't fill more than one or two sanitary pads, everything is probably all right. If the bleeding is bright red or has clots in it, call your doctor right away. And if there is cramping with the bleeding, call your doctor immediately and ask whether they want to meet you at their office or the nearest hospital.

Believe me, I know how hysterical you can feel if you are pregnant and you find blood in your underwear, but if it makes you feel any better, all four times my bleeding was bright red (but without cramps) and my doctor just had me rest with my feet up for a couple of days until it went away. My pregnancies were just fine after that. It is perfectly natural to call your doctor for reassurance, but it's not always a call for alarm.

Dizziness

Quite a few of my Girlfriends said that they were light-headed early in their pregnancies. Getting out of bed too quickly could give them tunnel vision and make them see stars. Bending over to tie their shoes could result in them having to lie on the floor until the blood returned to their head. A word of caution here: A significant number of women have gotten pregnant after too much to drink, and sometimes pregnancy and a hangover are hard to tell apart. The general rule should be that a hangover that lasts for more than a couple of days could be pregnancy, and it might be a good idea to give up the partying until you know for certain. Even if you aren't pregnant, if you have hangovers that last more than a couple of days it is probably a good idea for you to give up partying anyway.

If you are light-headed, it is usually nothing to worry about, but you could pass out and bonk your head or something, so move slowly and let your blood pressure adjust at its new, slower pace.

Nausea

Nausea is the Waterloo for many newly pregnant women, and it can strike at any point in the pregnancy, usually at the two-month point. They will either find themselves eating everything in sight in a desperate attempt to make the queasiness go away or they will gag at the mere thought of certain foods. You would think that a nauseous woman is a woman who cannot eat a crumb. Not true. Many of my pregnant Girlfriends experienced starving and vomiting almost simultaneously. Pregnancy can create a gnawing uneasiness in the tummy that is most easily compared to seasickness, and, as with seasickness, food is the only thing that can settle your stomach. The catch is that not *all* food is friendly food. The challenge is in finding just the right foods to soothe the nausea, because you will be amazed at how many of the old favorites, such as cheese, fish, broccoli or chicken, now make your stomach lurch uncontrollably when you simply think of them.

Some of my more unfortunate Girlfriends have had such extreme nausea that they would gag right in the middle of a sentence. My poor Girlfriend Maryann was so plagued by morning sickness that she would throw up spontaneously. There would be no warning signs, like a wave of nausea or a watering of the mouth. One moment she would be chatting normally, and the next minute it was the pea soup scene from *The Exorcist*. She just sat as quietly as possible with her mouth clenched tightly to try to keep the mess to a minimum. Then again, just as many other Girlfriends have never experienced a gurgle of nausea. This diversity is just another example of how nature gets a kick out of keeping us guessing and never letting us completely relax.

There is really no rhyme or reason in this area of food preferences and sensitivities. You might be like my Girlfriend Sondra, who when she was pregnant craved anything spicy. She would start her days with Mexican food drowning in salsa. By lunchtime she was begging her friends to go to sushi bars with her so that she could nibble on the green mustard, even if she couldn't eat the raw fish. Or you might be like my Girlfriend Shannon, who craved "comfort" foods like mashed potatoes, cereals and white toast. My Girlfriend Corki got on a fruit kick and lived for strawberries and nectarines, with a little chocolate thrown in every now and then for variety.

Obviously, the goal is to eat some foods from the five major food groups, if not at every meal, then at least once a day. DO NOT PANIC, HOWEVER, IF YOU FAIL TO EAT TEXTBOOK BALANCED MEALS EVERY DAY DURING YOUR FIRST COUPLE OF MONTHS OF PREGNANCY. No matter how vehement those other pregnancy books are about your needing eight ounces of protein, four glasses of milk and a bushel of green leafy vegetables every day, just do the best you can and KEEP TALKING TO YOUR DOCTOR. He or she may prescribe vitamin supplements to help carry you through the nauseous period and into the second trimester, when you will be thrilled to eat nearly anything that is placed before you. You may find that a calcium pill is as effective as the glass of milk that makes your eyes water and your throat close down. The bottom line this early in your suspected pregnancy is this: If you feel "green" and you haven't got a temperature, it's time for a pregnancy test.

Sensitivity to Odors

For a lot of women, including myself, the very first sign that they are pregnant is that the world begins to smell strange. Common aromas seem to get more powerful or cloying. My Girlfriend Mindy developed such an aversion to the smell of dairy products when she was pregnant that she couldn't walk into a grocery store or a delicatessen for fear of smelling the cheese and throwing up in the aisle. One morning she saw me pouring cream into my coffee and started making noises like a cat trying to get up a fur ball. Continuing with this cat theme, my Girlfriend Lynn had to beg her husband to take over the job of feeding their cat because the first waft of the "Seafood Surprise" when the can was opened sent her streaking for the sink.

By the way, if you do have a cat, and you are, indeed, pregnant, it is time to give your husband the job of changing the cat litter. Ask your doctor for details, but there is some virus that cat poopoo can give to pregnant women, so steer clear of it (like I have to twist your arm, right?).

During my first pregnancy, I was so certain that my bed pillows and comforter were mildewed that I wrapped them in plastic garbage bags and disposed of them. I immediately (and irrationally, according to my husband) replaced the pillows and comforter with brand-new ones, only to discover when I crawled into bed that night that they smelled exactly the same!

Insanity

Another indication that you might be pregnant can be the feeling that you are losing your mind, or at least some vague control of your emotions. You may feel as though you have a monster case of PMS. This is not something I am proud to share with you, but as your Girlfriend I will: Two different times, the first doctors to suggest to me that I might be pregnant were not gynecologists, but psychiatrists. One time my husband calmly put me in the car and drove me to his therapist right after I tried to knock his head off by throwing a book across the room. (Believe me when I say this behavior was not only uncharacteristic of me, it was absolutely unacceptable to him.) Another time, after I tried to steer the car *while my husband was driving* (because he wasn't taking the route I had so generously suggested), I ended up on a therapist's couch sobbing that I feared I was going through early menopause because I just didn't feel like myself and my periods had stopped. That menopause turned out to be my baby Jessica, a possibility that I had not even considered.

Even if you are not prone to violent outbursts, you may experience the hormonal irrationality of pregnancy in the form of weepiness or utter lack of humor. My Girlfriend Amy, who is normally the sweetest of southern belles, was so cranky when she was pregnant that she actually became funny. The contrast between her usual tiny-blond demeanor and her general pissed-off state during pregnancy was so great that it was comical, not unlike a toddler swearing.

One of the most important things to consider during this time of emotional whiplash (aside from putting off the cleaning of any handguns) is the probability that *you* will be completely unaware of your strange behavior. If your husband or friends dare to suggest to you that maybe you aren't yourself these days, you will certainly feel attacked and unfairly judged (and you will begin formulating plans to have them poisoned). As convinced as you may be of your rationality and of everyone else's irrationality, you really are not normal, and you should just accept it and allow for it. In other words, this is not the time to file for divorce, change your job, buy a house or, most important, cut your hair.

No Period

You might think that not getting your period is a pretty reliable indication that there is a bun in your oven, but that was never my first clue. Sure, there are millions of women who have regular twenty-eight-day cycles and know exactly when to expect their periods, right down to whether it will be before breakfast or after dinner. I, however, am all over the place. Not only am I irregular, I am usually too distracted by the business of living to have even a vague notion of when my "friend" (don't you just hate that term?) is coming. I have a hard enough time remembering to fill my car with gas, and it comes equipped with a gauge.

The fun part about this absentmindedness is that it can keep your life full of surprises; one day you wake up expecting the same old routine, and instead you discover you are going to have a baby! The troublesome part of this absentmindedness is that when you do confirm that you are pregnant, your doctor will invariably ask you for the date of your last period, and you will have to either lie (as I have always done) or give some lame answer like "I think it was on the morning that the Soap Opera Hunks were on *Regis and Kathie Lee*. (As if that narrows things down.)

My Girlfriend Mindy had missed two periods before she began to suspect that she might be pregnant. I think that she, like a lot of us, was not particularly upset about missing two weeks of tampons and cramps, so she accepted her lack of periods at face value: *A gift from God*. One thing, though, that I have learned from experience is that it is helpful to have a vague familiarity with your cycle, because the new home pregnancy tests are so sensitive that you can often know if you are pregnant as early as twelve to fourteen days after *the deed*. And since it only makes sense that you would want to protect your pregnancy from the earliest possible moment, a positive test result could inspire you to stop smoking or drinking or taking Prozac immediately.

Intuition

The last clue that you might be pregnant that I will discuss here is "intuition." We women are supposedly famous for it, and while it has never happened to me, I have a number of reliable non–New Age Girlfriends who swear they knew they were pregnant the instant it happened. They felt something come over them, like a shudder or an instant awareness that this particular roll in the hay wasn't like all the rest; something momentous had occurred. Scientist (or cynic) that I am, I have asked these women if they have ever felt that mystical sensation and *not* been pregnant and just never mentioned it to anyone. Of if perhaps the event wasn't heightened by the fact that they knew that they were having sex on day fourteen of their twenty-eight-day cycle and they weren't using birth control. (You don't have to be a member of the Psychic Network to know that one out of five times that you get sperm to egg you make Baby.) But, no, these Girlfriends insist that they felt different physically and emotionally from that climax onward. And you know what? I believe them, even if I don't understand or relate to any of it.

If you are feeling any of these symptoms, alone or in groups, and if you don't yet know for certain whether you are pregnant, then what in the world are you reading this book for? No, I'm just kidding. You must have a pretty good hunch that a baby is in your future, so you'd best get in touch with a good obstetrician and start taking special care of your baby and yourself right now.

2

Sharing the Wonderful News

Since the beginning of time, any woman who has gotten pregnant by a man who has a job and is not married to someone else has been congratulated and showered with best wishes. (One would hope that she gets showered with more than just wishes, and I will address a good husband's responsibilities in this area later.) The news that you are pregnant is BIG each and every time it happens. You know this already by the way you feel when your doctor's nurse comes out of the little lab room with a big smile on her face.

The general rule is, if this is your first pregnancy, you will tell your husband the glorious news before you tell anyone else (except your doctor, of course). If this is your second or third baby, however, you will tell all of your Girlfriends reachable by phone, fax or E-mail, then your mother, then your father, and then any stranger who happens to ask "How are you today?" and *then* your husband. And if this is your fourth or subsequent pregnancy, well, we really would need a whole other book to get into that.

If women and men were really emotional equals, then all prospective fathers would be with their wives, waiting anxiously in the doctor's office for this momentous news. There they would sit with you, flipping through old copies of *Working Mother* or studying the manuals on how to give yourself a breast exam. If this is your first pregnancy, there is a chance that your husband will indeed be there with you to see the nurse and her smile. But if he's not, remember, perfectly good husbands, including my own, are not always with their wives when they learn they are pregnant. They can still grow up to be wonderful and attentive fathers. Keep this bit of advice in mind: One good kind of husband is a husband with a job, and a husband with a job might not be able to get away for an afternoon sitting in the gynecologist's office. Be pragmatic; a busy man does not automatically equal a bad father.

Your Obstetrician

Let's not forget that the truly most important person who should know about your pregnancy is your obstetrician. So if he or she is the first person you share your wonderful news with, that's just fine. Although the chemistry behind the newest home pregnancy tests is nearly foolproof, especially when the result is positive, most first-timers do not consider themselves officially pregnant until their doctor tells them so. Even if you strongly suspect that you are, indeed, pregnant, the shock of hearing this news from a medical professional can be so stunning that even the most capable and stouthearted of us become weak and quite grateful that there is someone familiar with CPR in the room with us.

Your first response will be the slightly inane question, "Are you SURE?" And without a doubt, your next question will be, "When is it due?" Few things are more exciting than watching your doctor pull out one of those little cardboard wheels with the numbers all over them to compute your baby's expected arrival. That date becomes engraved in your consciousness, as if pregnancy were like booking a flight on an airplane: "If they tell me I am going on August 4, then that's when I'm going!" No matter how often your Girl-friends will advise you not to rely on it too much, you will embrace that date firmly and plan your entire life around it. And when that due date comes and goes with no baby in sight, as it frequently does with women expecting their first babies, you will become a directionless person without the slightest clue as to how to pass the time until you feel your first labor pain.

With subsequent pregnancies, you might choose to do what I did by my third and fourth pregnancies: You buy about three home test kits with the little sticks that you pee on (being careful to pee just on the end that's covered by the cap, not all over the entire stick and your hand! Believe me, this sounds easier than it is). Frankly, one test is reliable enough, but some of us need that extra validation that comes with mindlessly repeating the test. Here is one of the few times that a pregnant woman's constant need to urinate comes in handy. Anyway, line up all the sticks on your bathroom counter and wait for them to change color. If the results are unanimous, call your doctor to inform him or her that you are pregnant, *again*, and that you will drop by in a couple of weeks for some information, such as whether there is a heartbeat (they can often see a little flashing beat as early as six weeks with ultrasound) and whether it's time to start applying to preschools.

If your husband *is* in the doctor's office with you when you are given the glorious news, the two of you can rejoice together and cry and bury your heads in each other's shoulders, just like those couples do on the TV commercials for home pregnancy tests. If your husband can't be there with you, you can spend the next couple of minutes being patted and congratulated by the doctor's staff and figuring out the best way to tell your husband that he is going to be a daddy.

Telling Your Husband

Some of my Girlfriends are quite sentimental about how they share this delicious information. Candlelit meals with romantic music in the background are very popular in my crowd. But if my husband were to come home to a setup like that, he would think I had joined a cult and given all our money to the swami. He would be so relieved to hear I was *only* having a baby that my announcement would be anticlimactic.

Having watched far more TV than was good for me, I always imagined telling my husband as we walked hand in hand along the beach at sunset. I would turn to him and he would embrace me and we would look out to sea as we dreamed of our child's future. Perhaps he would even sing the *Soliloquy* from *Carousel*, I don't know. Anyway, it never happened. What did happen was usually something like this: I would call him from the doctor's office and hysterically scream at his assistant, "What do you mean, can you take a message? You just tell him to get out of that damn meeting and talk to me right now because I'm PREGNANT!" Remember, progester-one and I don't get along very well.

I did try the romantic-dinner approach when I learned I was pregnant for the fourth time (I was desperate after all), and this is what I learned: When you are telling your husband that he is going to be a father and looking directly into his eyes, it is almost impossible not to start crying before you even get the first word out. No matter how many times it has happened to you or how comfortable you may be about your new condition, the first couple of times that you say the words "I am going to have a baby," you can hardly form the words because of how much your chin quivers. I nearly choked to death before I could get beyond "Honey, guess what?" My poor husband imagined all sorts of disasters, like the dog died or I lost his baseball jacket, before I finally spit out the words. And when I finally did, his expression seemed to say, "Oh, is *that* all?"

As a matter of fact, this last time I distinctly remember him going on to say, "How could you do this to me?" (Of course, this *was* our fourth baby in five years). I mumbled something to the effect that my elementary understanding of biology indicated that this was something *he* had done to *me*, but this really wasn't the time to quibble. Before I dissolved into a puddle of hurt feelings, I recalled that my Girlfriend Mindy's husband had said something equally enthusiastic to her when she had gotten pregnant six years before. I believe his exact response was, "I'm sorry, but I'm just not ready." As a matter of fact, he wasn't certain if he was ready for most of her pregnancy, and was reading old issues of *Road and Track* while she was in labor for forty hours. But the minute their baby girl took her first breath, he became her devoted slave. A father couldn't love his baby more.

Keep these husbands in mind, because they both started out slowly and then became candidates for Father of the Decade. It isn't necessarily wise to take a husband's first response much to heart. Or, if you prefer, you can keep his lack of enthusiasm filed away for future infliction of guilt. For example, when our youngest baby does something that is so cute and loving that it brings tears to my husband's eyes, I have been known to toss out, "And *that* is the child you didn't want!" Then I run out of the room as fast as I can.

The telephone got better results for me. It was immediate, it was out of sight and it gave my husband some time to get used to the idea by the time he got home. A good husband can usually get over nearly anything in six hours. Plus, and perhaps more important to a bigmouth like me, once the formality of telling my husband was out of the way, I was morally free to tell everybody else in the world.

As you can see from Mindy's and my experiences, sharing the news with your husband that you are pregnant can be an emotional minefield, and it's best to know this going in. Almost all women, in their hormonally stimulated state, are deeply disappointed by any reaction other than just the right blend of joy, pride and adoration from their husbands. No matter how much the two of you have been looking forward to this (or not), stay light on your feet, because only Ricky Ricardo took his wife in his arms in front of the whole Tropicana Club and sentimentally sang, "We're Having a Baby, My Baby and Me." Far more husbands of my Girlfriends have responded with a dumbstruck expression and then the inevitable question, "Are you SURE?"

Chances are they will eventually come to feel all the things you want them to, at least occasionally, but most men initially trip the land mines by reacting with equal parts shock and fear. When they ask "Are you SURE?" what they are really saying is, "What happens if I change my mind?" Be honest—you must have asked the same thing of yourself at least once. If you didn't, I assure you, you will, either when your head is in the toilet and you are dry-heaving, or nine (ten) months from now after hours of pushing. (A lot of parents of teenagers report asking themselves the same question fifteen years later.) So give the guy a break. There are too many other female expectations that won't be met during the next nine months to get bogged down in this one; things like his not wanting to shop for the layette with you, his reluctance to sing to your belly, his unwillingness to spend a few hours each and every day obsessing about baby names and his refusal to watch educational videos of complete strangers giving birth.

It's not that he doesn't want this baby, it's just that he may feel that he has been given a life subscription to *GRW* (Guilt, Responsibility and Worry), and lost the one to *GQ*. Guess what—that's exactly what he *has* been given, but trust me it will be worth the price to him most of the time. Even he will admit it by the time the baby comes, and for several years thereafter. When my husband told his friend Larry that we were going to have a baby, Larry, the father of two grown boys, replied, "Congratulations, it will be the best twelve years of your life." And Larry had BOYS! Ah, But I leave further discussion of *teenagers* to another *Girlfriends' Guide.*

Telling Girlfriends

After about the age of twenty-one, any woman's announcement that she is pregnant with the child of any man outside of prison is met with great glee. We women don't usually respond by worrying if the couple can afford it or if it is too early in their relationship. We just like pregnancy, and rarely do we care about the practical aspects. Financial worries are the exclusive domain of fathers-to-be. (Don't you love dealing with the world in gross generalities? It makes life so much simpler.) Your friends who have never had children will welcome it as an enjoyable diversion: spending the next nine months watching you get huge. Your friends with kids will be deeply grateful for the opportunity to share with you every detail of their own pregnancies, especially their deliveries. In fact, one feature of *The Girlfriends' Guide* that you will come to love is your freedom to shut it up when you feel that you've had it up to here with pregnancy.

After your Girlfriends know that you are pregnant, you will never again have a conversation with them that doesn't include questions about the baby. Some pregnant Girlfriends start to feel like a vessel rather than a person, because their whole identities seem wrapped up in gestating. However, other Girlfriends can recount every detail about their pregnancies until the listener wants to shoot herself for asking in the first place. Your very empathetic Girlfriends will tell you how great you look and how you're hardly putting on any weight. Decide for yourself if you want to believe them. I never did.

Telling Mothers

Mothers, on the other hand, are often not quite so blind to your weight gain, because, as I mentioned before, they were taught that gaining any more than twelve to fifteen pounds was self-indulgent gluttony. Aside from that little issue, telling your mother that you are pregnant can be much more fun than you might initially imagine. This is especially true if your mother can say your husband's name without spitting on the ground or making the sign of the horns. Astonishingly, the further you proceed in your pregnancy, the more pleasant and reassuring it is to be around the very same person who, just months before, inspired you to buy an answering machine so that you could screen your calls and not answer if you heard her voice.

This could be the beginning of a beautiful relationship, because it is the official transformation from being mommy's little girl into being another woman, equal in stature. You, too, are going to be somebody's mother. You might find yourself thinking about the mother you remember from when you were really small, the way she took care of you and the things she said to you. You are already inclined to be sentimental in your hormone-jostled state, and you may suddenly remember things like the way she used to make a trail of jelly beans from your bedroom door to where your Easter basket was hidden so that you really believed the Easter bunny had been there, or the way she always bought you an ice cream cone after a dentist's visit, and you will sob (a response you will find occurring with much more frequency as the pregnancy progresses).

Or something quite the opposite might happen. You might have total recall of every unenlightened move you think your mother ever made raising you, and you could spend your entire pregnancy strategizing how to be as *unlike* her as possible. Several of my Girlfriends got quite panicky at the thought that they were doomed to become their own mothers. First of all, remember that there is an element of choice here; you are free to adopt or reject all sorts of models of behavior, including your mother's. Second, and much more valuable, is this advice: Take this time to get to know your mother better, because you will come away with a much more empathetic perception of her. For once in your life, you may understand why she publicly embarrassed you in high school because she caught you riding on the back of a motorcycle. All you have to do is picture your own baby strapped to the back of a Harley with a seventeen-year-old at the wheel to understand her hysteria.

Unless your mother is Joan Crawford, she will always be interested in your condition and deeply concerned for your well-being (even if most of her actual advice will sound inapplicable to birthing in the nineties). If you think that this is kind of nice, just wait until the baby is born. If you are one of the very many lucky ones, you will notice that your mother seems to love your baby as much as you do, and that is the beginning of the biggest bond in the world. Remember, husbands have been known to come and go in our society, but once your mother has that lovelock on your kid, she can be a great constant in your child's life. And you will begin to realize that maybe she didn't do as bad a job raising you as you'd thought. Not as good as the job you're going to do, of course, but not bad.

I spend this time talking about mothers for two reasons: First, I want to encourage Girlfriends who still have mothers around to take the necessary steps to allow them to share in this pregnancy. Second, for those of you who have lost your mother, or who have a relationship far too dysfunctional to repair in nine months, I want to speak out in honor of the mother-in-law. Remember, it is *her* baby's baby, too, and she might be just the person for you to bond with. Ignore her meddling in what you eat and whether you should be reaching for anything over your head. (There was an old wives' tale that when you reach over your head, you wrap the umbilical cord around the baby's neck. Forget about it.) Remember, this is a woman who would bite her own arm off to make your little baby more comfortable, OR EVEN BABY-SIT IF BEGGED. Even if she doesn't seem all that crazy about you, she will love her son's baby. And if you are a loving mother to her grandchild, she will probably learn to love you, too. Put it this way: If it's ever going to happen, now is the time.

The most reassuring feeling for a mother is to know that it is possible for you to let your guard down for a few hours with the knowledge that someone else is looking after your child with the same eagle eye and fierce protectiveness that you would. Baby-sitters are great, but you can never be sure whether in an earthquake they would remember to pick up your precious baby before sprinting out of the house to save their own life. A grandma would not only pick up the baby, she would make sure to grab the baby book and the antique christening dress (even if she had to trample you to do so). I know for certain that if my mother-in-law witnessed any sort of unkindness to my child on the preschool playground, she would either hit the inattentive teacher or burn the whole school down (but, of course, she's Sicilian).

The Girlfriends' advice pertaining to mothers is simple: LET THEM INTO THIS PREGNANCY. Contrary to all indications, they are not there to judge you or tell you what you are doing wrong in your pregnancy. And if they are, try to overlook it, because that kind of concern and commitment are impossible to find anywhere else.

Telling Daddy

Sharing the news with your father can be fun, but it is different from telling your mother. If you and your husband are together when you tell your father, you might feel Daddy's eyes come to rest on your husband, as if to say, "O.K. You got her into this fix and you better take care of her or I will have to kill you." Most of my Girlfriends agree that your dad is happy if you are happy, but that, like most men, he doesn't immediately fall into baby rapture; that happens when the baby actually arrives. Think of it this way: Some people can look at an outfit on a hanger and know just what it will look like on. Other people need to wear the thing for a while before they understand the fit. Same thing with babies: Most men can't imagine fatherhood or grandfatherhood until they are holding the little darlings.

You may notice that your father gets nervous if he hears you and your mother talking too much and too graphically about your pregnancy. It is important to remember that it is his job to be suspicious of anything that might hurt you. Remember, this is the guy who wanted to hit a doctor for making you cry when you got stitches, so this alien baby who might be making you vomit uncontrollably or who might take fourteen hours to get out of your body isn't sending your father into a tizzy of planning and daydreaming like it is you and your mother.

There is one other little thing about telling your father that you are pregnant: This may be the very first time in your entire life that you have boldly declared to him that you are no longer a virgin. I don't know about you, but I managed to live for over thirty years without any overt reference to my sex life in front of my father. Sure, he probably had his suspicions, especially after I started living with my boyfriend in college, but still we could pretend. There is no skirting the sex issue once you announce that you are going to have a baby. Dad's bound to know how that happened, which may be another reason his gaze shifts so quickly to your husband upon hearing the news.

When Should You Tell?

Quite a number of people believe that a newly pregnant woman should not announce her condition until most of the danger of miscarriage has passed, usually at about three months. In fact, if you are Jewish, there are "rules" about not bringing any baby clothes or furniture into the house before the baby is born safe and sound, for fear of jinxing it in some way. Being neither Jewish nor particularly reserved in nature, I have consistently told people I was pregnant from the moment I knew (but I must admit to feeling strange about buying baby clothes or toys before the baby was born). It's simply that I cannot keep a secret of that magnitude. I remember sitting at dinner one night with my Girlfriend Patti and a number of other people, blabbing about my new pregnancy with all the self-importance of a woman who had just invented the condition. I so enjoyed being the object of everyone's attention, surrounded by so much concern about whether I was eating enough and if my chair was comfortable enough. Two months later, Patti told me that she had known that night that she was pregnant, too, but that she didn't want to tell anyone at the dinner until she was sure the pregnancy was "a keeper." I guess I did feel a little sheepish about glomming all the attention when she was as deserving as I was of tender care and special congratulations. But, as my mother says, "It pays to advertise."

If you don't tell your closest friends that you are pregnant, how else do you explain why you no longer have the energy to lift your gym bag, let alone take a ninety-minute aerobics class? How else do you explain to your gracious hostess that those capers she so imaginatively tossed into your salad are making your eyes water and your throat spasm? And how else do you excuse yourself to a colleague who has walked into your office and found you asleep with your head on your desk, drooling on your blotter? I suppose you could give that Chronic Fatigue Syndrome a try, but then how do you explain the new upholstered look your body is taking on?

People give pregnant women wide berth (literally and figuratively), and it is a universally accepted excuse for all kinds of unforgivable behavior, so I would advise invoking it whenever possible. A word of warning, however: THIS EXCUSE LOSES ITS MAGICAL EFFECT ON HUSBANDS WITHIN A COUPLE OF MONTHS, AND IT HAS ABSOLUTELY NO POWER OVER THEM BY THE SECOND PREGNANCY. Your husband will look up from his football game to notice you moving the sofa across the room by yourself and do nothing, while a stranger who sees that you are pregnant won't let you lift your own grocery bags.

Of course, there is a very good reason why many women keep their pregnancies a secret, and that is that about 10 percent of all pregnancies end in miscarriage within the first twelve weeks. If such a disaster were to happen to you, it would undoubtedly add to your grief to have to repeatedly recount your tragedy. I have seen a few of my most cherished Girlfriends beginning to heal from the physical toll of miscarriage, then having to endure an uninformed person coming up to them and asking how the baby is doing. It was deeply painful for all concerned. I suppose the only solution is to tell just those people who would be puzzled by your bizarre behavior (or anyone who has the gall to suggest that you should consider dieting) and to save the megaphones and skywriters for later in your pregnancy.

Total Strangers

You will be amazed at how easy it is to drop your pregnancy into absolutely any conversation or circumstance. If you are a circumspect type and kept mum through the entire first trimester, you will nearly explode with the news right at the three-month mark. That kind of a secret is like rice in a pressure cooker: When it bursts, it flies everywhere. Telling people you are pregnant works like a charm when you want some special treatment, like permission to move to the front of the line in the ladies' room at the movies, which is far more useful than getting the proverbial seat on the bus if you drink large sodas with your popcorn.

In the beginning, you will have to be the one to declare your condition, because most people either are not too observant or are deathly afraid of congratulating you on your pregnancy only to learn that you aren't pregnant and have simply been eating your way through the universe. In fact, you are generally well-advised *never* to congratulate a woman on her apparent pregnancy until she shows you her positive pregnancy test, because if she is not pregnant, you automatically become the bonehead of the universe. It couldn't hurt to tell everyone from the checkout clerk to the policeman who stops you for speeding that you are in that exceptional state called pregnancy. Who knows—they might offer to bag your groceries for you or give you a police escort to the nearest clean public rest room. At the very least, they will give you a nice smile and a few kind words, which is more than most people give you these days. But be prepared—if the person you are telling has borne a child of her own, you may be in for a never-ending monologue about her labor and delivery. It's sad, but we really can't help ourselves.

The Girlfriends are unanimous in this warning regarding strangers: THEY WILL INSIST ON RUBBING YOUR STOMACH AND THEY

WILL NEVER ASK FOR YOUR PERMISSION TO DO SO. If you think that this is going to bother you, you might consider keeping your arms folded protectively in front of you. Don't forget, you are completely entitled to take a step back and announce the No Touching Rule. It's just that people feel you're not a very good sport if you don't allow them to manhandle you. I didn't mind it too much when I was cutely pregnant in the second trimester, but by the end, when I was so pregnant I had corners and my belly button popped completely out like on a butterball turkey, I really hated people touching me, especially if I didn't even know them.

3

Pregnancy Is a Total Body Experience

efore I actually became pregnant for the first time, I naively believed that the only part of my body that would be affected would be my tummy. I took great satisfaction in the fact that I had always been slim and active, and I knew that I would sail through pregnancy with just an adorable bump of a tummy atop my lean, athletic legs. Yeah, right. When I was pregnant, I was pregnant from my chipmunk cheeks to my water-retaining ankles. The legs I was shaving in the shower looked and felt like those of a stranger, so round and dimply were my knees. If I allowed my arms to lie flat against my sides, they looked as wide as my thighs. (Keep this in mind: Sleeveless and pregnant don't mix.) My wedding ring didn't spin on my ring finger anymore. And, worst of all, I had cellulite so bad it looked like I had been pelted with cottage cheese. It wasn't just me, I swear! I have a Girlfriend who is a professional model (she threatened to tell one of my secrets if I told you her name) who gained so much weight in her face that I didn't recognize her in the restaurant where we were meeting for dinner and I walked right past her. If you are like me, you have loving friends who will reassure you that your face hasn't changed at all, and that from the back you don't even look pregnant. They will say that you look healthier and more beautiful than ever. THEY ARE LYING!

Let's talk about the concept of gaining weight—how much is too much and how much is too little and what repercussions it will have on your body for the rest of your young life. I will begin by saying that if you are obese or anorexic, your weight is your own private issue, one for you and your doctor to deal with. I will also say that it should be understood that the baby's health is more important than any other consideration, and that any woman who starves herself or eats only trash foods should be permanently ostracized from the community of Girlfriends, if not from the universe.

That aside, let's talk about the rest of us. Those of us who read in popular books on pregnancy that the weight gain is supposed to progress something like this: zero to three pounds in the first trimester, ten to twelve pounds during the second trimester and eight to ten pounds during the third trimester. If we don't match up with those specifications, we live in dread of the weighing days at the doctor's office. There are a number of us Girlfriends who pass that suggested twenty-five-pound weight gain mark at about the seventh month, just when we are really getting good and hungry. In fact, I have been known to put on so much weight in the first trimester that when the nurse asks me on my first visit what my pre-pregnancy weight was, I lie and add five pounds so that she won't know I have already gained ten pounds.

Pathetically, most women learn to gauge their pregnancy based on what their weight gain was for a particular doctor's appointment. If I had a visit where there was no weight increase since the last visit three weeks ago, I would beam with pride, relief and self-satisfaction for days. I would call my friends to tell them how the baby was doing, and then *casually* mention that I hadn't gained any weight. Then on those visits that I was told I had gained seven pounds in less than a month, I would be so embarrassed and humiliated that I would cry, and I *never* told anyone that I had even seen the doctor, let alone been weighed. After four children I have finally learned two lessons, one vitally important and one just useful. The important lesson is: OUR SELF-ESTEEM ISSUES THAT ARE TIED TO WEIGHT, AND HAVE BEEN SINCE PUBERTY, ARE NEVER MORE INAPPROPRIATE THAN WHEN WE ARE PREGNANT.

Pregnancy is a great time to learn the life lesson of surrender. This body is not for your own personal enjoyment at the moment. It is cozy home in which a child is growing, and you can choose to fight it or to relax and enjoy the ride. *The Girlfriends' Guide* knows how hard it can be for a generation of superwomen to watch themselves transform in this alarming way, because we all felt that way (except my Girlfriend Sondra, but she never got cellulite, so she shouldn't count). That is why I tell you the straight information and then sit back and laugh with you about it, because your sense of humor may be the only thing to get you through these trying times.

The other lesson I learned, the simply useful one, is this: TURN YOUR HEAD AWAY WHEN THE NURSE IS WEIGHING YOU AND ASK HER NOT TO TELL YOU HOW MUCH YOU WEIGH. There is no law that says you have to have that information every visit. Trust me: If the doctor looks at your chart and notices a problem, he or she will tell you soon enough. Otherwise, what difference does it really make to you? You are getting fatter—so what? Get over it.

By the way, you might be as secretly gratified as I was to notice that women who are what I call "professionally thin"—meaning that because they are actresses or models, they *have* to be skinny—often really pack on the pounds during pregnancy. I'm talking sixty to seventy pounds for some of the most svelte women you have ever seen on television or in magazines. It must be the relief of not having to live on rice cakes and cigarettes for nine months. My girlfriend Shannon, who is a gorgeous actress, started each pregnant day with eggs, bacon and so much white toast that she would go through a loaf every other day. She just had a fabulous time, and after the baby was born, she dieted and worked out until she was thin and fit and even more beautiful than she had been before. That is precisely what the other beauties have done, and you can, too, so go ahead and EAT. Heck, you might as well; you can't get drunk, you can't slink around in a sexy black minidress, you can't even take medicine when you are suffering from a cold. What other joys are there for pregnant women?

The Upholstered Body

As any good subscriber to PMS already knows, the female body is capable of retaining up to five pounds of completely unnecessary (in my estimation) body fluids. The only relief is the arrival of the period. Unfortunately when you become pregnant, that period is postponed by about forty weeks. So, even before you begin putting on actual "baby weight," you might begin to grow, and you may continue to retain water until you find that your wedding band is uncomfortable and your feet spill out over your shoes toward the end of a long day. Your eyes may look a bit puffy, too. You would think that with all the peeing you are doing, there wouldn't be enough water in your body to make spit, but nature makes sure that no one is going to threaten your precious placental fluid and future milk factory. One Girlfriend used to eat only watermelon for the entire day before her monthly visit to her obstetrician because watermelon is a natural diuretic and she kept her water weight as low as possible for the loathsome chore of being weighed at each visit. *I am not recommending this to you*, but, hey, a little watermelon every once in a while might help keep the puffiness manageable.

The waistline is one of the first things to change in pregnancy. Especially if this is your first pregnancy and your stomach muscles have never been traumatized before, your waistline will *widen* quite a few weeks before your belly starts to look rounded. (If this is your second or subsequent pregnancy, your belly will pooch out about five minutes after you learn you are pregnant, and in ten minutes you will look five months pregnant.) Imagine a straight line from your armpit to your hips and you will get the basic idea of what this waist-widening looks like. You won't look fat or pregnant at this stage, but you probably won't be able to button your jeans all the way to the top. This is a good time to take your belts and all your shirts that need to be tucked in out of your closet and drawers and to put them in a box in the garage where you will never be tempted to touch them in pregnancy fashion desperation. Look at it this way—you will be gaining useful drawer space for your nursing bras and giant underwear.

The Breasts

Your breasts will also start to change almost immediately. They get bigger; much bigger. Those of us who were never particularly buxom look at our newly pregnant breasts wondering if these beauties will stay this big forever, and we silently pray to God that they will. Echoing our prayers are our husbands, who now think that maybe this pregnancy business isn't so bad after all. Sondra's husband, Ray, looks forward to the arrival of what he calls the "Titty Fairy" with the same enthusiasm most six-year-olds have for the Tooth Fairy.

The good news about the breasts is that they will continue to grow throughout your pregnancy. That aching soreness I talked about in Chapter One will disappear by the end of the first couple of months. You will really have yourself a nice set of knockers for a while—usually until your stomach gets so big that it dwarfs even your mammoth breasts. The most important bit of Girlfriends' advice regarding pregnant breasts is WEAR A BRA. You don't need to be allowing your ripe melons to strain their ligaments at a time like this. Pregnancy and childbirth are very hard on breasts, what with all the stretching and swelling and sucking that goes on, and you should coddle them as much as possible.

The bad news is that once you have finished gestating and nursing, you will be left with breasts that look like water balloons that have sprung a small leak. Not only do they not retain their pregnancy lusciousness, they are actually smaller and/or saggier than they were before you got pregnant. I know this is terrible news to give you, and you may want to insist that I don't know what I am talking about and throw this book to the floor. But I have made it my business at every opportunity to appraise the breasts of women after they have become mothers—at my gym, in the communal dressing rooms at Loehmann's, in the steam room—and I have yet to see any that truly remained unchanged after childbirth. I'm so sorry your Girlfriends had to be the ones to tell you, but it is better that you know it going in. Feel free to live in your disbelieving dreamworld now, but read this part of the *Guide* again in about a year and then talk to me.

Any woman who tells you that she was small-chested until after she had children and then developed a voluptuous body (like a certain Guess? model) either suffers from an inability to distinguish reality from fantasy or has neglected to mention a critical bit of plastic surgery. The following rule of thumb holds true for just about every woman who has borne children and yet has full and perky breasts that stand at attention without the help of underwire, whether she is a movie star or someone in your aerobics class. IF THEY ARE FULL AND ROUNDED AND STAND UP ON THEIR OWN, THEY ARE NOT REAL. If you know any substantiated exceptions to this rule, do us all a favor and keep them to yourself.

Any breast-feeding advocate who assures you that, after nursing your baby, your breasts will return to their pre-pregnancy loveliness either did not have very nice breasts to begin with or is a La Leche League recruitment officer. Many women, including several of my

Girlfriends, decided not to nurse their babies, and this concern about trashing their breasts was one of the reasons why. By the way, *The Girlfriends' Guide* thinks that breast-feeding can be wonderful if it suits your temperament and lifestyle (especially if it is given up by the time the baby can unbutton your shirt herself), and one reason we are so cavalier about this is because we are convinced that most breast-deflating comes from losing the weight after pregnancy, not from the act of nursing. So, go ahead and try it, and if it doesn't work for you, quit, because it's six of one, half dozen of the other where your breasts are concerned.

The Behind

You may ask yourself sometime during this pregnancy, "If the baby is in my belly, why is it my butt that's growing?" After a few visits to the zoo and a lot of Discovery Channel watching, I have developed my own hackneyed explanation for why our hips and butts get involved in pregnancy when it really doesn't seem to be any of their business. Have you ever noticed how the chimpanzees and orangutans walk around with their babies on the back of their hips? Who knows, maybe nature intended to provide a rumble seat for our little ones, since only kangaroos and other marsupials are blessed with those handy pouches to tuck their babies in. If my theory is correct, that this fat pocket is simply a holdover from our caveman days, then a few more evolutionary generations of using umbrella strollers should eliminate this problem entirely.

Then again, there is the traditional explanation that nature wants to ensure that the fetus won't starve, so it forces your body to carry around emergency food supplies in the form of fat on your hips, butt, upper arms—and let's not forget the face! That might explain the existence of the fat, but it doesn't go far in explaining why the butt takes on the roundness of a bubble. Remember this anatomical fact when we get to the chapter on maternity fashion, because there is nothing worse than a too-short shirt hiking up over that bubble to make you look like the Queen of the Wide-Asses. Even if you don't get very fat, your backside will take on a new silhouette.

Hair (and Nails)

One last area of accelerated growth is your hair. It's as if the protein button is permanently pushed on in pregnancy, as most pregnant women find that their hair seems longer and thicker than ever before. Not only does your hair grow faster than usual, but your body is also signaling your scalp not to release old hairs as frequently as it used to. Therefore you get *more* and *and* longer hair. This is one of nature's consolation prizes: You get big as a Volkswagen, but you have more lustrous hair than a Breck Girl.

If that was all there was to this hair business, it would be a dream come true, but there always seems to be a catch, doesn't there? The first catch is your scalp, which we will discuss shortly. Another problem is that sometimes it's not just the hair on your head that accelerates in growth when you are pregnant; it can be the hair all over your body. Some women find their pubic hair stretching farther up their bellies and down their thighs. Others sprout a hair or two along the outline of their nipples. And some find a downy fuzz growing on their jawline and cheeks or on their backs between their shoulders.

The texture of your hair and its personality will also change during pregnancy. Because of this, another cardinal rule from *The Girlfriends' Guide* is: NEVER GET A PERM WHEN YOU ARE PREGNANT! Chances are good that if you do, you will find that only some of your hair "grabs" the perm, and that other huge portions remain straight and unaffected, leaving you looking like Edward Scissorhands.

A big dilemma for the pregnant woman is whether to continue coloring her hair during pregnancy. As opinionated as the *Guide* can be, we will control ourselves long enough to present both sides about hair color. This is a decision that you must make after consultation with your doctor. There are some people who would no sooner put chemicals on their hair when pregnant than drink a Diet Coke. They wish to protect their unborn children from as many toxic substances as possible; in the world teeming with pollution, malathion and radon, the last thing they want to do is voluntarily ingest more chemicals. There. That said, we can get on with other opinions, namely mine. Being an older mother, I was certain that my natural hair color was probably not only boring brown, but boring brown streaked with gray (YIKES!). I am not sure, because I haven't seen my natural hair color in nearly two decades, but it seems like a reasonable assumption. Therefore, it would take nothing short of a nuclear disaster for me to show the world my real hair. Then again, I was known to drink a Diet Coke now and then, too. So shoot me!

Before you reach for that peroxide bottle, however, there are a couple of things you should know. First, because your hair will be growing so much faster now, you will need to color your roots more often than before. Unless you color your own hair at home, this will soon become very expensive. If you are, like Madonna, a platinum blonde of brunette descent, you could have a stripe down the middle of your head every two to three weeks. Second, the smell of ammonia and bleach will be unbearable early in your pregnancy; after all, they are nearly unbearable when you're not pregnant. And, third, you may just be too plain old tired to get to the beauty salon as often as before. These are all good reasons to change your hair to a shade that is closer to the one God gave you so that you can get away with less frequent coloring, or to consider alternatives to permanent hair color, like rinses or vegetable dyes.

The last, and perhaps most important, rule about hair during pregnancy is this: DO NOT CUT YOUR HAIR OFF WHEN YOU ARE PREGNANT! This advice may sound like it's out of left field right now, but trust us, there will come a time when you will consider cutting all your hair off. This is never a good idea, because a very pregnant woman who wants to cut her hair is not really looking for a new hairdo, she is looking for a new, *nonpregnant*, look, and I'm afraid that's too tall an order for a haircut. I know how simple and carefree a short, boyish bob can sound at about seven months, but pregnancy is not the time to try it out. Don't forget, your face is pregnant now, too, and you need bone structure to pull off that Linda Evangelista look. Sure, Mia Farrow looked adorable with short hair when she was pregnant in *Rosemary's Baby,* but remember, that was a *pretend* pregnancy; she didn't have to really get pregnant to get that role, and besides, remember *that* baby? Between us Girlfriends, you may end up looking more like a Pinhead than Mia Farrow if you cut your hair when you are ripe with child. And your husband, whose nerves are already pretty raw at this point, will probably snap if you cut your hair, since we all know most men prefer long hair under any circumstances, even if it makes you look like Fabio.

To let you know how overwhelming this haircutting urge can be, I provide my own experience. I have always known this prohibition against changing hairstyles in pregnancy, and I was able to withstand the temptation for three whole pregnancies! Then, during my fourth pregnancy, I decided to test the rule. Perhaps I thought it was a stupid rule, or that it didn't apply to me. Who knows what insanity was racing through my brain? So in I went and lopped all my hair off, and never did a human head more resemble a coconut. Trust me, it wasn't a bad haircut. If you are puffy and overtired, there is no haircut in the world that will make you look better.

The other protein in your body that will be growing as fast as your hair will be your fingernails and toenails. If you have previously had the flimsy kind of nails that bend and peel, you will love the new nails you get to enjoy during pregnancy. They are not only growing faster, they are harder and healthier. In fact, if you notice your nails getting worse rather than better at this time, you should discuss it with your doctor immediately, because it could indicate that your body is not getting enough protein to keep you and the baby healthy.

This is a good time to pay more attention to manicures and pedicures. If you can find the time and the money, have them done in a salon. You could use an hour or two of someone massaging your hands and feet. Besides, as pregnancy progresses, only the most limber and determined of us will still be able to cut and paint our own toenails. You will enjoy having pretty hands, expecially when you have a sense that everything else about your appearance is questionable. Around the third trimester, you will be tempted to ignore the pedicures, not just because they become impossible to do yourself, but because you so rarely see your own feet anymore that you never notice if they look groomed. But this is when pedicures become particularly important, because your toes are usually right in your obstetrician's face during internal exams and even more so during the long hours of labor and delivery. I gave up the bikini waxes about seven months into pregnancy, mostly because I couldn't see my pubic hairs from any angle, but I ferociously kept up appearances where my feet were concerned. One Girlfriend took this advice so much to heart that when her water broke, she immediately ran for the nail polish. She sat on a staircase to paint her toes so that she could reach them all. Then, she slipped on some rubber sandals and left for the hospital. By the time she finished checking in and getting to a room, her pedicure was dry. Now that's a woman with standards!

Your Skin

Pregnancy can be a very trying experience for your skin. First there is the obvious challenge of stretching enough to allow for the growth of another human being within your body. You may sometimes wonder, too, whether your skin will be able to encompass your gigantic breasts without suffering some kind of permanent damage. The bottom line, of course, is that the skin will stretch to meet these challenges. Have you ever heard of anyone who just spontaneously rips open under the pressure of pregnancy, even in the *National Enquirer?* But this stretching will not be entirely without incident. Let's talk about some of the specifics, shall we?

Stretch Marks

Stretch marks are lines on your skin that look like runs in your stockings, if you can imagine your breasts, behind and belly wearing stockings. They occur when the skin stretches more than it wants to. During pregnancy, they look rather reddish or purplish, but long after the baby is born they will look almost white or silver. All Girlfriends ask each other if they got stretch marks, as if to determine whether God was fair when he made it happen. It's sort of like, "I got them, and I will be pretty disappointed if I'm the only one in our gang who did, damn it!" Here's the news on stretch marks: THE ONLY SURE WAY TO GUARANTEE THAT YOU WON'T GET STRETCH MARKS IS TO MAKE SURE YOU ARE BORN TO A WOMAN WHO DIDN'T GET THEM, AND WHOSE MOTHER DIDN'T GET THEM EITHER. In other words, it is largely a matter of heredity whether you will get stretch marks. What about all of those lotions and oils that are for sale, you ask? Useless! Go ahead and massage them in if you like the smell or if you are one of those who believe that it doesn't hurt to cover all the bases, but they cannot fight genetics.

Those creams, lotions and oils *can* come in handy for another reason. They might help soothe the itchiness that comes from skin being stretched mercilessly. Some women really suffer with this itchiness, and their temptation, especially when they get undressed for the day, is to scratch their bellies and sides until there are fingernail marks on their skin. If this gets really out of control for you, tell your doctor, because there are creams and antihistamines that can be prescribed to keep you from tearing yourself to shreds. But if you are only mildly itchy, it might be pleasurable to massage yourself with these magic salves. If you can get your husband to play along, you can use the lotions and oils to lubricate all sorts of things, if you know what I mean.

By the way, I have never really found stretch marks to be the odious things that some people think they are. I suppose if you put on a bikini and go out for a sunbath, they can be a tad imperfect, but after you have children, you will probably find that bikinis just don't cut it anymore (be honest now!), and everyone knows a suntan is a terrible idea. Stretch marks hardly show if you keep them out of the sun.

Your Complexion

Quite frequently, newly pregnant women get pimples for the first time since they were teenagers. As you know, hormones are very potent chemicals, and they can mess up your skin almost as much as they mess up your emotions. There is not really anything you can do about this zittiness; it just has to pass on its own. Trust us—it will pass as soon as your body equalizes its hormonal seesaw. In the meantime, you can help matters by keeping your skin clean and *not picking!* Perhaps if you take extra time making your hair look great, no one will notice your bumps.

Again on the subject of hair, you may find it heavy and dull early in pregnancy. This is because your scalp, which, being skin, is subject to the same hormonal haywire that is affecting your face. You may find that your scalp is oily or flaky for the first time in your life. The Girlfriends offer this general rule: Always have scrupulously clean hair when pregnant. If you think you can go one more day before you need to shampoo, you will generally be wrong. Heavy hair that hugs your skull will do absolutely nothing to draw attention away from your face and its problems.

Another way in which your skin might tick you off is by getting little red dots or broken capillaries. They are small and not particularly unattractive, but they may bug you. The red pin-dots usually come during the pregnancy and the broken capillaries are usually the result of a lot of long, hard pushing during delivery. You usually have to have them removed by a doctor after the pregnancy, since they tend to stay with you long after the child has grown up and gone to college.

In keeping with your general condition of overall fertility, you may find strange things growing on your skin. Lots of my Girfriends got skin tags, which are little teeny flaps of extra skin. Two popular places for a tag is under your arm, and on your eyelid. Perhaps this is because there is skin rubbing on skin in these locations. One of my Girlfriends even got one on her labia. They aren't dangerous at all, unless you pick them, in which case they could become infected. Just leave them alone, and later they can be easily removed.

Changing Colors

Pregnancy does a very interesting thing to your pigment, and this is a subject that is not often discussed by anyone other than your Girlfriends. You will change colors in all sorts of places. The first change you may notice will be that your nipples get darker. If they were pink before, they will look more purple when you are pregnant, and if they were beige before, they will turn brown. The nipples and the surrounding pigmented area also get substantially larger, so that what was once the size of a half-dollar may grow to be about the size of a small pancake. The Girlfriends have found that after pregnancy, the nipples may return to approximately their former size, but they will never regain their former color.

Here's a news flash that your doctor will probably never point out to you (unless you live in Berkeley·) Your labia (in other words, the "lips" of your vagina) change color, too, when you are pregnant. They get darker and more engorged with blood. Take a hand mirror and look for yourself if you don't believe me. Just as your nipples get bigger, so do your sexual organs. This change might sound a bit alarming to you at first, but nobody really sees it besides your husband and your doctor, so don't be embarrassed. Of course, you may want to reassure your husband that this is a completely natural state of affairs, because oral sex could seem to him like an athletic feat at this time. The best news about the changes "down below" is that many Girlfriends feel like they live in a state of constant sexual arousal because their organs are engorged with blood. My Girlfriend Tracy says that she became nearly orgasmic if she walked very far because the action of her legs rubbing together was like never-ending foreplay. Kind of makes a trip to the mall an entirely new experience, don't you think? But there is one minor drawback to the swelling down there, and that is the sudden inability to aim your urine stream. I know that might sound like a meaningless complaint, but you will often be asked to pee in a specimen cup, and it would be nice if you could do so without getting your hand wet. (Incidentally, my Girlfriend Shannon says that the lips on her face, not just her vaginal lips, also got fuller and darker. Wouldn't you just love to have that happen to you? I don't know; my lips stayed pretty much the same and I still lived for my lipstick pencil, but who knows, you may be as lucky as Shannon.)

Pigment can also play nasty tricks on pregnant women. Some Caucasian women get what is diabolically described as "The Mask of Pregnancy" on their face, which usually looks like you got a skier's tan on your cheeks and forehead, but that you had sunblock on the rest of your face. This irregular coloring goes away after pregnancy, but it can take a while. Stay out of the sun, because it only makes matters worse, and try foundation makeup to blend everything together.

Almost every pregnant woman will eventually get a pigment stripe that extends from the top of her pubic hair toward her belly button. We have no explanations for this; we just know it happened to all of us. It was less noticeable on the Girlfriends with more olive or brown in their skin, but on the Irish girls like me, it was pretty obvious. People will tell you that this irregular pigmentation goes away after pregnancy, but I don't think it ever really does for some of us less fortunate types. Maybe it is just my imagination, but I think I can still see that trail when I slouch and my baby belly folds over itself. I also think the fine hair that covers my belly has remained darker in the middle. Of course, my belly has not seen the light of day since my first pregnancy seven years ago, so the contrast between light skin and dark hair is glaringly apparent. No wonder six million people (almost exclusively men) are fans of *Baywatch*. A really good stomach is rarely seen by the father of young children, especially in the privacy of his own bedroom.

4

"I Never Imagined My Body Could Feel Like This!"

People tend to concentrate on the millions of external physical changes that occur to pregnant women, but the internal changes, not even including those in your uterus, are equally dramatic. As we have pointed out, pregnancy is not limited to your womb, it is a full-body experience, and you may be shocked by how strange and different your body will feel. Everything from stuffy noses to burping can be pregnancy-related.

Your Digestion

A pregnant woman's digestive processes are slowed way down by the pregnancy hormones. Evidently, nature wants to ensure that every last vitamin and mineral is extracted from every morsel of food that you eat, so it lets the food sit in your stomach longer than usual. What that means for you can be reduced to two words: *burping* and *farting*.

You may be loath to admit it, but if you take a poll of husbands of pregnant women, they will be unanimous in their astonishment at how much free-floating gas there is. All that food just sitting around in your intestines ferments, and you become carbonated. The indelicacy of this condition suggests to me that pregnancy is one of life's best reminders that we are just a few generations removed from dragging our knuckles on the ground when we walk. But if you start thinking that life is unfair for making women endure such a humiliating experience as pregnancy, remember this: It is men who go bald.

Let's start with the flatulence. It isn't much of a problem if you spend a lot of time alone or with children under the age of four. In fact, young children are deeply respectful of people who can pass wind on command. It will shock and offend your husband, but even the most fastidious pregnant women soon tire of leaping out of bed or fluffing the sheets surreptitiously, and they soon just let it rip with little regard to whether their beloved mate is present or not. But, in our inimitable way of caring more about what near strangers think of us than about what our spouses think, being out in public can be fraught with anxiety for those of us with gas. Unfortunately, most of us are not as well-adjusted as my Girlfriend Corki, who will stand up in a small gathering of people and leave the room, announcing over her shoulder, "Excuse me, but I have to fart now." The rest of us feel the slightest intestinal pressure and rush to the ladies' room, praying the whole way that no one else is in there.

Burping is equally hard to control. You can be in the middle of telling an interesting story and out sneaks a little belch, as if it were an exclamation point. These burps often come out of nowhere with no warning, leaving the burper as shocked as her audience. And pregnant burps are usually not the short little gasps that most women insist they make; they are long, ripping sounds that would make any adolescent boy jealous.

Unless your doctor will allow you to take antacids, which we will discuss later in more detail, there really aren't that many things you can do to relieve all this gas. You should probably avoid carbonated drinks and see if that helps. It seems to the Girlfriends, though, that the biggest gas offenders are precisely the foods that you are supposed to eat to make a healthy baby—things like broccoli, spinach and cauliflower. What's worse, these foods give an aroma to the burps as well.

Another effect of this relaxation of your digestive muscles can be heartburn. Heartburn, in case you have never had the joy of experiencing it, feels just like it sounds. It is a burning sensation at the base of your esophagus—usually on the left side, it seems—and it can often go hand in hand with burping. It's like an upset stomach, but it's up higher, closer to your chest.

Some women suffer from heartburn throughout their entire pregnancy. Others don't succumb until the baby has grown large enough to put pressure on the muscle that keeps food down in the stomach where it belongs and interfere with it closing tightly. This can result in stomach acids leaking out. Certain foods seem to make heartburn worse, much like the burping agents, but while I personally was willing to forgo my ration of legumes and brussels sprouts in the name of keeping the burn and gas down, I could not give up my daily ration of peanut M&M's, and they were the worst culprits of all.

If you are lucky, and if you have selected your obstetrician well, you will be allowed to take antacids. Antacids become a pregnant woman's best friend, and it is wise to have them with you at all times. My Girlfriend Julee had huge bottles of the chewable kind in her car, beside her bed and at work. When you want an antacid, you *really* want one, and you want it *now*. They are chalky and disgusting, even if they do now come in a rainbow of fruit flavors, but, believe me, they actually begin to taste good after a while. A Girlfriends' tip, always check your mouth in a mirror after eating an antacid, because they can leave you with white chalky stuff on your lips or at the corners of your mouth.

One last important bit of information regarding heartburn: No matter what people may try to tell you, HEARTBURN DOES NOT MEAN THAT YOUR BABY WILL BE BORN WITH LOTS OF HAIR. I had heartburn so badly in all four of my pregnancies that I could have spit fire, and all my kids were born as bald as Uncle Fester.

Morning Sickness

As soon as a woman announces that she is pregnant, people ask her if she is feeling sick yet. This is because the stereotypical pregnancy includes a good season of nausea. This nausea, with or without vomiting, is called morning sickness. The Girlfriends and I think that it should be called something more accurate and suitably dramatic, like "progesterone poisoning." Calling it morning sickness is particularly misleading because it can strike you at *any* time of the day or night. Some women even find that they feel seminauseous all their waking hours.

There is some good news about morning sickness. First, not everyone experiences it. Second, if you do have it, it should go away by the end of the first three months, never to return again (please don't hold me to this). And third, there is a popular, old-fashioned belief that the worse your morning sickness is, the less likely you are to have a miscarriage. I guess it is because it is believed that those babies of particularly green mothers are already exercising such control over their mothers' systems that nothing is going to get rid of them. All I know is, every time my doctor's nurse asked me how I was feeling and I answered "Sick," she smiled and replied, "Good!"

The first and foremost Girlfriends' rule about morning sickness is this: IF YOU GET MORNING SICKNESS, IT DOES NOT MEAN THAT YOU HAVE DONE ANYTHING WRONG DURING YOUR PREGNANCY OR THAT YOU ARE AMBIV-ALENT ABOUT HAVING THIS BABY! Remember how PMS and cramps used to be considered psychosomatic, and doctors told women that they were only experiencing these manifestations be-cause they were weak or crazy? Then they realized that the massive hormonal fluctuations that women experience each month would bring Hulk Hogan to his knees. There are still some assholes who will suggest that you are barfing your brians out because you are not sure if you are ready to become a mother. Heck, if that were the case, then all women with half a brain would be vomiting all the time, because any fool is smart enough to know that motherhood is a very scary business. If you feel nauseous, it's probably because you and progesterone just don't get along. That's it; nothing more.

Morning sickness and seasickness have a lot in common. I have had the nausea that comes with pregnancy, and I have been on a round-bottomed ship in a storm at sea, and the experiences were really quite similar. For example, they both strike an otherwise healthy person. They also have what I call a "head component"; your equilibrium is affected and you might feel dizzy or spacey. Also, I found that there was no relief from seasickness or morning sickness in throwing up, as there can be with stomach flu or food poisoning. Some of my Girlfriends felt otherwise about this, but my experience was that I barfed, I continued to feel sick and I barfed some more. For this reason, it really doesn't pay to stick your finger down your throat in a desperate attempt to rid your body of the offending poison.

Since "progesterone poisoning" has little to do with what you have eaten, you don't stop vomiting simply because you don't have any more food in your stomach. You just move on the dry heaves or, worse, spitting up stomach bile. Yet even though most women do not get sick *because* of something they have eaten, the sight or smell of particular foods can accelerate the gagging. That, too, is true of seasickness. A whiff of cottage cheese can send a victim of either malady running for the toilet, even if she hasn't actually eaten any of it.

You may be asking yourself right now, "How do I know if I will have morning sickness in my pregnancy?" The answer is, "You can't predict." Even if you have been pregnant before and sailed right past morning sickness, it doesn't mean you won't get it this time or some other time. Some of my Girlfriends suggest that there is a link between the sex of the baby and whether you will be nauseous. They seem to feel that carrying a girl might make you sicker than carrying a boy. I have no idea if this is true, and I was ill with all four of my kids, so it sounds a little like hoodoo talk to me. I would imagine that the "scientific" explanation could be the presence of the extra female hormones that a baby girl might share with your body—a sort of estrogen overload. But for every Girlfriend who has told me that she was sicker with her girl babies, I have another who swears that pregnancies with boys were more nauseating. By the way, another wives' tale is that baby girls make your face distort more, and I *swear* that was true with me.

Morning sickness is not necessarily one of the very first physical signs that tell you that you are pregnant. What usually happens is, you find out you are pregnant and you feel pretty normal in the digestive sense for another couple of weeks. You will be tempted to start congratulating yourself that your superior health and positive attitude (or the power of your prayers) have conspired to spare you the nausea that lesser mortals have to endure. Then, one morning you walk downstairs in your nightie to get some orange juice from the refrigerator. You open the door of the fridge and get a whiff of last night's meat loaf. Next thing you know, you are puking in the kitchen sink.

Morning sickness does not strike all its victims with equal intensity. Its severity can almost be measured on a sliding scale. At one end are those lucky ones who have one green moment and then never feel a bit of nausea for the rest of their pregnancy. At the other end are those who vomit so much that they actually lose weight in their first trimester. Some of these poor women actually end up in the hospital, where doctors can make sure they don't become dehydrated. You want to know how demented I am? I actually felt a pang of envy for those women who were staying thin, even if it meant that they vomited frequently, while I was getting fatter by the day. Then over the course of time I learned that even those pregnant women who were sick as dogs in the first trimester ended up gaining as much weight as those who never met a meal they couldn't force down. I guess it pays to be careful what you wish for.

I have one Girlfriend, Mary, who was so used to being in a constant state of nausea with all three of her pregnancies that she just decided to go on with her life as if nothing were unusual. She would go about her daily business, stopping to vomit when it became necessary. She said that she did not go anywhere without knowing in advance where the nearest bathroom was so that she could streak to it should the need arise. She also kept towels on the passenger seat of her car so that she wouldn't vomit all over herself when she was caught in some traffic jam and feeling ill. I was always so impressed with her matter-of-factness when I would see her at Mommy and Me classes with two kids and pregnant with a third. She would calmly, but very quickly, excuse herself from a verse or two of "The Wheels on the Bus Go Round and Round," go vomit, rinse and come back to the group in time for the part about the wipers on the bus going swish, swish, swish. We all knew where she had been and what she had done, but she never mentioned it, let alone complained about it. She became a sort of hero to the rest of us, who were complaining about everything all the time.

In the middle of the spectrum is where you will find most of us. We have our good days and our days when we want to die. On the bad days, even staying in bed doesn't provide relief, because we feel just as horrid lying down as we do standing up. So, we generally get up and face the day, just counting the hours till we can go to sleep and start a new—and, we pray, better—day. For those of us in the middle, morning sickness doesn't necessarily mean constant vomiting. In fact, I only vomited a few times with each pregnancy, but I felt mildly ill much of the time. It wasn't unusual for me to have to leave meetings or luncheons to get some fresh air during the first trimester of my pregnancies because I was afraid of either fainting or gagging in front of people who I didn't think would understand.

I wish that I could tell you about a secret remedy that would make all pregnancy-related nausea disappear, but I haven't found it in years of looking. What follows, however, is a list of my Girlfriends' guidelines:

The **10** Commandments of Morning Sickness

1 Eat Small Amounts of Bland Foods All Day Long.

2 Don't Eat Anything That Doesn't Smell Appealing to You.

3 Eat Something at Around 4:00 A.M., or After Your Last Middle-of-the-Night Visit to the Toilet.

4 Take Your Prenatal Vitamins at Night, or Stop Altogether Until You Are Feeling Better. (Your Doctor May Want You to Take Folic Acid Supplements in the Meantime.)

5 Do Not Take Your Vitamins With Citrus Juice.

6 When Nothing Sounds Appetizing, Try a Bowl of Cereal With Milk or a Piece of Sweet Fruit.

7 If the Thought of Chewing Any Kind of Food Makes You Sick, Try Sucking on Natural Licorice Drops (They Can Be Soothing).

8 Try Wearing the Elastic Wristbands That Are Sold in Pharmacies to Prevent Seasickness.

9   Skip the Saltines Unless You Have a Real Craving for Them (Which I Can't Imagine Unless You Are a Parrot).

10   Follow Your Cravings. If You Really Want Some Particular Type of Food, There Is a Good Chance It Will Actually Make You Feel a Little Better If You Eat It. (Just Be Careful If Your Cravings Are Consistently for Chocolate and Ice Cream, Like Mine Were.)

Most women find that morning sickness disappears at right about the three-month mark. It is truly a magical feeling the day you wake up, brush your teeth without activating your gag reflex, get dressed without having to pause to put your head in the toilet, and go to the kitchen eagerly thinking of breakfast. And it happens just like that: One day you are miserable and cooling your cheeks on the bathroom floor, and the next day you've never felt better.

Your Bowels

As I have said before, there is really no aspect of your physical being that is unaffected by pregnancy, and this even applies to your bowel movements. First of all, if you are taking one of the popular brands of prescription prenatal vitamins, you may find that your poops are the color of tire rubber. I think it has something to do with all the iron you are taking, but I don't really know. It's just one more thing about your life that will seem strange—even your bowel movements become unrecognizable!

And, as if you don't feel full enough down there already, with the baby and the fluid and the placenta and God knows what else all jammed into an area that you once were proud of to show off in a crop top, pregnancy adds one more ingredient: lingering poopoo. Yes, you may notice that you just aren't the same "regular" gal you were before you were pregnant. Perhaps it is the iron in your prenatal vitamins again, or it may just be the relaxation of your entire digestive tract, but constipation can be a real annoyance for pregnant women.

How upsetting you will find this unpredictability of bowel movements will depend on a variety of factors. My Girlfriend Andrea, for example, determines the mood of her entire day based on a successful b.m., in the morning, whether she is pregnant or not. Constipation can also be particularly upsetting if you already feel uncomfortable about how round your stomach is becoming. And if you are begining to feel more than a little pissed off at how unfamiliar your body is in so many ways, then this can be the straw that breaks the camel's back. Constipation is one area where I remained fairly relaxed, probably because I had never heard of anyone succumbing to a poop explosion, and because anal issues are generally not where my neuroses lie. What goes in must eventually come out, no matter how hard and dark, is my philosophy. Many of my Girlfriends disagree, however, and they were willing to try anything short of scheduling colonics to rid themselves of that "full of shit" feeling.

Traditional books on pregnancy will tell you to increase the amount of fiber you eat and to drink more water. I believe, however, that you can eat bran and drink water until you're ready to explode and your bowel movements will not really get any more manageable. I think that ingesting something more akin to WD-40 and dynamite would be much more effective (but not particularly nutritious for the baby).

Talk to your doctor if you are constipated. Don't be ashamed to have such an indelicate conversation with him or her; believe me, far more indelicate things are going to happen in your relationship in the near future. Ask if you can take fiber tablets like psyllium husks, or a fiber drink. If things get really stopped up, ask about taking a stool softener. I took one that was a small gelatinous pill, and it really got things moving after three or four days of use (plus, it was a cinch to swallow, which is much appreciated on those gagging days).

JUST MAKE SURE THAT WHATEVER YOU TAKE CONTAINS NO LAXATIVES. Laxatives can really screw up your digestion, you can get "addicted" to them and they can make your stomach cramp up as in labor. Not to mention that that last thing your little baby needs is something to make *him* poop uncontrollably.

My Girlfriend Denise reminded me of one of the most disconcerting aspects of pregnancy: "elimination" and the public rest room. Sometimes pregnant women find they must work very hard to accomplish a bowel movement. In fact, some of my Girlfriends have said that they remember times they pushed so hard to "move" that they got sweaty at their hairlines and made humilating grunting noises. This can be horrifying enough in the privacy of your own home, but it is much, much worse if you are at work and using the employees' bathroom. It isn't so bad in a very public place like Disney World or the beach because, honestly, what do you care what complete strangers think? (Unless, of course, they tap on the door to see if you are all right, or worse, shout from their place on the line forming outside your door asking if you plan to spend the day in there.) But to have the office gossip or your own secretary in the stall next to you can be so inhibiting that you would rather succumb to fecal poisoning than do what it takes to poop.

There is a bright side to this difficulty in pooping, which is that you can consider those big-effort eliminations to be practice runs for delivery, because a proper delivery push feels *exactly* like the most difficult bowel movement you have ever had in your life. Keep this sensation in mind, and you will know what to do when the doctor tells you it is time to push.

This description of forcing a movement may run afoul of everything your good, overly attentive mother has told you since you stopped wearing diapers. Remember, they said, "Don't push too hard or you'll get hemorrhoids." And guess what: This time Mother may have known what she was talking about. Nonetheless, pushing too hard sometimes happens without our realizing it until it is too late, which leads us nicely to:

Hemorrhoids

If you are like me, you have grown up seeing "those" commercials, but you never really paused to think about *where* those people were putting that miraculous cream—or *why* they were putting it anywhere, for that matter. Well, my innocent little Girlfriends, they were putting it around their anuses, and they were stooping to that indignity because they had little protrusions like peas down there that hurt and itched them to distraction. Don't you just want to scream? It is almost too horrifying to talk about, but as your Girlfriend, I will.

There are various ways to get hemorrhoids, so it is rather like running an obstacle course: You may have successfully leapt over the fence, but you may still fall into the mud pit. First, you can get hemorrhoids (or what colorful older folks call "piles," for reasons I don't even want to speculate about) from pushing too hard to move your bowels. We have just discussed this, so you know that I am not blaming you. Too much pressure down there can cause some of the anal tissue to herniate and stick out, either individually or in little clusters like grapes.

Another way you can get them is just by virtue of being pregnant, hard poops or not. You see, the weight of the baby and all the other stuff in your abdomen that is supporting it gets so heavy that it can cut off the circulation in the veins and arteries down there, much like a car tire driving over a garden hose will stop water from coming out. When the rosy area down there gets its blood all pooled up, it's grape time again.

Then, just when you think that you have dodged all the hemorrhoid bullets that nature can shoot your way, it's DELIVERY TIME! That was it for me—my Armageddon, my Alamo, my Little Bighorn. I was just fine, black poops and all, until I pushed my first baby out—and evidently, part of my rectum as well. After the epidural wore off, I hurt in that general area, but I had an episiotomy and a small tear that required some stitches, so I attributed the pain to those things and didn't do any investigating for the first couple of days. Besides, I was not particularly eager to touch any stitches down there anyway.

When I got home from the hospital and took a shower, I absentmindedly soaped up to wash my "privates," and I nearly fainted dead away with the shock of what I felt. In the soft tissue around my anus were these grapelike clumps of tissue. It felt as though my insides were on the outside.

I immediately went to bed and cried. (At least until a certain newcomer started wailing even louder.) I had no idea what I had felt, but I was certain that no one else had ever experienced anything like it before and that I would probably die of it (or at least require a rectum tuck). I was so mortified that I didn't mention my condition to anyone—not my husband (who doesn't have the stomach for such things anyway), not my Girlfriends (who I was afraid would pity me and know that I was disfigured) and certainly not my doctor.

Finally, after not having heard from me since the delivery, my doctor called to see how I was doing, and I blurted out, "There is something growing out of my behind and it hurts worse than my stitches!" I was shocked and relieved to learn that he knew exactly what I was talking about, and that he even had some suggestions to make me feel better. I couldn't believe it—there were actually prescription creams to shrink the hemorrhoids and to lessen the pain and irritation. My doctor also prescribed suppositories, which I suppose were intended to do the same shrinking and relieving on my insides, but I can't tell you if they worked because, five years later, they are still in my medicine cabinet, unopened. My doctor was crazy if he thought I was going to try to shove something up there in my condition.

My Girlfriend Jaye had such a bad hemorrhoid problem after the birth of her first child that she saw a proctologist during her second and third pregnancies. Evidently, he gave her cortisone shots in her you-know-what. While the thought of that procedure makes me go numb, Jaye assures me that they didn't really hurt and that they saved her from a shower horror like mine. (She giggles when she describes having sat in the proctologist's office, since everyone else in the waiting room was concerned about his prostate and/or was over the age of seventy. Everyone had a pretty good idea of what part of her anatomy was being treated because, let's face it, no one goes to a proctologist for a second opinion about open-heart surgery.)

Here is a Girlfriends' list of things to try for relief of hemorrhoids (subject, of course, to your doctor's approval):

Ask for a prescription cream or ointment to help shrink the hemorrhoids and relieve the discomfort.

Use witch hazel on cotton pads or use medicated hemorrhoid pads whenever the opportunity arises, and certainly every time you use the toilet. They will keep the area clean and contribute to the shrinking process.

Take lots of baths. The warm water is not only soothing (and the weightlessness of your body a relief), but it keeps the area scrupulously clean, which helps prevent infection. Someone may suggest that you take a *sitz bath*. What they are referring to is sitting in a few inches of the hottest water you can stand for twenty to thirty minutes at a time. But my personal feeling is that if you have that kind of time on your hands, go to sleep instead. You will forget all about your hemorrhoids while in slumberland.

Have some kind person go to a pharmacy and buy you a hemorrhoid pillow, which looks like a large firm donut. In fact, if you live in a two-story house, have the kind person buy you two so that you don't have to try to carry both your baby and your donut up and down the stairs at the same time. Better still, invest in one of those circular baby pillows, which you can find in many of the mail-order catalogs. You know the ones: They are covered in bright and cheerful cotton, and the baby is supposed to sit in the hole in the middle and be propped up by the surrounding pillow. I have never yet seen a baby who wanted to be seated in one of these contraptions, but they sure are great for the moms.

If all else fails, there is always very successful surgery in this area. It is even covered by most insurance policies.

5

Pregnancy Insanity

he physical changes brought on by pregnancy are numerous and extreme enough to give a woman whiplash, but they would probably be ultimately manageable if they were not accompanied by some pretty hefty emotional changes. The inner life of many pregnant women is scary enough to make their husbands anxious and vigilant and their friends impatient and annoyed. I was so bitchy during one of my pregnancies that my friends finally stopped trying to spare my feelings and just told me to "shut up" whenever they had heard enough. Some pregnant women become short-fused and extremely rigid. For example, if we were to ask my Girlfriend Janis out for lunch, she would have all sorts of rules, like we had to eat at 12:15 exactly, no sooner and no later, and the restaurant chairs had to have arms or she wouldn't be comfortable enough to digest her food.

Keep this Girlfriend rule of thumb in mind as you read this chapter: CRAZY PEOPLE ARE OFTEN THE LAST TO KNOW THEY ARE CRAZY. Therefore, if you are tempted to skip to the next chapter because you don't see how this one applies to you, think again; you may be crazier than you look (at least to yourself). In fact, ask around, because you may be surprised to learn that you, too, are a victim of the Body Snatchers.

One aspect of Pregnancy Insanity feels quite like PMS. The answer to the question "How long will this feeling last?" is "About forty weeks." Like everything else in pregnancy, its severity varies not just from person to person, but from day to day. This will be good news to those of you really feeling the effects of the Insanity, and not-so-good news for those of you who maintain that you have never felt better in your life.

Here is another bit of Girlfriend advice: If your friends who have been pregnant tell you that it was the most emotionally fulfilling and happiest time of their life, don't believe them. Those kinds of comments invariably make you feel as if there is something wrong with you if you don't feel equally ecstatic, and they are undoubtedly inaccurate. There is some strange biological force that gives women amnesia about the pregnancy experience, so that they forget the less savory details and see the whole thing in a sort of rosy glow. This is just nature's way of making sure that women get pregnant more than once; if you remembered too much, you might never repeat the experience.

What follows are various manifestations of Pregnancy Insanity. You probably will know them all at some time during gestation; let's hope you won't feel them all at the same time!

"I Can't Concentrate Anymore!"

At no time this distant from the onset of Alzheimer's disease will you experience such forgetfulness and lack of logical thinking. Part of this feeblemindedness can be attributed simply to the overloading of the pregnant woman's brain circuitry: there is just so darn much to think about! You have to decide who your doctor will be, what hospital you want to deliver the baby in, whether you want to know the baby's gender in advance, whether you should get prenatal genetics testing, how to tell your boss that you will be needing a maternity leave, how to tell your husband that your mother will be staying with you for a few weeks after the baby comes, and so on and so on. It is only rational and natural that you should feel confused and out of control at a time like this.

But there is more to this aspect of Pregnancy Insanity. Many pregnant women also exhibit a sort of foggy, daydreamy behavior. You know what I am talking about: the state of mind that allows you to drive all the way home from work with your dry cleaning on the roof of your car, or to sit in a meeting for hours and not remember a single thing.

Perhaps you and your baby are already talking to each other: planning, imagining one another's face, being shy about your first meeting. Perhaps you are wondering what a son will be like or whether your daughter will be nicer to you as a teenager than you were to your mother. You wonder if your child will ever do anything to make you burst with pride, like Bill Clinton did for Virginia Kelley. You worry that they may do something to totally embarrass you, like Roger Clinton did for Virginia Kelley. These reveries are so compelling that other people's chatter may seem irrelevant to you and you may want to shake them by the shoulders and shout, "Don't you know the universe is being forever altered because I am having a baby?" You might become a bit worried about how this lack of concentration will affect your ability to care for your baby when it is born. This is not the time to fret. This absentmindedness is small potatoes compared with how distracted you will be once you have a child in your home to worry about until the day you die. Enjoy how low the stakes still are, because once the baby is born, you will have to worry about more realistic catastrophes, like setting the baby down someplace and driving off without it.

"Diaper Commercials Make Me Weep!"

One of the more harmless aspects of the emotional spin cycle of pregnancy is how sentimental Girlfriends become. Nearly every mother has a recollection of crying at diaper or formula commercials on television when she was pregnant. I used to love the commercials for health care plans that showed babies being born to deliriously happy couples. One night, toward the end of my first pregnancy, I sat in my son's waiting nursery and played a cassette of lullabies and sobbed until my husband worried that I might need to seek professional care.

My Girlfriend Maryann, who recently found out she is pregnant, tells me that she is frequently overwhelmed by her affection for her parents and her husband. She can sob buckets simply by imagining that one of her loved ones might get hit by a truck or struck by lightening before the baby is born. It's as if she is dealing with how vulnerable she feels over the fragility of all life, and particularly the lives of the members of her family.

A particular emotional crisis can occur if you happen to be pregnant during a publicized catastrophe involving a baby. Years ago, when the little girl from Texas called "Baby Jessica" fell down a hole in her backyard, my Girlfriend Amy got so upset that she was a mess for days. She felt such empathy for the parents that she was unable to eat, sleep or even talk on the telephone until the child was rescued. Those television news segments on starving children in Third World countries are so psychically painful for pregnant women that they often react as if they have sustained a personal loss. Even the pictures of missing children on milk cartons seem like a special call to action for all pregnant women.

The other amusing part of this sentimentality is the kinship you immediately feel for all mothers of the world, from Donna Reed to the woman yelling at her whining child at Toys "R" Us. The world becomes divided into two groups: those who have children and those who do not. And at this stage in your life, you will be most interested in the subgroup of *women who are pregnant when you are.*

When you are pregnant, it seems as though the entire childbearing population is pregnant, too. You can't swing a loaf of bread in a supermarket without hitting a pregnant woman. You check each other out with uncontainable curiosity but with the friendliness of comrades. You try to guess how pregnant your new comrade is (and whether she is looking as good or as bad as you are at this point), and you will have no qualms about asking this complete stranger her entire gestational history.

If you happen to be pregnant at the same time as a celebrity, you will develop a familiarity with her pregnancy that will make you feel "related" to her in some way. For example, I have been pregnant with Kathie Lee Gifford, Linda Carter, Demi Moore and Fergie, and I feel maternal about their children, even though I don't know them. (Though I can't help but feel I know Cody.) If Kathie Lee woke up one day and complained about retaining water on her show, then I pinched myself the rest of the day to see if I was doing so, too. When I saw on the 11:00 P.M. news that the star of a successful television series suffered a miscarriage very late in her pregnancy, I had my husband get out of bed immediately and take me to the hospital to make sure that our baby was still safe and alive in my stomach.

Later, after you have all had your babies, you will keep an eye on these women to see how they are doing getting back into shape. I was deeply traumatized by the fact that Kathie Lee Gifford was in a slinky gown hosting the Miss America contest while I was still struggling with maternity underwear and nursing bras, and my husband's baseball shirt as the cover-up. I particularly loved tabloid magazines for all their unflattering photos of brand-new celebrity mothers caught off-guard getting off an airplane after a seven-hour flight with a new baby.

"I Want It and I Want It Now!"

Immediate gratification is the goal of most pregnant women. It may appear to the unenlightened that pregnant women are just whimsically indulging themselves and taking advantage of their condition. This is not entirely true. Certain sensations take on a ferocity when you are pregnant that they never had in your nonpregnant state. And God help the person who stands between you and your satisfaction.

For example, a nonpregnant woman can find herself unexpectedly needing to peepee when driving in a car with her husband. When this happens, she might calmly mention to him that she wouldn't mind stopping at the nearest clean bathroom if they should happen to pass one. And she'll probably add that if they don't happen to pass one, she can hold it until they reach their destination.

The scenario changes when the woman is pregnant. Her voice takes on a twinge of hysteria as she blurts out that she has to go to the bathroom. She immediately sounds so desperate that you would swear she is so full that she has started to float. Her husband begins to look for an appropriate stop. The next thing he knows, her hand is on the door handle and she is preparing to hurl herself out of the moving car. She has to relieve herself so badly that she is willing to do it anywhere but the front seat of the car. She would consider doing it there, too, but then she would have to sit in it for the rest of the trip.) The husband's inability to completely comprehend the urgency of his wife's request to stop can be the ground-zero point for a good hormonal fight, so our best advice to husbands in this situation is this: Don't Ask Questions. Immediately Pull Over and Run Around to Your Wife's Side of the Car. Help Her Out and Into a Hiding Place Behind a Tree or Road Sign. And Watch Out for Your Shoes. Remember, Extreme Times Call for Extreme Measures!

If that sort of display of impatience regarding urinating is apt to shock your husband, just wait until he sees the pregnant you when you discover that you are hungry and you have no food within your immediate reach. A pregnant woman's hunger is no small appetite. It isn't a moderate or simple hankering. It is a hunger so ferocious that if the car isn't parked in front of some food-selling edifice within thirty seconds, the husband will find himself face-to-face with a sobbing woman who is tearing through the glove compartment trying to find the peppermint candy she spotted a couple of months ago.

Perhaps there is some medical explanation, like a rapid drop in blood sugar levels or something, for what happens when a pregnant woman gets hungry. I do know that it makes you feel anxious, cranky and desperate. That is why we Girlfriends suggest that you plan ahead for these hunger crises by carrying food in your car, in your husband's car, in your purse and in your office. By the way, mark any food stashed at work with the words "Pregnant Woman's Food—Do Not Touch" because there is nothing worse than reaching for your last snack only to find that the receptionist ate it. Bags of nuts and grains, granola bars and bananas are great rations, and they will keep you from streaking into a fast-food drive-through line in a frenzy. Thirst, too, is immediate and gripping for a pregnant woman (just wait until you try nursing if you want to know what "dying of thirst" really means). So, in addition to the snacks, you should have several bottles of water strategically placed.

"I Think I Hate My Husband!"

Let's start with the simple premise that, by virtue of being a non-female, your husband will have absolutely no idea what it feels like to be you right now. He will not know your anxiety, your ambivalence, your insecurities or your near-toxic hormonal state. That's enough right there to qualify him for the title of World's Most Annoying Man. Trust your Girlfriends when we tell you that even if he denies it to your face, your husband thinks that pregnancy has made you irrational, emotional and unpredictable—all of the things most husbands hate in a person, especially a wife. I have found in my interviewing that when wives are present, their husbands regale me with stories of their brave and pioneering wives who selflessly gave themselves over to pain and sacrifice to produce their precious angel babies. Get these men in a group without their wives, however, and the stories of Pregnancy Insanity grow like the legend of

Paul Bunyan. Gary remembers the time his wife lay down on the floor of the frozen-yogurt store because she felt nauseous. He recalls with agonizing embarrassment how the other shoppers had to step over and around her to get to the counter. Then there is Michael, who describes the quantities of food his pregnant wife ate as if she were a human garbage disposal. He goes on to piteously explain how he was never allowed to finish his own meal because his voracious wife attacked his plate with a shovel. All of these husbands roll their eyes and nod in unison when one mentions the impossibility of coming up with the correct answer to the pregnant woman's favorite question: "Do you still love me even though I'm fat?" This one throws them all, because they don't really know whether they are supposed to tell their wives that they would love them no matter what—since that implies that they do, indeed, think their wives are fat—or if it is wiser to say no, they only like thin women, like her.

There are few things more irritating than losing your mind and having someone point that fact out to you at the same time. Get prepared for comments from your spouse like, "Aren't you overreacting, just a little?" or "Is this the real you or the pregnant you talking?" How about, "You used to be a lot more fun before you got pregnant," or "My chiropractor's wife didn't need any medication when she delivered their baby, and I don't think you should take any either," or "I know you have the flu, but do you really need that antihistamine?" (that the doctor recommended)!

The chief complaint among the Girlfriends seems to be that our husbands don't find this pregnancy business as overwhelmingly important as we do. They are able to think of other things for hours, even days on end, while a pregnant woman (especially if it is her first pregnancy) can think of nothing else. To a pregnant woman, even war in the Middle East becomes about her baby in some way: Maybe Saddam Hussein will invade Kuwait and there will be an oil shortage and she won't have enough gas to get to the hospital when she goes into labor. Husbands, on the other hand, tend to look at pregnancy as something that makes their wives spin out a bit, but largely a nonevent until the baby is actually born.

I once called my husband, who was in New York on business, to complain that he clearly did not want the new baby as much as I did. When he rationally asked what evidence I had for this presumption, I told him that, even though I had been pregnant for seven months, he had not spent one single minute thinking about what we were going to name the baby. I thought about the baby's name at least twice a day from the day I found out I was pregnant, and more often than that after the doctor told me I was going to have a little girl. My husband seemed to work on the assumption that names were handed out at the hospital.

There is one way that many husbands can and do share the pregnancy experience with their wives, and that is by matching them pound for pound in the weight-gaining department. So many of my Girlfriends report that their husbands put on ten to twenty pounds when they were pregnant. Who knows—maybe they are eating from nervous stress, or maybe they are just keeping their wives company at the feed bin. Some of them actually get cravings along with their wives. I don't think this is really a grand display of empathy, but rather a case of "If you get something I want it too"—as in, "If you are going to have a banana split, I deserve to have one too." My husband took this "me too" business a bit further when he insisted that he caught every malady I had, only he had it worse. In other words, if I took to bed with bronchitis, he was sure that he had pneumonia. This is a very clever ruse, because no one would ever expect a man with *pneumonia* to be able to take care of a chubby, crazy woman with a little bit of a cough.

What can be really infuriating to a pregnant woman who feels that she is enduring her pregnancy with little or no genuine support or understanding from her husband is the gnawing thought at the back of her mind, "It's all his fault. He *did* this to me in the first place." He comes away from a roll in the hay with a satisfied glow and the promise of a good night's sleep, and her life is changed forever. At no time is this feeling of blame greater than during delivery. There is something so infuriating about lying in a hospital bed with your uterus contracting like a bucking bronco and seeing your husband eating something from the cafeteria and watching television. Life's just not fair sometimes.

"I'm Scared to Death!"

Fear is a common denominator among all pregnant women. It is neck-snapping, the speed with which you can go from feeling joyous to feeling terrified upon learning that you are going to have a baby. First there is a sort of general sense of alarm at the whole prospect of growing a baby inside you and being responsible for it until the day you die. This is when you might start looking for an escape.

Shortly after this, the fears become more specific. You don't just feel a huge, undifferentiated sense of worry, but you can list the individual things that terrify you from moment to moment. The fears usually break down in the following manner:

Fear of Miscarriage

Once you have come to terms with the shock and excitement of learning that you are pregnant, you will discover that sustaining that pregnancy becomes the single most important goal of your life. This fear of losing a pregnancy is not completely irrational. Statistics say that something like one out of five diagnosed pregnancies do end in miscarriage, and the odds vary according to such factors as how old you are. And if you have ever endured a miscarriage or had a close friend go through one, you know that it is far more than a particularly painful menstrual period. To a woman who is eagerly awaiting the birth of her child, the loss of that child, no matter how early on it is, is agonizing.

For some women, especially those who conceived without much trouble and who have never experienced any threat to a pregnancy, such as bleeding or actual miscarriage, sustaining their pregnancy means little more than using a lower step in their Step Reebok class. For other women, like myself, who tried for years to get pregnant or who for some other reason think that their pregnancy is more fragile, the first three months are characterized by far more precautions.

Almost every pregnancy book on the market will tell you that there is absolutely no reason for a woman with what is known as a "low risk" pregnancy (ask your doctor to classify yours) to curtail her fitness activities in any way. Intellectually, I will begrudgingly accept this wisdom, but emotionally, especially for the precarious first three months, I reject it wholeheartedly. I know that the vast majority of miscarriages that occur in the first trimester are the result of a genetic malformation of the embryo, but I just cannot understand why anyone would want there to be one scintilla of a chance that her taking that ninety-minute kick-boxing class was partly to blame. If you can take it easy, why not do so?

The only reason why not is to live up to some current notion of being a superhuman who can gestate and swing from a trapeze at the same time. Sure, we have all heard of women who have done just that, but what do they have to do with you and your baby? The most important rule of pregnancy is THIS IS NOT A CONTEST! YOU JUST DO WHAT YOU CAN TO SURVIVE THE NINE (TEN) MONTHS AND HAVE A HEALTHY BABY.

I have already told you how many times I turned white as a sheet and ran to the bathroom in dread of seeing blood in my underwear. As I mentioned earlier, I actually did bleed in all four of my pregnancies, and it was terrifying every single time. I took the bleeding episodes as messages from God to go right to bed. I had a new respect for how fragile all life can be. That is why the Girlfriends advise that you cut yourself some slack when you find out you are pregnant. Miscarriages, tragically, do happen, but there is absolutely no reason for you to wonder whether there was anything you could have done to help save the pregnancy, like give up the cigarettes or the bench-pressing.

Another biological reason that some women worry about miscarriage is a cramping sensation that often occurs in the early part of pregnancy. This cramping feels just like menstrual cramps, and if you feel them in the early weeks, you will swear that this pregnancy business was all a dream and that your period is starting within minutes. I must have been ten weeks pregnant before I stopped tucking sanitary napkins in my underwear every day, just in case those cramps meant business. If you are feeling them, relax—they almost always mean nothing. If they are painful and accompanied by any bleeding, ignore everything I have just said and contact your doctor.

Fear of Something Being Wrong With Your Baby

Your sometimes uncontrollable fear that your child may be born less-than-perfect is your first inkling of how vulnerable you will be regarding the well-being of your baby. From now until the day you die (or gratefully succumb to senility), you will fret over the condition of your child. If your baby is not happy and well, neither are you. Here it is, not even born yet, and already you are suffering from the sense of dread about how you would cope if something were to happen to your child.

We all know that, unfortunately, babies are sometimes born with health problems, just as we all know that older children sometimes get sick or break their bones, need emergency appendectomies or, God forbid, have even worse things happen. But our fears almost always exceed the probabilities of these things ever occurring. The vast majority of children are born with ten fingers and ten toes, and they manage to survive childhood disasters so successfully that the greatest threat to their well-being is the very real chance that we will kill them ourselves when they are teenagers.

Even with all this in mind, it is impossible to stop rerunning the brain tape that plays out what you would do if something were less-than-perfect with your baby. This is because you are certain that if something were to happen to your child, you would have no other option but to die yourself. This kind of intense love and identification with your baby surprises every woman when she first recognizes it. When you recognize its power, you will begin to understand why you will want to smack a two-year-old who throws sand in your child's eyes, or slap a schoolteacher who suggests that your child might not be ready for first grade after all.

Anyway, back to the irrational fears that something will be wrong with your baby. I think that one of the reasons we play out every disastrous scenario in our minds during pregnancy is to toughen our psyches in the event such a horrible thing should happen. It is as if we think that if we have imagined it already, the shock or sadness might not be as great as they would be if we were caught blissfully unaware. I don't need to tell you that this is hoodoo thinking at its finest; you know it, too, but it is something most of us need to do.

Many women choose to have various tests to eliminate some of the worries about birth defects. Many states require that mothers give a blood sample for what is known as an alpha-fetoprotein test, which checks for spina bifida and can indicate whether the fetus has a statistically higher chance of being born with Down's syndrome. There is also a new blood test with genetic markers for Down's syndrome.

Ultrasound, which many pregnant women get at least a couple of times during pregnancy, can also reassure you that your child has a heart with all four chambers, a brain and all the arms and legs it is supposed to have. If the baby is feeling particularly brazen on the day of your ultrasound (or "sonogram"), you may even see its sex organs and know with reasonable certainty if you are having a boy or girl.

If you are age thirty-five or older, you will probably have a genetic test that actually samples some of the pregnancy matter or the amniotic fluid. These tests are called CVS (chorionic villi sampling) and amniocentesis, respectively. (They will be discussed further in another chapter.) A good result on these tests eliminates the possibilities of your baby being born with a number of birth defects.

But if you think the worry stops there, you are pitifully mistaken. As soon as you think that your baby is spared the traumas of Tay-Sachs disease or Down's syndrome, you creatively come up with other things to obsess about, like whether it is going to have crossed eyes or ears like Prince Charles's. Worry seems to be a necessary exercise for pregnant women, and for every bit of reassurance you get, you will substitute one more thing to worry about.

Guilt provides all sorts of material for uncontrollable worrying in a pregnant woman. We become convinced that now is the time to pay the piper for all of the terrible things we did to ourselves in our carefree youth. If you, unlike a certain president, actually inhaled when you smoked, you will feel faint at the prospect that your chromosomes were forever altered and your baby will have twelve toes. Imagine those of us who did worse things in the way of chemical experimentation. Unless we take the Girlfriends' advice, we have more than thirty-six weeks of worry ahead of us. The most common fear of retribution comes to those of us who were drunk or high when we conceived. What a double bind; you get loose enough to take the chance of getting pregnant, and then you spend your entire pregnancy wishing you had been stone-cold sober that night.

Eventually, God willing, the baby is born in robust good health. But for those of you who are not completely distracted by the outrageous experience of having a full-size baby come out of your insides, there will be a moment after that last push or when the doctor reaches into your cesarean section when you steel yourself for the possibility that you are going to be presented with a baby that looks more like Bubbles the Chimp than the Gerber baby. Believe your Girlfriends: The moment you hear your baby cry and you see its squishy little face, you will feel like all the angels of heaven have smiled on you.

Then hold on to your seat, because you will be entering the Major Leagues of Worry. If you thought you obsessed about the little baby in your stomach, wait until you see how you wig out over the little baby you are now holding in your arms, who has immediately become the most important person in your household. (Remember how the Shirley MacLaine character in *Terms of Endearment* hovered over her baby's crib to see if she was breathing? When she wasn't sure she'd heard a breath, she gave the baby a good pinch that woke her up howling.)

You may think that this is hyperbole for the sake of drama, but you couldn't be more wrong. My Girlfriends and I were all convinced (primarily with our first babies) that we were keeping our newborns alive through the sheer force of our wills, that if we did not concentrate on them, they would stop breathing. We all held small mirrors under the baby's nose to see the moisture clouds which indicated that respiration was indeed taking place. And those baby monitors that no mother can live without? Most of us kept the volume turned up so high in the early months that not only could we hear every breath and coo, we could hear the baby's fingernails grow.

Fear of Getting Ugly

Some women, like my Girlfriend Shirley, have never been so beautiful and happy as when they are pregnant. They feel fulfilled as women, they glow with health and they revel in their ripe, round figures. As I have said many times, "Goody goody for them." Call me alienated from my role as a woman or as a reproducing creature, but I found the changes in appearance mildy disturbing at times, and sometimes downright horrifying. It's not that I look at pregnant women and find them unattractive. On the contrary—I think other pregnant women are adorable. I just have a hard time reconciling my own pregnant dimensions with the size-four clothes in my closet.

I also wondered whether my husband would still find me sexy, or equally important, whether I would find myself sexy. The completely honest answer to both of these questions was "No," but there are just as many Girlfriends and their husbands who found the whole experience erotic as those who did not. (More about this in the chapter "Sex and Pregnancy.")

I know, it is boring and trite to condemn our society for promoting a notion that thinliness is next to godliness, but there is no denying that a pregnant woman may have an identity conflict in such a society. She may wonder whether she will lose her standing as a "babe" because she is growing a babe inside of her. To make matters worse, most of the clothes offered in maternity stores look like something worn either by a clown or a flight attendant.

All pregnant women pray fervently that they will somehow be able to reclaim their former selves after the baby is born. But I must tell you, society sends mixed messages in this regard. On the one hand, you see people like Vanna White restored to her former beauty minutes after her baby is born, and you think that is what is expected of you. On the other hand is the universal comment, "She looks so good . . . for having four children," as if having children were a justification for something distinctly less than perfection. I must confess, however, that I will take a compliment any way I can get it, no matter how left-handed.

Fear of Turning Into Your Mother

It is scary enough to make the transition from sweet young thing to MOTHER, but it is even scarier to contemplate turning into your *own* mother. It happens to all of us—we catch a glimpse of ourselves in the mirror and notice that we are beginning to look just like our mothers. Whether it is the set of the jaw or the way we crinkle our eyes when we smile, we recognize someone in our face who is not us.

For many pregnant women, this transformation can lead to a full-fledged panic attack. Will you become a bossy, judgmental, rigid and fretting person like you always thought your mother was? You are sure that the mother you have always known never acted wildly and impetuously, never had sex in a Jacuzzi and never dreamed of having an affair with Mel Gibson. (Or if she did, you never, ever wanted to hear a word about it.) The fear that you may go from being Holly Golightly to becoming June Cleaver is just too frightening to contemplate.

As you grow to love the baby that is inside of you, you will have a new understanding of how much your mother must have loved you. You will begin to understand why she can't help herself when she butts into your life and is hypervigilant concerning your well-being. Just wait until the baby is two or three years old and you hear yourself yell, "Get down from there—you'll break your neck!" exactly like your mother used to. My own epiphany occurred when I caught myself spitting on a tissue and trying to clean my daughter's face before she walked into a birthday party.

Fear of Turning Into Your Husband's Mother

I don't mean this transformation as literally as I described turning into your own mother. I am not talking about the fear that you will transform into a physical replica of your mother-in-law. I am talking about changing from your husband's lover and friend into his asexual nurturer. Sometimes, in our determination to learn to mother before the baby is dumped in our laps, we start behaving like the mothers we grew up with, or worse, like the mothers our husbands grew up with. You'll know you are succumbing to this when you suggest that your husband wear a jacket because he might catch a chill or when you begin making his dental appointments.

This change is not usually made unilaterally, but with the cooperation of your husband. After all, who wouldn't want someone fussing over him? While most men maintain that their mothers drive them crazy, they also love how their mothers devotedly cared for them. You know how it goes: They want the Thanksgiving stuffing that their mothers used to make, they want their shirts hung with the buttons facing the left of the closet, à la Mom, and they want you to make them a bed on the couch when they are sick, just like you-know-who always did.

Husbands encourage this mothering not just because they want to be babied, but because they, too, are intimidated by impending parenthood, and the only models they have for how mothers are supposed to act are their own mommies. It is amazing how many men develop an opinion about whether their wives are tidy enough or organized enough only when they learn that a baby is on the way.

There is only one thing more troublesome than being held to the romanticized standard of motherhood that your husband has been burnishing for the last twenty years, and that is being compared with his *first wife*. This is where you really must put your foot down. I don't care (and you shouldn't either) whether his first wife had her Christmas cards addressed by Halloween and made her own apple pie, she is no role model for you. If she were, her name would still be on the credit cards. Right?

Fear of Not Doing Pregnancy Right

Out of our overwhelming desire to be judged perfect and the biological imperative to do everything we can to protect our unborn child from all the mishaps described in the above section, we have set standards of proper behavior for pregnant women. If these standards were established on an individual basis between you and your doctor, I would applaud them. Unfortunately, many of us, through our inexperience and insecurity, buy into a whole litany of rules that are not only burdensome and unnecessary, but also guaranteed to make any woman feel inadequate.

If your own self-control and guilt aren't enough to keep you on the path of perfect parenting, you will soon learn that the world is filled with people who feel it is their responsibility to monitor your performance. The Girlfriends have dubbed these "oh-so-helpful" folks the Pregnancy Police. There is only one thing I hate more than a Pregnancy Police person; and that is a MALE Pregnancy Police person (as if a person without a uterus, or at least a medical degree, has any right in this universe to comment on how a pregnant woman lives her life).

Pregnancy Police come from the same school as those complete strangers who feel free to pat your belly when they run into you at the grocery store. Pregnancy Police can be relied on to share all sorts of bullshit information. They always seem to know of a woman who had a fifty-hour labor and then needed an emergency C-section because the umbilical cord was wrapped around the baby's neck or some such horror story. Of course, the Pregnancy Police have an explanation for this crisis, and it almost always involves some shortcoming on the mother's part; either she was sleeping on her back rather than on her left side, or she took the epidural too early for the P.P.'s taste, or some other bogus thing.

Pregnancy Police get tremendous satisfaction out of telling unsuspecting pregnant women that they should throw their microwave ovens into a toxic dump site, that they are being poisoned by the hidden formaldehyde in their mattresses, that they are exposing their baby to cancer by eating peanut butter, and that drinking a diet soda is tantamount to shooting heroin. The more distressed the mother-to-be becomes, the more fulfilled the Pregnancy Police feel. You would swear that they must have had perfect labors and deliveries and flawless children to have earned the credentials to tell you what you are doing wrong, but it never works out that way. It's like the child psychologist who lived next door to us when I was a kid; he was dispensing child-rearing advice on the phone in his study while his twins were lighting the living room draperies on fire.

One of my Girlfriends remembers a time that she was in a beauty salon getting her roots touched up when a complete stranger approached her with a look of tremendous concern and inquired, "Don't you know you are not supposed to use chemicals on your hair when you are pregnant?" My Girlfriend, who already had half her head wrapped in aluminum foil with hair dye in it, went into an internal panic. She finished the coloring, but she left the salon near tears with the fear that she had ignorantly harmed her beloved baby. This hair-coloring business is something you should bring up with your doctor and decide for yourself, but my babies were all subjected to my hair dying in utero and they seem just fine to me. My theory was this: If I were to have let my hair return to its natural brown and gray condition every time I was pregnant, my children might have been spared some indirect contact with chemicals, but they would also have been born to a single parent, because my husband surely would have left me after the first two inches of the "real me" had grown out. So, if my kids didn't run the risk of biological imperfection, they would have run the risk of societal imperfection, along with their insane mother.

If my beauty salon story sounds extreme, just wait until you run into the Pregnancy Police at a party or restaurant. God forbid if you should have a glass of wine with dinner or participate in a champagne toast, even with a notarized letter of permission from your doctor. The P.P. will either look witheringly at you or actually come up to you and lecture you about fetal alcohol syndrome. Almost all of the Girlfriends—none of whom, I hasten to add, drank more than a total of four or five glasses of wine or champagne over the course of their entire pregnancies—found themselves lamely trying to defend their imbibing to total strangers more than once.

Naturally, doctors will have their opinions about drinking during pregnancy, and I am neither condoning nor condemning drinking. I am just saying that pregnancy is hard enough; what with the societal stigmas against hot tubs, aspirin, coffee, and artificial sweeteners, not to mention your own compromised sex life and your comical physical proportions, a single drink once every couple of months seems allowable, if not outright deserved. But, hey, I'm no doctor. Life is a series of calculated risks, and you and your doctor should work together to chart a course of behavior that is healthy for the baby *and* livable for the mother.

One last hangout of Pregnancy Police is airports. They congregate near the security clearance areas and will comment that you are nuking your baby if you walk through the X-ray machine. Now here, I have absolutely no complaints about their concern, but that is for my own personal reasons rather than any evidence I have heard of regarding the danger of this kind of exposure to an unborn baby. I always made a big fuss about the danger of these X-ray machines so that I could be excused from passing through them. I was then hand-patted by a female security officer; and while I wasn't crazy about the patting part, I did like the fact that I usually got to cut to the front of the line. For someone who is chronically late for flights, this could make or break my travel plans. While we are on the subject of air travel, always check with the individual airlines to learn their policies regarding when they deem you "too pregnant" to be allowed on their planes. You know how fussy those flight attendants can be about labor and delivery on board. (And then you'd have to do some ridiculous thing like name your child after the airport.)

Fear of Being a Bad Mother

This fear usually comes from one of two possibilities: Either your own mother was so extraordinary, loving, patient and selfless that you know you could never in a million years be as good a mother as she was, or your mother was such a selfish, neglectful and undemonstrative person that you are terrified you may be genetically predisposed to act just like her. As in most aspects of pregnancy, there appears to be little middle ground.

Much as we would like to, we Girlfriends cannot predict what kind of mother you will be (although we have all the faith in the world in your mothering instincts). What we have all noticed is that pregnancy is the time to settle your issues with your own mother. Now is the time to look at your mother with a grown-up eye, as a woman with the same demands, insecurities and hopes that you are feeling right now. You may emulate your mother, but *you are not your mother.* You have the opportunity to appraise your own childhood and pick and choose the parts that you want to share with your child and the parts you want to spare it. Motherhood is a work in progress. You have nine (ten) months to prepare for some aspects of it, but you won't really understand what it feels like to be someone's mother until you have taken your child out of the hospital and into your home. It will be a love affair, but whether it will be love at first sight or a gradual thing varies from mother to mother. And you won't really know how good a mother you have been until your child sends thrilling and literate letters home from his Peace Corps job or sends postcards from his mobile home in the desert, where he collects roadkill and puts it in his freezer. You just love away and hope for the best—all the while coming to the rude awakening that this unbelievable love you have for your baby could just possibly be how your mom felt about you!

Fear of Labor and Delivery

See, I have saved the big one for last. This is the mother of all fears for a woman pregnant with her first child. At first, the fear of labor and delivery is really just the simple fear of pain. You have no doubt that it will hurt; just a rudimentary understanding of simple physics will tip you off that a vagina that has never experinced anything larger than a super Tampax or a very well-endowed fellow is going to balk a bit at passing a watermelon through its dainty corridors. But you have no idea how *much* it will hurt. More than a bikini wax? More than a broken leg? More than a root canal?

After you have had enough time to hear the birth story of every woman you have ever met (roughly two weeks from the day you announce your pregnancy), your terror will expand to include the fear that you will be a wimp; the fear that you won't be able to push hard enough to get the baby out; the fear that you will make poopoo instead of pushing the baby out; the fear that you will faint or cry when they give you an IV (intravenous) needle; the fear that you will faint or cry, period; the fear that the epidural will hurt more than labor; or the fear that the anesthesiologist will have a bad aim and you will be paralyzed for life. We won't go into the details of labor and delivery and what they feel like here (there is an entire chapter devoted to them later), but we will discuss the essence of the Fear of Labor and Delivery, as we, your Girlfriends, see it.

The terror, in its most fundamental form, is that you will be in a vulnerable position; in pain, with your legs spread; scared of the creature that is insisting on coming out of you; AND NO ONE WILL DO ANYTHING TO SAVE YOU! Can't you just imagine yourself limping into the hospital with the nagging suspicion that you are facing the trial of your life with a pitiful arsenal of Lamaze breathing, a Yanni cassette and your hapless husband to help you?

You don't really consider other options because the Pregnancy Police of the world (especially those nazis in your prepared childbirth class) tell you that you are doing it wrong if you vary from this prescription. To them I say, with all respect, BULLSHIT! A healthy mother and baby, achieved under *any* conditions necessary, is the ultimate goal of labor and delivery.

We Girlfriends want to let you in on a secret. THERE IS NO AWARDS CEREMONY FOR MOTHERS AFTER DELIVERY. No announcements are made over the loudspeaker; no medals are presented to those mothers who managed to deliver their children without pain medication, without crying and without making a mess on the delivery table. First of all, very few victors would emerge. Second of all, the other mothers in the audience would throw their hemorrhoid pillows at the medalists.

Here it is, Girlfriends: Epidurals are *great*. Cesareans can save lives and curtail unnecessary suffering. THERE IS NO SUCH THING AS A SECOND-CLASS BIRTH. Willingness to suffer or to put the baby or yourself in jeopardy, especially when you are frightened and tired, is a sign of questionable judgment, not heroism.

You have a choice: You can lay on a bed of nails to deliver your baby or you can lay on a bed of downy feathers. No matter what you choose, neither your doctor, your nurse nor your baby will think any better of you for suffering because of some possibly misunderstood notion of what is best for your child. And trust us: Your husband will think that you are a goddess for at least forty-eight hours for enduring what you have endured to give him a child, with or without medication.

Keep this in mind: Those of us who took a little nip from the epidural tap are usually the life of the champagne celebration in our rooms after the baby is born, while our American Gothic counterparts are sound asleep with every capillary in their cheeks broken.

One last bit of advice about fear and worry: Learn to roll with it, because it doesn't ever really end. Even when you have the relief of holding a perfectly healthy baby in your arms after nine (ten) months of agitation, you are just warming up for serious worrying. You will wonder, "Is he getting enough to eat?" Or, "Is he eating too much and getting fat?" Then it's on to whether your child is the last one to be toilet-trained in your Mommy and Me group or whether she will make any friends. Then, as they get even older and have plenty of friends (and are using the potty with great ease), you start to worry about whether those friends are good influences on your child—whether they take drugs, whether they're in a gang. Add to all that the abject terror all parents feel when their children are given driver's licenses and turned loose on America's highways, and you get a pretty good idea of why your own parents looked so distracted most of the time you were growing up. But I digress. . . .

6

You and Your Doctor

s you may already have deduced, the person you have known for years as your "gynecologist" transforms into your "obstetrician" on the day you find out you are going to have a baby. Your obstetrician (or o.b., in pregnancy lingo) is the person responsible for caring for a pregnant woman during gestation, delivery and postpartum recovery. I guess that means that when they give you estrogen pills for menopause, they magically transform back into gynecologists.

Doctor or Midwife?

Nowhere is it etched in stone that you need a medical doctor to assist you in childbirth. There are many certified nurse-midwives, or lay midwives, who can be the primary assistant to a delivering mother, either at the mother's home or at a birthing center that is usually affiliated with a doctor and is near enough by ambulance to a hospital should an emergency arise. Quite a few of the more forward-thinking doctors are now sharing their practices with certified nurse-midwives, and their patients see the doctor and the midwife on alternate visits. Since the vast majority of midwives are female, you get the Girlfriend factor built right into the relationship, and you may find yourself more comfortable asking certain questions of a midwife, like "Is is normal to have so much gas?" that you would never ask your doctor (most of whom still are men, as of this writing). There is also a belief that midwives might be less inclined than an overbooked obstetrician to hurry a delivery along through the use of pitocin or an eventual cesarean section.

My Girlfriend Kathy opted for a home birth with a nurse-midwife, and the midwife did everything from make her herb teas to walk with her in the hills outside her house to help bring on regular contractions. The nurturing and reassurance was extraordinary. Unfortunately, Kathy found labor longer, more painful and more frightening than she had anticipated, and she ended up falling into the tiny backseat of her sports car and being whisked to a hospital to deliver her son. The biggest disappointment for her was that she had waited so long that the doctors decided not to give her any pain relief because it was time to push anyway.

There are three lessons I gleaned from Kathy's story. First, you can never get to the hospital too early, even if you end up spending the next twenty-four hours just walking the halls of the maternity ward. Second, save the home births, midwives and underwater deliveries for second, third and fourth babies. There is no way you can make an informed decision about how you want to manage your delivery until you have some realistic idea of what in the world to expect. We Girlfriends guarantee that you will be surprised; perhaps pleasantly, perhaps not so pleasantly, but YOU WILL BE SURPRISED, even *after* reading this book. And third, never elect to have a child where you have no access to medication or, God forbid, real doctors.

You will tell yourself from now till labor begins that you intend to try delivering without an epidural, but I can't think of a Girlfriend who didn't take it when it was offered. Well, I take that back. My Girlfriend Jillian never took pain medication, but perhaps if her husband had not been there promising her jewelry if she could make it through, she too would have found the epidural a relief. (I wonder how it would go if she were to stand beside him with diamond cuff links while he was getting a vasectomy.) Nor was there any medication for Corki, whose baby had a heart problem that might have been adversely affected by it, or Amy, who just labored too fast for the doctor to have time to get the epidural into her without slowing down her progress. But both Corki and Amy maintain that they would have been forever grateful for such medical intervention.

A postscript to this home delivery section: Childbirth is as messy as a pig slaughter. Why in the world would you want to sacrifice your beautiful sheets, not to mention your mattress, to such a thing? If you just can't stand the thought of going to a hospital, perhaps you should consider delivering at a four-star hotel; it's still cheaper than a hospital, and the food and maid service are infinitely better. (Wouldn't you just love to be in the room next door to that?)

How to Select Your Obstetrician

Did you notice how quickly we have made the decision for you that a medical doctor will delivery your baby? We apologize if you think we are taking too much for granted, but that's what Girlfriends do. If you wanted something more statistical or analytica', you could have read any one of a million other books on pregnancy. Our job is to give you the inside scoop, based on what we tell each other, and our unanimous vote is that you go for the traditional hospital birth with a godlike medical doctor for your first go-round on this birthing carousel. Remember, we are creatures of popular culture, we revere doctors as if they were the heroes and heroines we grew up watching on TV. It's the *doctors* who are so honorably portrayed on everything from *Dr. Kildare* to *Dr. Quinn, Medicine Woman.* Poor innocent midwives never have their own series. In fact, they were tried as witches in colonial Salem!

So how do you find that perfect person? Well, you can do one of two things: You can stick with the person who has heretofore been your gynecologist, the person who fitted you for a cervical cap and treated your yeast infections. Or you can pick a new doctor on the presumption that your needs are different now and that perhaps your gynecologist isn't necessarily the right person to get you through this pregnancy.

It can really be a mistake to think that the gynecologist you have had for the last ten years must automatically be the person to deliver your child. Choosing the person who will deliver your baby is subject to different criteria than choosing the person who does your Pap tests. There are many reasons to rethink your choice of doctors.

First of all, YOU SHOULD ASK YOUR GIRLFRIENDS WHAT THEY THINK OF THEIR OWN DOCTORS OR LOCAL DOCTORS. There is a real o.b. grapevine in existence, and in most communities a few doctors' names come up over and over. I

found my doctor when I was seated next to a Girlfriend of a Girlfriend in a salon. She had four children, and positively glowed when
she talked about her doctor. When another Girlfriend spoke of the
same person in the same affectionate and reverent way, I knew I
had found my man. I am still a satisfied customer.

It is also important that you engage in some serious soul-
searching to discover what kind of patient you are likely to be. If
you are assertive and full of questions, you will need a doctor who
doesn't resent making big allowances of time for you. If you are
frightened about the entire prospect, you absolutely must select a
doctor who is protective and understanding. Those of you who are
eager to attempt a pregnancy that is "natural" and "organic" would
be well-advised to find a doctor who not only supports your choice,
but who has a special understanding of nutrition, environmental
hazards and treating colds with little more than hot water and
lemon.

It is particularly important that you and your doctor share the
same expectations for your birth experience. If you have your own
private reasons for wanting a scheduled C-section, under any circumstances, then you and your doctor had better be in agreement
about that from your first handshake. It also wouldn't hurt (no pun
intended) at this time to discuss with you o.b. candidate your feelings and his regarding pain medication; not just *whether* you will get
it, but *when* and *how much*.

When my first ultrasound showed pretty clearly that I was going
to have a baby boy, I actually asked my Girlfriends with sons how
they felt their doctors did on the circumcision. You may be surprised
to learn, as I was, that it's the obstetrician, not the pediatrician, who
does the tip clipping if you want your son circumcised in the hospital. If you don't think this is an important skill, just ask your husband's opinion. Some doctors seem to leave too much foreskin, some
clip too far back, and it is still quite variable as to whether a topical
anesthetic is used to mitigate the pain. Of course, not every one
circumcises these days, and most Jewish parents make a party of it.

Should Your Husband Be Consulted?

I don't think I know of a Girlfriend who ever consulted her husband
about her choice of a gynecologist, unless, like my Girlfriend Kelly,

she happened to be married to an obstetrician. Many of us have known our gynecologist far longer than we have our husband, and we never asked them what they thought of our then fiancé.

We Girlfriends believe when picking who will see you through this pregnancy, you should include your husband in the decision-making process. He will, after all, presumably be far more involved in the pregnancy and delivery processes than he was in your Pap tests. And for many reasons, it is critical that your husband feel almost as safe and comfortable with your doctor as you do. First, his child's entry into the world is in this doctor's hands. Second, your husband will presumably be at your side throughout most, if not all, of your labor, and it would be awfully nice if he liked the person who had his arm inside you up to his elbow. And third, he should feel as free as you do to call the doctor throughout the pregnancy to ask any questions he might have or to secretly report any examples of your insanity. Any suspicious or alarming symptoms that I experienced during pregnancy I tearfully reported to my husband, and he was the one to call the doctor for me. When I started spotting, I was so panic-stricken that I couldn't form the words to speak on the phone, and my sweet husband called and described my condition. Labors, too, often tend to be reported to the doctor by the husbands. Either the wives are too involved with the contractions to carry on conversations (a reliable sign that a woman is in productive labor is her inability to get out any fluent sentences when a contraction strikes) or they are worried that they might not really be in labor. At a moment like this, a good husband will step in and remind you that you are entitled to call your doctor at any time, whether the baby is hanging down to your knees or not.

We are not saying this to alarm you, but it will blow your husband's mind even more than it blows yours when a baby emerges from your interiors, whether via your vagina or a C-section incision, since he's the one with the bird's-eye view, and he might really need someone to lean on at that time. Let's not forget that your husband loves you very much and doesn't want anything bad to happen to you. Or more to the point, he doesn't exactly want to have you die in childbirth and leave him with this baby that he hasn't even met yet. He will insist on a doctor who'll guarantee that you will come out of this ordeal alive and well. Ultimately, however, your needs are paramount, and the final decision should be yours.

Male or Female?

Should your doctor be a man or a woman? Need I even say that we Girlfriends see absolutely no difference in technical expertise between men and women? It goes without saying that nearly any obstetrician in your community who has been recommended to you (and who is in good standing with the American Medical Association and hasn't been investigated on *60 Minutes*) will be competent to care for you during pregnancy and delivery of your baby. The decision about whether you would prefer a female or a male doctor is a purely emotional one. That is not to say, however, that it isn't a crucial decision. We Girlfriends uniformly believe that your emotional safety and well-being are as critical to a successful birth as your medical support.

This is certainly a time to throw political correctness aside and honestly appraise what type of person elicits your respect and trust and, in turn, trusts and respects you. This probably should be a private evaluation of your preferences, so that you are not swayed by a mother who thinks all good doctors are men or a sister who says she has never met a man who treated her as if her brain and spinal cord were connected. Are you the type who prefers a male doctor because he seems fatherly and physically able to protect you from harm? Or perhaps you prefer a female doctor because she is more likely to empathize with you. As one Girlfriend asked, "Would you ever hire a mechanic who had never driven a car before?"

Then there is the whole issue of sexuality. Many of my Girlfriends, including Mindy and Maryann, were very happy with their choice of female obstetricians because they felt less inhibited during physical exams and delivery, and they were freer to express their emotional concerns. These Girlfriends also mentioned the not-unimportant fact that their husbands were reassured by their having female doctors for such an intimate relationship. In addition, there can be real pressure on a woman to maintain her attractiveness around men, since many of us learned this lesson very early in life, and there are some aspects of pregnancy that can make a woman feel less than attractive when exposed to her male doctor. This can create additional headaches, which is the last thing a pregnant woman needs.

On the other hand, you may ascribe to *my* philosophy that you grab your harmless pleasures where you can because pregnancy can be a long, dry spell. The doctor who delivered three of my children is a man, and I had a great time flirting with him and taking special care with my appearance for my monthly visits. Of course, this doctor looks like Clark Kent, so I was not the only pregnant woman in town making a fool of herself. Especially in your last couple of months of pregnancy, your male doctor may be the only man on earth who is still interested in how you feel. A good many husbands have fallen by the wayside by that time. Remember, nine (ten) months of pregnancy will lead to about twelve visits to the doctor's office, and labor will involve hours of intense bonding between you and your doctor, so you had better pick carefully.

Sole or Group Practice?

Delivering babies pays well and is certainly the cheeriest medical specialty, but the hours suck. Except for scheduled inductions or C-sections, babies' births are unpredictable and often tedious, and always seem to involve middle-of-the-night calls to the doctor. Chiefly for this reason, two or more doctors often band together in a group to divide up the number of sleepless nights they will have to endure, and to try to get a vacation or two in each year.

The way a group practice works is that each time you go for your monthly checkup, you are examined by a different member of the group. This ensures that you and all the doctors have at least shaken hands before you are called upon to deliver a baby together. Then, when you go into labor and call your doctor, whichever member of the group is on call at that time will meet you at the hospital. So, not only can you look forward to the surprise of "It's a boy!" or "It's a girl!" but you can have the added surprise of hearing that "It's Dr. Hammill!" who will be attending your delivery.

For my first pregnancy, I chose a doctor in a group practice. My favorite doctor happened to have the most seniority in the group, and he never got out of a warm bed to deliver a baby. That task always went to a newer member of the group who was still earning his or her stripes. Since I had a scheduled C-section, I not only had my favorite doctor on hand, but another doctor in the group, since there are usually two doctors attending this type of surgery. The other doctor was a woman he happened to be dating at the time. It was really a sweet experience, watching the two of them work together. They worked with great professional skill, but they kept making goo-goo eyes at each other across my gored abdomen.

My next three children were delivered by a doctor in a sole practice. About two of my pregnancies ago, he brought in a nurse-midwife to help take some of the pressure of the routine examinations off himself, but he did the delivering. In the rare event that he was unavailable to deliver a baby, he had an arrangement with a doctor in another practice to step in for him. The fact that, at least in this one respect, I knew what to expect was a real blessing.

All of my doctor's patients ask two questions when they find out they are pregnant, "When is it due?" and "Will you be in town to deliver it?" One Girlfriend was so terrified that the doctor's wife would insist that he take a family vacation when the Girlfriend was due to deliver that she offered her parents' plush (and within-driving-distance-of-the-hospital) beach home to the doctor and his family just so she could keep him near.

This is not the place to speculate about the personal toll a sole practice takes on a doctor, since we are talking about someone you are going to have deliver your baby, not marry. But the decision about whether to select a doctor in a group or sole practice is an important one. It all boils down to this: In a group practice, you will never be sure who will join you in the delivery room until the moment arrives. On the other hand, a sole practitioner may have intestinal flu when you go into labor (or worse, be skiing with his family in Colorado), and you could end up having a stranger's hand on your cervix when you least want it there. At least in a group practice you have shaken that hand.

D*o Not Be Afraid of Your Doctor!*

Doctors in general can seem too important, too busy or too intimidating for us to bother with all of our questions and concerns. We might want to ask the doctor something of great importance to us, but worry that we will be wasting his or her time, or worse, *looking stupid*. This applies when we are being treated for anything from chronic heart conditions to bunions, but it is particularly problematic when we are dealing with pregnancy.

A pregnant woman's relations with her doctor is uniquely complex because, in the vast majority of cases, she is not *sick*. Except for supervision of her condition and the growth and development of her pregnancy, the pregnant woman offers relatively little to treat medically. The only *cure* for her condition is delivery, and until that thrilling time, she and her doctor are basically waiting for the proverbial watched pot to boil. This basic condition of good health is usually cause for gratitude on the pregnant woman's part, but it can make her feel sheepish when she needs some emotional support or reassurance from her doctor. Since our view of doctors is that they are in the business of saving lives, we are often reluctant to intrude on that mission unless we are convinced that we are at death's door.

My Girlfriend Whitney sat for nearly twenty hours with another Girlfriend who was going through an early miscarriage. The Girlfriend suffering the miscarriage had been through this ordeal before, and since she knew what was happening to her physically, she saw no reason to bother the doctor with her news until it was over. What she needed was reassurance (a good painkiller wouldn't have been a bad idea either), but she was reluctant to be unnecessarily demanding of her doctor's valuable time.

I am sure her doctor would agree with me when I say *this was a big mistake!* All good obstetricians are fully aware of the emotional nurturing that a pregnant woman requires, and if they aren't you should drop them like hot potatoes. I once had a gynecologist who was treating me for infertility (can you believe it, four children later?). One day he walked into the examining room and asked, "How are you?" I started to cry and say that I was feeling pretty blue and frustrated. He did an about-face and called over his shoulder as he walked out the door, "I will send in a nurse to talk to you." Not only did I immediately stop seeing him, but I wrote him a very pointed letter. Most gratifying of all was my pleasure in trashing this particular doctor all over the Girlfriends' Grapevine. Hell hath no fury . . .

If *The Girlfriends' Guide* accomplishes little else, I will be satisfied if it succeeds in encouraging you to get your money's worth out of your relationship with your doctor. Trust me when I tell you that it takes a long time to get over a disappointing pregnancy. If you feel ill-prepared, frightened or slighted in any way, you will still be talking about it twenty years from now. I have a Girlfriend who still talks about how inadequate she felt during labor, and I think it was her doctor's job to bolster her confidence. Women who end up with C-sections when they had their hearts set on a "natural" childbirth can be filled with grief unless they are confident that it was a mutual decision and that it was the best thing to do. So go ahead and call your doctor or go visit him or her whenever the urge arises, because I promise you that you are no more neurotic or insecure than the rest of us.

What If You Think You Are Falling in Love With Your Doctor?

Sometimes, the combination of dependency and admiration that you feel for your doctor may make you think that you are falling in love. Relax—it is strikingly common for a pregnant woman to fall in love with her doctor, especially when her doctor is a man. Perhaps it is a form of the syndrome known as Hostage Identification, like when Patty Hearst fell in love with her Symbionese Liberation Army kidnapper. The theory goes that utterly helpless people identify and develop a relationship with their captor because that person is all that stands between them and certain death. Sounds about right for a woman pregnant with her first child and her doctor, don't you think?

Another reason why you may get a crush on your doctor is that you are desperate for any kind of attention, and your obstetrician joins you in your obsession at least once a month. (As unique and special as your pregnancy is, it can tend to lose its fascinating and compelling aspects to everyone but your mother and you about half-way through. And unfortunately, a pregnant woman's need for attention is about as deep as the Grand Canyon.) I hate to be so blunt, but it is important for you to remember, YOU DID NOT INVENT PREGNANCY, AND EVENTUALLY YOU WILL HAVE TO RESORT TO PAYING PEOPLE TO REMAIN CAPTIVATED BY YOUR CONDITION. Your friends have their own lives that will occasionally distract them from your crucial project, and, if your husband is like mine, even he will eventually tire of waking up to touch your belly every time the baby moves. Your doctor, however, will continue to be solicitous and inquiring right up until the bitter end—assuming, of course, that you have selected your obstetrician based on *The Girlfriends' Guide* criteria. Plus, he or she will eventually become the only person you encounter who does not irritatingly ask you, "Haven't you had that baby yet?"

7

Prenatal Tests

There once was a time when the only medical test routinely give to a pregnant woman resulted in a dead rabbit. It's true—the old-fashioned way of diagnosing early pregnancy was to administer a serum of the woman's blood to a rabbit, and if the rabbit died, the woman was pronounced pregnant. (PETA would just hate that, and thank heavens it is no longer the method of choice for doctors in the free world.) Well, a test to establish pregnancy is no longer the only test that is given to pregnant women. Depending on your age and some other factors, such as how comprehensive your medical insurance is, there are a variety of medical procedures that might be recommended or even required of you during the next few months.

Once again, let me make it clear that this is not a medical book. My purpose is simply to make you aware of the basics of pregnancy. Think of this chapter as an introductory foreign language course where you learn how to ask where the bathroom is and how to order dinner, so that you don't look like a complete imbecile. Once you get the lingo, you'll know how to ask a doctor for the real information.

The following list is not to be considered comprehensive in any way; it is just the collection of the Girlfriends' most commonly experienced tests and procedures.

The Pregnancy Test

You have probably taken this already, but just in case you haven't, there are basically two kinds of pregnancy tests: the kind that require urine and the kind that require blood. As you might assume, the ones you do yourself at home require urine, not blood, thank God. The home pregnancy tests and the urine tests performed at your doctor's office look just the same to me. They used to require some mixing and a lot of waiting, but now the results are in within minutes. Many home tests and the doctor's office will require you to pee in a small cup. Until recently, doctors wanted this urine to be as pregnant as possible, so they recommended that you collect your first pee of the morning. Evidently the chemicals of the test are more sensitive now, because both the doctors' tests and the home tests say any old pee will do.

If this is your first pregnancy, or if you have never had a vaginal delivery, the task of peeing into a small cup may be simple. If you have had a few children, however, it can be more difficult. First of all, you may no longer be able to pee where you aim. Second, it may be harder to stop peeing once you have started, and you run the risk of filling the cup to overflowing and dropping the whole thing into the toilet. Whether it is your first test or your tenth, a rule of etiquette always applies: Wipe off the outside of the cup after you have put about an inch and a half of urine in it, just in case it's wet. Not only would a wet cup be disgusting for the nurse, but it could make the cup slippery and one of you could drop it.

My Girlfriend Lili, who discovered she is pregnant during my writing of this book, took the cutest home pregnancy test I have ever heard of. A positive result is indicated by the appearance of a little heart. Couldn't you just weep? My favorite urine pregnancy tests are the sticks. (But then, I had never heard of the hearts before.) You simply remove the cap from the end of the stick and urinate on it. No need for perfect aim, and no need to stop the flow just when it was beginning to provide relief. You can all read the information included with the home pregnancy kit to learn its accuracy rates and disclaimers. The basic rule of thumb is, a positive is a positive is a positive. And, a negative is a maybe, but a probably not. The problems arise, according to my Girlfriends, when they think the stick has turned "a little pink, but not real pink," or when they see "a faint line, but not a clear blue line." Sometimes this uncertainty arises because you are not yet making enough pregnancy hormone to activate the test properly. Other times—and I speak as a person who was unable to conceive for three and a half years—sheer hopefulness makes you see a result that really isn't accurate. If you are unsure of your results, go to the doctor and get a blood test. Knowing whether you are pregnant or not is not the same thing as knowing whether you will be picked for jury duty; if it is possible to find out right now, why not go and do it. I never understood it when people said that they were going to wait until they missed their second period or got a certain result from the home test before calling their doctor. If you are indeed pregnant, find out now, so that you can clean up your act accordingly.

The blood test to determine pregnancy can, if you have a cooperative doctor, also test to measure your hormone levels and to test for HIV. This test is usually done in the doctor's office, and involves the same old rubber band on the upper arm and poking for a vein that any other blood test involves. Does it hurt? Well, that usually depends on three things: your doctor's or nurse's skill, your available veins and what you consider painful. I think it's fair to say "Ouch!" but silly to cry, if that gives you any indication. Feel free to look away while they stick the needle in, and ask if you can lie down if you have any premonition that this procedure might make you light-headed. You will not be perceived as any more of a baby than anyone else. Is it dangerous? Not as long as you use a clean needle and aren't allergic to Band-Aids.

Vaginal Cultures

Once you and your doctor are reasonably satisfied that you really are pregnant, he or she will want to swab some gunk out of your vaginal canal and off your cervix to test for a bunch of things. This is pretty much an all-purpose Pap smear, and feels just about the same. The doctor will insert the dreaded speculum into your vagina, crank it open, take a look to see if your cervix is tightly closed like it should be (and taking on the new, rosy colors of pregnancy) and then stick a large Q-Tip in to wipe out some of the secretions. These will then be wiped on a number of glass slides and sent out to a lab, which will make sure that you are not getting cervical cancer and that you don't have any sexually transmitted diseases.

Urine Tests

From your first visit till your very last, you will begin every exam in a doctor's office by peeing into a cup. Gradually, you will lose any inhibitions you may have had about walking around with a container of your own body waste. A nurse or nurse's aide will then stick a paper strip in the urine and you will walk into an examining room without giving it a further thought. The nurse will, however, see if the paper strip changes color to indicate whether you have unusual protein levels. You probably do not, because if you did, you would hear about it immediately. The reason why anyone cares whether you have protein in your urine is that it can indicate you are heading for toxemia (see a real medical book), and your doctor will want to head this usually manageable condition off at the pass.

Blood Pressure Tests

A pleasant little ritual that you will join in every single time you visit your obstetrician for a checkup will be the measuring of your blood pressure. The most important thing you need to know initially when having this test done is to stop talking and allow the nurse to count without distraction. Other than that, just sit there, because nothing is going to hurt or break the skin. The motivation for the test is the fact that pregnant women have an increased risk of high blood pressure. (And who wouldn't, under these circumstances?) I always liked this test, because I didn't have any problems with blood pressure and because it had nothing to do with passing or failing, like the weighing did. You must go to the doctor and have it done frequently, however, because it, like the protein-in-the-urine test, will warn you of any predisposition toward toxemia.

Ultrasounds

These used to be referred to as sonograms, and you will often find the two names used interchangeably. Even when you still look unpregnant on the outside, through this technology you will be able to see a recognizable human on the inside, getting ready to become the core of your being, the love of your life, and the burr in your behind.

The test involves you lying on your back on an examining table and the doctor using one of two instruments to send sound waves through your belly. A computer then interprets these sound waves and their echoes and creates a picture of your pregnancy on a monitor that looks like a television screen or a computer monitor. At first the image on the screen is nearly impossible to interpret, but with your doctor's help you can see the major bones, the heart, the brain and sometimes the genitals of your little baby. The doctor and you can also see how many babies are in there, often a nice little surprise that is good to get out of the way early in pregnancy rather than on the delivery table. Your doctor can also see your placenta, where it is placed in your uterus and how much fluid is in there for the baby to swim around in.

It is a truly wonderful test, and most people consider the only reason not to use it is its cost. Insurance companies and HMOs think that ultrasounds should be reserved for critical diagnoses, not just to look for a penis between those bony legs or to see if there is a heartbeat at six or seven weeks. You will probably get one or two ultrasounds during your pregnancy (assuming there isn't anything extraordinary hiding in there, like twins, or puppies), and this experience may be the very first time you really "get it" that there is a human being growing inside you. More important, this will be a reality check for your husband, who up to this point has only taken your word for it that you are, indeed, pregnant (and who may have secretly had his doubts about the reliability of the home pregnancy test). He may need to sit down or be given a hankie at this moment; that's how staggering this introduction between parent and child can be.

One of the greatest moments in pregnancy is when you are having an ultrasound and your baby moves for you, or better still, sucks its thumb just like a *real* baby. In fact, the entire ultrasound experience is so thrilling that the Girlfriends recommend that you ask someone, like your husband, to videotape it. If the video idea doesn't pan out, rest assured that you won't come away empty-handed in the posterity department, because the doctor or ultrasound technician will give you some Polaroid photos of your very own little E.T. to take home and confound your friends and relatives with (since they won't be able to tell the baby from first base in the fuzzy photo).

To work, ultrasounds depend on water. Early in the pregnancy, before there is a lot of amniotic fluid in your uterus, the transducer (which I'll call the microphone) that your doctor scans over your belly will not get a good reading unless you have a full bladder. This fact is almost always casually offered, but I am here to tell you that a full bladder when you are pregnant and lying on your back is *very* uncomfortable, if not desperation time. Do you have any idea how much water it takes to fill your bladder sufficiently? Judging from my own experience, it took more water than any normal person could bear to drink in one sitting. I never thought I would see the day that water would make me nauseous, but it did on ultrasound day. If your doctor doesn't mention it, ask him if he has a *vaginal* "microphone" he can use instead. The vaginal instrument is more accurate when there is no extra fluid because it is able to get in there closer to the uterus, so you don't have to fill yourself with water to the point of bursting. Believe me, you will relax and enjoy the show on the screen a lot more if you are not petrified that you might pee all over the table.

Does it hurt? No, but if you are one of those women who hates any sort of internal vaginal exam, you won't be crazy about this one either, because the doctor not only puts a dildo-resembling instrument in you, but he points it in quite a few directions to "see" everything he wants to see. If you know any Lamaze breathing, use it during a vaginal ultrasound where it can really help you stay relaxed, because it will be virtually useless during delivery. Feel free to try puffing away, but don't come crying to me if it doesn't really take the edge off; in my opinion, that's what epidurals are for, but I digress.

Later in the pregnancy, when you are holding so much water in your uterus that you could float a ship, your doctor or technician will be able to get a good picture by using a flatter, more rectangular "microphone" that he or she will slide all over your belly. First, however, they will smear some gel on your abdomen to help conduct the sound. Recently, doctors have gotten humane about that gel, and they often keep it in a dispenser that warms it. But if your doctor hasn't yet invested in that marvelous invention, get ready for a shock because, that gel is *cold* on your poor exposed tummy.

Gestational Diabetes Test (Glucose Tolerance Test)

Even if you don't normally have diabetes, you might develop a condition of it during your pregnancy. This is called gestational diabetes, and it almost always disappears after the baby is born. It is also quite common in pregnancy, and as long as you eat carefully and do what your doctor tells you to do, you and the baby will be fine. The test to see if you have gestational diabetes is called a glucose tolerance test. I have had a doctor who sends patients to a lab for the test, and I have had a doctor who routinely does the test in his own office. You will be asked to drink a small, soda-sized bottle of a liquid that tastes like soda pop with an extra half cup of sugar thrown in for good measure. So cloying is this taste that it can make you queasy if you don't follow a couple of instructions. First, definitely refrigerate the liquid before you drink it; the cold seems to numb your taste buds somewhat. (Either your doctor will give the bottle of sugar drink to you before your test visit, so you will have ample time to refrigerate it, or the lab will have it already chilled for you.) And, second, don't gulp it down too quickly. I know you will want to down it as rapidly as possible, but your unsuspecting stomach may rebel, and then you will vomit all of it up as quickly as you swallowed it—and have to drink it all over again.

If your doctor has given you the liquid to drink at home, you will need to time it so that you are at the doctor's office one hour after you drink it. If you do it at a lab, you will have an hour to kill between drinking the foul potion and getting a blood test.

The most critical bit of Girlfriend advice we can offer regarding the glucose tolerance test is this: Bring something healthy and substantial to eat after the test, like a sandwich, a piece of fruit or a bag of trail mix, because you won't have eaten anything before it and pregnant women get *very cranky* when they have skipped a meal.

Amniocentesis

Amniocentesis is a procedure to test the genetic health of your unborn baby. It is usually performed at the end of your fourth month of pregnancy, and it takes about two weeks to get the results back. It is generally done to eliminate the worry of a child being born with Down's syndrome, but it can also detect the existence of several other genetic problems. The fun element of amnio is that it can tell you with almost absolute certainty whether your baby is a boy or a girl.

Not only is this an expensive procedure, but it presents a slight risk of harm to the pregnancy—in a word, miscarriage. Therefore, it is not usually done frivolously, but rather by women who have reason to suspect that they might have a higher-than-normal risk of genetic problems with their babies. Traditionally, and because most HMOs and insurance companies have decreed it so, amnios are generally given only to women who will be thirty-five or older when they deliver or who have a history of genetic abnormalities in their family. If you are having an amnio just to find out the sex of your baby, you might be a bit overcurious for your own good, and the baby's.

This test involves a doctor sticking a needle into your belly and through your uterus to withdraw some fluid from your placenta. That fluid is then sent to a lab, where it is cultured for the next ten days to two weeks. You can well imagine how long that needle must be to get to its goal, and you are right. If you have fainted at this point, don't worry; when you have recovered we will give you our words of advice and encouragement to get through this. WE PROMISE YOU THAT THE AMNIO WILL NOT BE AS BAD AS YOU THINK.

Almost everyone who is advised to get an amnio is terrified. I know this for a fact, because in my first pregnancy I was lying on the exam table with my belly draped and swabbed with disinfectant, and I chickened out. Yep, I got up in tears, put my clothes on and went home without having done the test. Now, am I recommending that you, too, let fear prevent you from getting the information your doctor thinks you should have? Absolutely not. I am just illustrating my empathy for you and your insecurities as you anticipate this event.

The reasons why we are terrified of amnios are threefold. First, we think that it will hurt like a son of a gun. Second, our genetics counselors or doctors have been legally obligated to tell us that there is a very small chance of causing the miscarriage of a healthy fetus through amnio. And third, and most agonizing, if the amnio should, God forbid, tell us that our baby is genetically abnormal, we would have to decide whether or not to terminate the pregnancy. This is one of the most difficult decisions a couple will ever have to make, and the prospect of facing it is brain-numbing. After all, if you are absolutely against abortion, why get an amnio in the first place, unless you just feel that forewarned is forearmed?

There, now that I have you ready to slit your wrists, let me rush to reassure you that your odds are incredibly good of having a perfectly normal baby, especially if you are under forty years old. Even after the age of forty, the odds are still overwhelmingly in your favor. As my father told me when I fretted to him during my fourth pregnancy at the age of thirty-nine, "I would play your odds at the racetrack any day of the week." All amnio will do for you, in all likelihood, is relieve you of some of your phantom worries about your unborn baby. I wish I could tell you that a good amnio result makes the rest of the pregnancy worry-free, but it doesn't work that way. After you have eliminated Down's syndrome and other *testable* genetic abnormalities from your worrying itinerary, you will simply and certainly replace them with fears of cleft palates and strawberry birthmarks, so get used to it. Pregnancy, remember, is the beginning of the slippery slope of worry down which you will careen for the rest of your life.

So, let's talk about whether it hurts. The answer is, yes, a little bit. (I would like to interject here that, having given birth, I chuckle when I speak of pain, so this is for you "virgins." After you have delivered a baby, pain will take on a different meaning.) More than being painful, the amnio rates high on the "creep factor index." Some doctors offer a shot of Novocain in your belly before the amnio needle. Others will say, "Why take two needles when you can get away with taking just one?" Here is why: Because the Novocain needle is about two inches long and has the circumference of a hair. The amnio needle is about seven inches long and is substantially thicker than the other. I can't speak for everyone, but I liked the sense of security that the shot of Novocain instilled in me. I was in the room holding my Girlfriend Amy's hand during her amnio, and she went straight for the big needle with no Novocain first, and didn't flinch. That is consistent with what a lot of Girlfriends tell me—after the initial prick of the skin, there is nothing to it. They insist that you don't feel anything inside of you, which makes sense anatomically since you don't have nerves in those organs. Nonetheless, if someone is offering a shield of any sort against any discomfort, real or imagined, I am first in line.

After the amnio, you will probably feel much like you felt when you went in, except a lot more relieved and extremely tired from the emotional ordeal. The Girlfriends and I, not to mention your doctor, recommend that you go right home and get in bed. I don't know what this does for the health of the baby, but I do know that anyone who has gone through what you just went through deserves a day of soap operas and Oprah. Take advantage, because this is one of the few days during your pregnancy that everyone in the universe will agree that you need to take it easy.

Chorionic Villi Sampling (CVS)

This was my procedure of choice. For three pregnancies I opted for the relatively new procedure called CVS. One of the reasons I was interested in CVS, which tests for the same genetic abnormalities as an amnio with the exception of spina bifida and determines the sex of the baby, was that the test is performed at eleven or twelve weeks of pregnancy, and the results can come back as quickly as twenty-four hours later. One of the biggest drawbacks of the amnio is that you are about five months pregnant before you get the results. By five months, you are halfway through your pregnancy and already feeling the baby kick, so a decision to terminate the pregnancy could be particularly horrible. With a CVS, however, you can have the test and the results several weeks before anyone really even needs to know you are pregnant in the first place. Then, whatever decision you make, you can make without the approval or disapproval of friends and family.

A CVS is done in conjunction with an ultrasound. Since it is done early in pregnancy, you will be asked to drink a lot of water before the procedure and a technician will do an ultrasound to see if your bladder is so full that it is getting in the way of the picture, not to mention making you feel like a water balloon; if it is, they will have you pee some off. After the technician has determined the age of the fetus and that it is alive and apparently healthy, the person performing the CVS will begin. Your legs will be in stirrups like during a Pap test, and the doctor will use gigantic Q-Tips dunked in a brown disinfectant called Betadyne to clean your vaginal canal and your cervix. That is usually the most uncomfortable part; it feels like you are having your insides cleaned with a Turkish towel.

After you are rendered scrupulously clean inside, an assistant will use an external ultrasound "microphone" to locate the baby and its chorionic villi, which are things that stick out from the fetus. Using the ultrasound picture as his guide, the doctor will insert a very thin plastic tube through the tiny cervical opening to the uterus. When the monitor shows that the doctor is at the chorion, a needle is slid up through the plastic tube to take out a tiny portion of it. In my experience, all of this is entirely painless. It even registers low on the creep factor, because it is so enthralling to watch the baby on the ultrasound monitor that you kind of ignore everything else that is going on.

After my third CVS, I started to bleed pretty heavily, and I was ready to kill my CVS doctor and myself. I had never had as much spotting the two times before, and I was convinced that I had tempted fate one too many times. I called the doctor's office, nearly unable to talk from the paralysis of fear, but they stayed in touch with me and reassured me that this was not unusual and that everything would be fine. Indeed, it was, and when I got a telephone call the next day saying that this thirty-nine-year-old was pregnant with a healthy daughter, I nearly did a backflip for joy.

This procedure is still controversial among obstetricians. Since it is relatively new, there are not that many doctors who have had a reassuring amount of experience performing it and who feel that the risks are acceptably low. For this reason, I would discuss the genetic testing options with my o.b. and make the decision together. There are tremendous advancements in this particular test, but there are still a few kinks, especially outside the domain of major teaching and research hospitals. For example, a few years ago there was some speculation that babies who underwent CVS as fetuses were missing fingers or toes as a result of it. I cannot discuss this as a professional, but I can tell you what I was recently told. The newest wisdom is to do the test slightly later in pregnancy than was originally thought advisable, say at twelve weeks rather than nine. This has successfully been shown to eliminate the threat to the baby's limbs. Still, as I said, this is a decision you will have to make with your husband and your doctor (and any Girlfriend who has the patience to discuss it with you for the billionth time). I should add that one of the reasons I felt secure getting a CVS rather than an amnio was that the doctor who performed it was the teacher of the technique at two major hospitals and had done the procedure thousands of times. He did nothing else in his practice but CVS and amnios. I don't think I would have been so willing had he been a regular ob/gyn who dabbled in the occasional CVS on the side. If you decide on this procedure, find the doctor in your community who has performed it more often and more successfully than anyone else and go to *that* person.

A CVS, like an amnio, is universal permission to go straight home to bed for a day of reading tabloids or watching television. You and your cervix have been through a lot, and your psyche is probably even more traumatized, so you all need a rest.

Alpha-Fetoprotein Test

This test is primarily done to detect abnormalities related to the spine. It can show whether the spinal column and brain are developing normally. It involves yet another blood test, taken about four or five months into the pregnancy. Sometimes, when the level of alpha-fetoproteins are suspicious, a woman will be advised to get an amnio as well, even if she is under age thirty-five and has no other recognizable risk for genetic problems. Studies have shown that the new "triple marker" AFP tests show a statistical relationship between certain levels and possible Down's syndrome. My Girlfriend Mindy got low results back on this test, and we all suffered for nearly two weeks while we awaited the results of her amnio. Her baby was not only genetically perfect, but one of the most beautiful little girls that the world has ever known. Still, we all had our lives shorted by the worrisome wait.

Does this procedure hurt? Not any more or any less than any other blood test. But it could lead to further tests like amnio which, if not painful, rank high on the creep factor index. Just because you get suspicious results back from this test doesn't mean that there is anything wrong with your baby. In fact, most of the time, nothing at all is wrong, so don't leap off a bridge if your doctor tells you your results require further testing. Still, it is a valuable warning flare, so get the test.

Non-Stress Test

The name of this test has nothing to do with *your* emotional state when it is taken. It refers, rather, to the fact that your baby is being electronically monitored in its natural, nonstressed condition of floating carefree in your huge belly. Your belly will, indeed, be huge if and when you have this test, because it is generally used to check on babies who are near term or past their due date, just to make sure that they are still groovin' in the womb.

This test is usually performed by a trained technician, since a medical doctor rarely wants to sit around watching your baby's heartbeat repeatedly graphed on endless strips of paper for up to an hour, riveting though you may think it is. The nurse or technician will put a fetal monitor belt around your tummy with the microphone portion as close to the baby's heartbeat as she can get it. She will then turn around and walk out of the room, leaving you completely alone. *(This is good preparation for what often happens to women in labor.)* The point of the test is to see if the baby's heartbeat responds properly to its own movement and to any contractions your practicing uterus may be doing. As you approach or pass your due date, doctors may want to make sure that the baby isn't overstaying its welcome and doesn't need to be encouraged out. The odds are very good that you will never have this test, but I mention it because I don't want you to worry if your doctor suggests it. This, by the way, is a good time to catch up on your reading.

It has always been my experience that my baby fell asleep during the non-stress test, and I was invariably given fruit juice to drink in the hopes that the sugar rush would wake it into activity, or I was prodded in the stomach to wake the little darling up. I am not complaining about this, however, because a lazy kid is a mellow kid, and when you have four kids you begin to admire mellowness as a desirable character trait.

Weighing In

O.K., so stepping on a doctor's scale doesn't seem like any technical medical procedure to you. So sue me. Still, you will be weighed every single time you visit your obstetrician, and this weighing is considered a tool to monitor both your health and that of the baby. So I say it stays right here in the prenatal testing chapter of this *Guide*.

If there is no real crisis with your pregnancy, the most painful medical procedure that you will be asked to withstand may be the monthly weighing in. I consistently dreaded this part of an otherwise lovely visit to my obstetrician, because I consistently gained more weight than I thought was good. When I only gained a pound or two between visits, I would be so proud and happy, but when I gained six pounds between visits, I felt like I had no self-control and was not handling my pregnant urges properly. Eventually, after the first two or three pregnancies, I noticed something that my Girlfriends had also pointed out to me: We all tended to put on the same amount of weight with each pregnancy, give or take a few pounds, without much regard to different activity levels and eating habits. In other words, I put on as much weight with Jeremy, when I was raising two toddlers, working full-time and rarely eating, as I did with Jamie, during whose pregnancy I stayed in bed for over four months and ate every bit of protein, carbohydrate and calcium that the pregnancy books recommended. We are of the conclusion that each woman's body has its own personal style of doing pregnancy. Whether your body's style is to get huge or to gain only ten pounds, it will probably stick to that style from pregnancy to pregnancy.

This seems to me to be a good reason to take it easy on yourself where weight gain is concerned. Sure, if you live on Boston cream pies for nine months, you can expect to get extraordinarily fat. But if you just eat when you are hungry and eat as nutritiously as you can (give or take a chocolate or cookie binge every now and then), you will probably put on an almost predetermined amount of weight, and it will stay constant from baby to baby.

8

Exercise and Pregnancy

I have always thought of pregnancy as divine permission not to exercise. For that reason, this chapter will be even more opinionated than the others, it will focus on some exercises that you have never even dreamed about and it will fly in the face of all the current notions that a woman should be able to grow a baby and run a marathon simultaneously.

Don't get me wrong: I am not antiexercise. In fact, I am quite keen on doing all sorts of fitness activities. When I am not pregnant, I jog, I lift weights and I engage in whatever other fad is popular in my neighborhood, from kick-boxing to stationary cycling. But I am a firm believer in the maxim IF YOU WANT TO DO SOMETHING WELL, GIVE IT AS MUCH ATTENTION AS YOU POSSIBLY CAN. In other words, you are trying to grow a healthy baby without sustaining too much damage to yourself during the process, and that deserves all the attention you can give it. Working, taking care of your other kids and doing all the other things that constitute living your life will be distractions enough (especially when you are lugging around an extra thirty pounds). If you find yourself with extra time on your hands, like my Girlfriend Shannon, who is an actress and who was unable to work once her pregnancy started showing, spend it needlepointing a Christmas stocking, organizing your photo albums or alphabetizing your CD collection. I guarantee you that you will never have time to do those things again once the baby is born.

Here are the biggest reasons why we Girlfriends don't think you need to keep up your aerobics membership while you are pregnant:

1 You Will Be Too Tired.

2 You Will Not Look Good in Your Leotard.

3 You Will Get Fat Anyway.

4 Exercise Will Not Help You in Labor or Delivery in Any Way.

5 You Might Endanger the Pregnancy.

6 Even If You Don't Endanger the Pregnancy, If Something (God Forbid) Goes Wrong, You Will Forever Wonder If Your Exercising Caused It.

7 It's "Nine Months Up and Nine Months Down" in the Weight-Gaining Department, No Matter What You Do. (Give or take a few months on the down side.)

8 Our Compulsion to Exercise When We Are Pregnant Is a Reflection of Our Inability to Surrender and Let Nature Run Its Course.

I can just feel the controversy that will arise over these statements. Doctors, fitness gurus and women who successfully exercised throughout their pregnancies are going to come looking for me, their water bottles poised for combat. I feel so strongly about this that I am willing to take them on. I realize that a large number of you will want to dismiss me outright, especially if you are very newly pregnant. That is all right, but read this chapter anyway, if only for the enjoyment of trashing me afterward. You just might see things my way in the end.

POINT 1 *You Will Be Too Tired.*

If the brain-numbing fatigue of early pregnancy has already struck you, then I don't need to go any further. You already know what it is like to sit on the side of your bed to tie your shoes and wake up two hours later. You have already made your peace with missing the rest of the season of *E.R.*, and have promised yourself you will catch up during summer reruns. You have already humiliated yourself by falling asleep during a staff meeting and awakening so suddenly and awkwardly that you nearly fell off your chair.

If you are like the rest of us during our first pregnancies, you keep telling yourself that as soon as the first three months are over you will get back to that aerobics class. Like the rest of us, you will be quietly disturbed that you are such a weakling that you let a simple thing like pregnancy get in the way of your supreme fitness. You will be certain that other women—who "do" pregnancy "better" than you—are up at dawn for a quick five-mile sprint instead of vomiting and then eating an entire pecan loaf for breakfast. Here is the news, Girlfriend: Even those jocky girls, the ones who were born with lean, muscular legs and lungs the size of all outdoors, tend to get soft and fat during pregnancy. If they don't, then they are either in the microscopic minority or they are depriving their babies and themselves of extremely valuable nutrition and rest.

Here is a novel concept for the nineties: If your body is tired, you should listen to it and rest. I am the last one to judge anyone poorly for being activity addicts in their nonpregnant state, but I sound the alarms when you have a human being growing in your abdomen. Think about it. From one little egg that you have had in your body since you were born, and one little sperm that your husband manufactured on the spur of the moment, you are expected to create an entire person. I'm talking arms, legs, heart, lungs, eyelashes and your uncle Harry's big ears. If you don't think that can be tiring, then you are a pretty invincible woman, and not someone I yearn to spend much time with.

The Girlfriends' recommendation is that you sleep whenever you possibly can during your pregnancy. You will not know this freedom again for several years.

POINT 2 *You Will Not Look Good in Your Leotard.*

At some point right around the three-month mark, you will probably begin to get your energy back. Not only will you get your old energy back, but you may actually feel *more* energetic than before you were pregnant. I call this the Wonder Woman Trimester. You probably aren't nauseous anymore. You may have regained your interest in sex (and then some, judging from the Girlfriends' reports). And you may consider taking up where you left off on the exercise regimen.

So, you dig through your drawers for your dusty old tights and leotards, and slip them on for a tentative visit to the gym. On your way out of your bedroom you catch a glimpse of yourself in your exercise attire. You do a double take. "Who is that squishy being, anyway?" Then you realize that that "squishy being" is you, and you run frantically to your bed to lie down before you faint.

Let's be brutally frank here. Everyone knows that skintight exercise clothes are primarily intended to show off our bodies. The manufacturers might insist that sleek Lycra is the most aerodynamic exercise fabric, and they might be right. But for the vast majority of us who haven't sprinted fifty meters since junior high school, aerodynamics are not all that crucial. We wear all that tight stretchy stuff because we think we look good in it.

These sleek little outfits take on a whole new identity when they are stuffed with pregnant breasts, pregnant bellies, pregnant thighs and pregnant knees, and topped off by pregnant arms. If you don't take my word for it, rent yourself one of those home videos of exercise programs for pregnant women. I don't mean to be nasty, but the women in these videos look swollen and uncomfortable. And *those* are the women who looked good enough to volunteer to be on TV in their little striped leotards in the first place! Those of us who would get dressed in absolute darkness to avoid having to inspect ourselves if we could would rather have natural childbirth than have anyone see us in spandex at this point.

I have seen some die-hard pregnant women in the gym with their husband's T-shirts over their exercise clothes to camouflage things, but I am one of those who would rather just sulk and stop exercising.

POINT 3 *You Will Get Fatter Anyway.*

I don't know about you, but I exercise in a constant effort to lose those last five pounds or to keep my derriere from resting on the backs of my thighs. Talk to me all you want to about endorphins, about restored energy, about cardiovascular fitness. I maintain that if we could all look like Naomi Campbell if we only lived on candy and Marlboro Lights, nearly all of the gyms in this country would close overnight and be replaced by more 7 Elevens and ashtrays.

In pregnancy, the whole idea is to acknowledge that your body is now a baby-making machine. It needs to expand to allow for the growth of the baby. It also needs to fulfill its biological imperative against starvation of the species by adding stores of fat to itself to make sure the baby doesn't starve even if the father fails to kill a boar for dinner one night. This is the opposite of what exercise fanatics are trying to do. Doesn't it make sense to you that you are making nature's job harder by following your quest for fat-burning activities? Why go through all that hard work when you won't look like Naomi for at least another year, if ever?

I have noticed in those home exercise videos for pregnant women that a big deal is made of lifting very light weights to keep the arms and upper body in shape. Since I have never seen "ripped" arms on a pregnant woman in my life, I have to assume that they are doing these wussy little exercises in hopes of keeping some sort of muscle tone so that it won't take so long to get back in shape after the baby comes. I am not a physiologist, but my personal experience suggests that lifting two-pound weights or two cans of soup for twenty repetitions every day has little or nothing to do with how strong your arms will be after the baby is born. If lifting two soup cans is all it takes to keep a pregnant woman's muscles toned, why does the guy at my gym make me struggle with two fifteen-pound dumbbells when I am *not* pregnant? He certainly does not get paid by the pound!

POINT 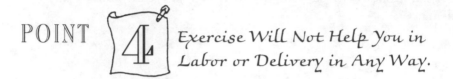 *Exercise Will Not Help You in Labor or Delivery in Any Way.*

The trendy logic goes something like this: Exercise builds strength and stamina. Labor and delivery require strength and stamina. Therefore, exercise must help during labor and delivery. Sounds reasonable, doesn't it? Well, we are here to tell you that it doesn't work that way. Labor is a series (seemingly endless) of *involuntary* muscle contractions. All of these involuntary contractions are supposed to result in the opening of the entrance to the uterus (the cervix) to a size of about ten centimeters. Then the mother is supposed to push the baby out of that opening.

You can do sit-ups from here till next Tuesday and they will not do one single thing to make your uterus stronger. Your uterus sits safely *behind* all of the muscles that are involved in the sit-up, and except for a Braxton Hicks contraction every now and then, it sits pretty quietly, minding its own business. If you think that you have come up with an exercise that can prepare your cervix to open quickly and on command, please let me know.

You can also stretch, lunge and lift light weights all you want, and you will not become any more efficient at pushing. If you really want a preparatory exercise for pushing a baby out of your uterus, then have a lot of bowel movements, because they are probably as close to replicating the sensation as you are going to get. In fact, it could hurt you or your pregnancy if you were to consistently do exercises that forced you to do the bearing down and grunting that remind most of us of pushing. This tendency to hold your breath or grunt while exerting a particular muscle is called the Valsavic maneuver, and most doctors are in agreement that it isn't good for you or the baby. Evidently it unnaturally raises your blood pressure and momentarily slows the oxygen passing to the fetus.

I have watched many of my Girlfriends labor and deliver their babies, and one thing that never ceased to interest me was how irrelevant their fitness levels were to the ease of their delivery. I have one Girlfriend who smoked cigarettes until the day she found out she was pregnant, and then ate until the day she went into labor. She labored for three or four hours and then pushed the baby out in a matter of minutes. I have another Girlfriend who was a college track star and had maintained her fitness ever since. She labored for forty hours and never dilated past four centimeters. To my nonmedical eye, it almost looked like the looser and less muscle-bound a woman was, the easier it was for the baby to get out. There is a certain poignancy here, because many Girlfriends work hard to stay physically fit and active and then have problematical deliveries, while many women who were petrified that they would never have the strength to make it through labor and delivery because their fitness regime consisted of walking briskly to the refrigerator are pleasantly surprised by their brilliant performance at getting that baby out. Once again, life illustrates its fundamental unfairness.

POINT 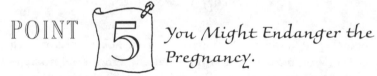 *You Might Endanger the Pregnancy.*

Now I am just speaking for myself. I may be the only woman on the face of the planet who experienced this, and if I am, just indulge me for one moment, then forget I ever said anything. Very early on in two of my four pregnancies, I tried to maintain my traditional exercise program of running and weight lifting, and two times I ended up with small tears where the placenta connects to the uterus. Apparently the strain of lifting heavy weights applied too much pressure on my uterus. And two times I took to my bed crying and frightened for a day or two until the bleeding stopped. Who knows how much I endangered my babies? Heaven knows, I was too terrified to ask my doctor that question—or more to the point, too terrified to hear his answer. I do know, however, that my doctor did a number of ultrasounds to monitor the healing, and that he was relieved when he saw that there was no more blood pooling up in there, so I guess he had been somewhat concerned, too.

A point could be made that I was exercising too strenuously, and that I should have modified my exercise routine rather than ended it. Most of the current wisdom says that a pregnant woman can continue exercising to her full capacity, but that she should not take up *new* or *more difficult* regimens after becoming pregnant. To be completely candid with you, I did not know how to exercise moderately. If I wasn't working out to achieve strength or to stay trim, I would just as soon skip the whole thing. Since the stakes were so high, I wasn't willing to gamble with how much was too much. And since there comes a point when exercising lightly becomes a waste of time, I just gave the whole thing up.

POINT  *Even If You Don't Endanger the Pregnancy, If Something (God Forbid) Goes Wrong, You Will Forever Wonder If Your Exercising Caused It.*

When we become pregnant, we become obsessed about taking care of the pregnancy. We invest so much physical and emotional nurturing because we start to love that baby when it is no bigger than a lima bean. Tragically, not all pregnancies result in the delivery of a healthy baby. The most common threat to a successful pregnancy is miscarriage. It happens more often than you might think; estimates say about 10 percent of all known pregnancies end in miscarriage, and more if the mother is older or very young. The vast majority of miscarriages occur during the first three months of pregnancy. It is widely believed that about half of all miscarriages occur because the fetus was not normal. Thus comes the most common, and least comforting, comment that a woman who has just miscarried will receive: "Don't worry, dear. This is just nature's way of weeding out the imperfect ones."

It is also widely believed that exercise, stress, intercourse and jumping off a chair will *not* cause miscarriage. So I guess that big scene when Rhett pushes Scarlett down the stairs and she loses their baby is biologically inaccurate. It is definitely true that when you are seventeen and have missed your period, all of the jumping, douching and praying in the world won't seem to do anything to interrupt a pregnancy. I don't know, however, if it is completely true in women who, like me, had a bleeding episode or used fertility drugs to get pregnant. If frequent exercise and intercourse have no bearing whatsoever on miscarriage, then why do so many very good doctors prescribe "full pelvic rest" (no sex) when the woman seems at risk for miscarriage?

My big question is, how do you know you are having a risky pregnancy until you push yourself and something goes wrong, like when I started bleeding after bench-pressing? What if I'd lost that baby? My doctor could have sworn on his own children (although I doubt he would have) that my pumping iron and the loss of the baby were purely coincidental, but I would never have totally believed him. How could I, when I would have always wondered if I should have relaxed a bit and been more protective of the pregnancy? I find the mantle of guilt a very easy one to don, and just like I won't stand within three feet of working microwaves when I am pregnant (I know, this is inconsistent with my cavalier attitude about hair coloring, but indulge me) just in case all the scientific evidence is wrong and they *are* dangerous, I won't exercise either, just in case. Nine (ten) months, give or take a few weeks for recovery, is not really very long to give up strenuous exercise if it can help you maintain a clear conscience. Besides, it could be a well-deserved vacation.

POINT **7** *It's "Nine Months Up and Nine Months Down" in the Weight-Gaining Department No Matter What You Do.*

Some of you will hate me for saying this, and some of you will be grateful and relieved. It usually breaks down like this: Those of you who are newly pregnant will hate me for telling you that it will take so long to get your old self back, because, in essence, I am telling you to be patient with your imperfect figure for almost a year and a half. On the other hand, those of you who have recently given birth will be grateful and relieved, because you will realize that you are not alone in your inability to wear your favorite clothes four months after the baby is born. (Please don't start in with me about your friend who wore her jeans home from the hospital. I know that there are miracles, but I think it is safer not to count on them happening to us mortals. If it makes you feel any better, speculate about the eating disorders they may be secretly harboring.)

When the baby is born, assuming it is of average size, you will lose about ten or twelve pounds during and shortly after the delivery. If you are like my Girlfriend Monique, you will then retain water so badly that you will regain about five water pounds within twenty-four hours. After you pee and sweat away another five to seven pounds over the next week, you will be left with at least ten to fifteen pounds that you didn't have before pregnancy. Or, if you are like my Girlfriend Lisa, you will have about forty unfamiliar pounds upholstering your little bones.

There is a biological reason for this extra weight. Food is the biggest and most obvious one. But the more pertinent question might be, why are you so much hungrier when you are pregnant and nursing? One answer might be that you need to bulk up to sustain this baby inside you and to feed it when it is born. You might also need extra food for a while postpartum to help your body regain its strength after pregnancy and delivery, neither of which is a day at the beach. My big gripe is that we get so hung up on the F-word (as in "fat") that we fail to understand that there is some greater wisdom governing our weight gain and loss.

As an experiment, I started working to lose weight when my fourth child was six weeks old. Usually, it had been my style to take it easy until four to six months postpartum, but after being pregnant and or nursing for nearly seven years without much of a break, I decided to wean the baby and aggressively try to reclaim my former self. I exercised like a lunatic.

Really—no matter how hard you are used to exercising, I did it harder and longer. I ran, mountain-hiked or StairMastered a minimum of sixty minutes, and more frequently ninety minutes, a day, at least five days a week. I lifted weights with a trainer who felt that repetition had to be so intense that you saw stars and whimpered during the workout. And, yes, I did lose weight pretty quickly, but I *did not* get my old figure back, truly, until my baby was more than nine months old.

Then there is my Girlfriend Amy, who was so busy with her baby and traveling because of her husband's work that she never really exercised until the baby was nearly a year old. *And she, too, had her old figure back at about nine months postpartum.* Something magical just seems to happen around that time that makes your body ready to let go of the fat it has been hiding under your arms, between your legs and around your middle. As long as you are no longer eating like a pregnant or nursing woman, you will drop the weight. An exception, of course, is if you are still nursing after nine months. People will tell you that nursing burns up a lot of calories, and it does, but it also encourages your body to hold on to an extra five to ten pounds to keep that milk factory in operation. Heck, your breasts alone are probably five pounds heavier than they ever were before. Therefore, you should not expect to drop down to your sleek former self until you have stopped nursing entirely.

Another change in your figure on which exercising has absolutely no effect is the loosening of your ligaments. In order for you to pass that baby out between your hips, your pelvic bones have to widen and separate. This means that, even if the scale says you have lost all of your weight, you still may not be able to fit into your old pants. Here, too, it is just a matter of time. After about nine months, or even up to a year, you will find your bones going back to where they used to be.

It would be a good idea of women *(and their doctors)* stopped thinking that the time required for recovery from pregnancy and delivery is the traditional notion of six weeks. That is absolute bullshit, and it really does a disservice to women to lead them into believing there is something wrong with them if they are not back to their old selves a month and a half after creating and birthing a complete human being. You won't feel the same, and you shouldn't expect to *look* the same, that quickly. If nature didn't keep you a "little bit pregnant" until your baby was old enough to eat something other than mother's milk, you might be tempted to wander off and get pregnant again. See, it's not you, it's *nature* that makes you have to still wear maternity leggings five months after the baby is born!

POINT 8 *Our Compulsion to Exercise When We Are Pregnant Is a Reflection of Our Inability to Surrender and Let Nature Run Its Course.*

"SURRENDER, DOROTHY!"

Get ready now: I am climbing onto my soapbox for this one, because it is the foundation for the philosophy of this entire book. The greatest lesson in life, and particularly in pregnancy, is to BE NICE TO YOURSELF. It is time to *really* understand that your body was intended for more than just being a vehicle through which you amuse yourself, promote yourself or abuse yourself. It is designed to gestate a baby. Nature has wisely put you on automatic pilot because She knows that, if left to your own devices, you might mess the whole thing up. All you have to do is behave moderately and surrender; nature will do the rest. Try as you might, you don't control whether you will have a boy or a girl (unless you're a subscriber to the sperm-spinning theory), you don't control when the baby will be born (unless you induce labor) and you have absolutely no control over your body. And really, when you come to think of it, why should you? You don't know anything about making babies. If having a baby required a preparatory degree, the species would have died out eons ago.

My observation is that a lot of my Girlfriends who continue to exercise rigorously during pregnancy are frantically trying to take back control of a life that they think is spinning out on them. Their bodies are distorting in more ways than they ever imagined, their emotions seem out of control and they are frightened of giving birth and becoming a parent. No one can blame you for trying to get a grip on things by acting as if nothing strange is happening. I remember how people used to try that when they experimented with LSD in the seventies. They just told themselves to act "normal" to try to keep from freaking out. The truth is, it didn't work then, and it doesn't work now. You can get out your *Buns of Steel* videotape every day, and it won't make you any more in charge of what is going on with your body. You can Jane Fonda or Kathy Smith your way through pregnancy, but if you think that you are guaranteeing yourself a more "perfect" pregnancy, you are deluding yourself. If, however, you are continuing to exercise (and ignoring the *Guide*) because it makes you feel good and you enjoy it, then knock yourself out—within reason.

Exceptions to My Tirade

There. Now that I have made my basic points about exercising, I want to back off in a couple of areas. First, there are two benefits to some forms of *moderate* exercise that I have neglected to mention in my tirade, and those are *relaxation* and *flexibility*. You might want to dance, swim (if you are brave enough to put on a bathing suit), do yoga or (my personal favorite) walk. These activities oxygenate your blood and help get the kinks out without making you overheated or exhausted. As I have mentioned, pregnancy can have its stressful moments, and getting "out of your head" in some physical way can be very helpful. Pregnancy is also quite demanding on your body and can lead to all sorts of aches and pains. My Girlfriend Patti, who wasn't keen on exercising for its own sake during pregnancy, took it up in her third pregnancy with a certified trainer to help ease the soreness in her sciatic nerve (which runs from your spine all the way down the back of your leg, and can become inflamed during pregnancy). She still gained a respectable Girlfriend's amount of weight (at least thirty-five pounds), but her back felt better. The best advice I can give you if you are going to continue with your exercise program is to move it outdoors whenever possible. First of all, there are fewer mirrors outdoors, and second of all, there are fewer gym odors outdoors (and we all know what havoc foul odors can wreak on a nauseous pregnant woman!).

A lot of pregnant women really enjoy swimming. About halfway through your pregnancy you will begin to realize the attractiveness of buoyancy. My Girlfriends found that swimming was a tremendous relief because it provided a respite from lugging all that weight around. I, too, loved that buoyancy, but I chose to experience it in my bubbly bathtub, not in the local YMCA pool. Walking is also great, because you get your circulation moving and get a chance to think at the same time. One of the best things about walking is its value during labor: It gets that baby pressing down on the cervix and can help move your dilation along. But more about that later.

Kegels—the Most Important Exercises You Can Do

Kegels are a series of exercises that are designed to strengthen an area known as your "pelvic floor." I have absolutely no idea where my pelvic floor is, but I do know that committing to a regimen of Kegels can help with such things as bladder control and sexual enjoyment after pregnancy. The reason why you might need to tighten up that pelvic floor is that it gets mighty stretched out during a vaginal delivery.

One of the deepest, darkest secrets about pregnancy is the amount of stretching and loosening your vagina and surrounding tissues will endure. The reason it is a secret is because women are embarrassed by the legacies of this wear and tear, which are conditions known as incontinence and flaccidity. In other words, a woman who has vaginally delivered a baby or two might find that she pees a little when she sneezes or jumps, and jogging can be a real bladder breaker. Flaccidity refers to a weakening of the vaginal muscles that makes it harder to reach orgasm because they aren't "gripping" the partner's penis with their former strength. I think it is pretty easy to understand why most mothers don't talk about their pelvic floors. Who wants to say that they wet their pants and have moved from a regular to a super-sized Tampax—and that even *that* slips out when they sneeze? The feminine mystique stands to take a real beating here.

I can just hear the groaning going on now and the exclamations of disbelief. But if your Girlfriends don't tell you, then how can we help you avoid or cure the problem? If what I am saying were not true, why are the majority of obstetricians so willing to "take a couple of extra stitches" when they repair your episiotomy to "tighten things up a bit down there." They certainly are not trying to sew your vagina *closed!*

Here's how you learn how to do your Kegels: You sit on the toilet with your legs apart and stop and start the flow of urine several times. Whatever muscles you are using to stop the flow of urine are the muscles that you use to do Kegels. In fact, while you are learning your Kegel fitness program, you should practice this "stutter peeing" whenever you use the toilet. Once you have gotten stronger and more familiar with the sensation, you can move on to the party-tricks section.

It is the Girlfriends' experience that "stutter peeing" is not rigorous enough on its own to really make much of an improvement in the strength of your vaginal muscles. What you are looking for is strength and endurance. Therefore the next Kegel exercise that you should master is the tightening-and-holding technique. Try this: The next time you are sitting in your car at a red light, see if you can keep those vaginal muscles tight without stopping until the light turns green. Or, if you are watching television, see if you can stay "flexed" throughout an entire commercial. Just don't forget to keep breathing.

The way you will know if you are doing the tightening-and-holding maneuver correctly is if you begin to feel anxious and uncomfortable. Honest, when this exercise is done correctly, my Girlfriends Amy and Shannon and I agree, it makes you feel slightly nervous inside. You can even feel light-headed. It's like orgasm without the O.

As you near the end of your pregnancy, you may find Kegels harder to do. This is because all of the soft tissue in and around your vagina starts to swell as the baby puts more pressure down there. Don't worry if you feel like your Kegels are completely ineffective— just keep doing them. As soon as the baby is born, start up again and do them whenever you think about it for the rest of your life. You will thank me for sharing this, and your husband (or any future sex partner, for that matter) will thank me, too.

9

Sex and Pregnancy

ince you are probably already pregnant if you are reading this book, you may smugly presume that you don't need to read the chapter. After all, if you didn't know at least a little something about sex, you wouldn't be in this predicament in the first place, right? (On the other hand, if you knew all that much about sex, maybe you wouldn't be in this predicament either!) If you are feeling a little smug, you will "labor" under that delusion for a very short time, because most women realize within the first few weeks of pregnancy that pregnant sex and regular sex are two *very* different things. We will all agree that under normal circumstances, our sexuality involves our bodies and our minds. In fact, really good sex is almost always more emotional than physical, at least for us Girlfriends. It is clearly no news flash for you when I mention that a pregnant woman's body is changing radically, and that this change is matched twist for turn by her emotional changes. These changes will most definitely affect how you feel about sex, and how your husband feels about it, too. And while not everyone feels the same about "pregnant" sex, everyone *can* be put in one of two different categories: Those Who Enjoy Sex *More* When They Are Pregnant, and Those Who Enjoy Sex *Less* When They Are Pregnant. (Things get problematical when one member of the married couple is firmly in one category and the other member is unshakably in the other.)

Physically, your body is already different, and if you are like me, it will continue to change until it takes on cartoonlike proportions. "Big" is the operative word here; big boobs, big belly and, like most Girlfriends, big butt, big arms, big thighs and even big face. In fact, one of the greatest sexual challenges is just figuring out how to negotiate the hills and valleys of the pregnant body to reach the mother lode, so to speak. How you feel physically and emotionally in this expanding body will deeply affect your sexuality. And if you think it's a trip for you, wait until you read about some of the reactions of the husbands I have talked to. Some of them are aroused by the fecund body, and some of them are terrified by it. (You will probably already have some idea as to which reaction your spouse is going to have.)

"Hormonal" is another very important adjective. The progesterone poisoning that we discussed in Chapter Four has an emotional component as well. Not only must you cope with the emotional whiplash of going from a nonpregnant to a pregnant state, but your libido is also going haywire. One minute you might feel as lusty and sexy as Jessica Rabbit, and the next you feel as ungainly as Baby Huey. Then there are times that you are so uninterested in sex that you vow to kill anyone who tries to approach you (think of the Tasmanian Devil for the cartoon analogy here). Unless you do something quite overt, like change colors, when your mood changes, your husband might not ever know who is lying in wait for him. My poor husband began to try to avoid making any eye contact with me until he was able to determine if I was rational enough not to endanger his health or safety.

As if you didn't have your hands full already, what with trying to deal with your physical and emotional adjustments to sex as a pregnant person, nature really complicates matters by asking you to contend with your husband's emotional adjustments, too. If nurturing your husband's emotional health as well as your own at this precarious time seems like an overwhelming task to you, do what Girlfriends have been doing for years: IGNORE YOUR HUSBAND'S NEEDS AND LOOK AFTER YOURSELF.

"And Baby Makes Three"

You may not even look pregnant yet, but still, it is no longer just the two of you in bed. Both you and your husband are keenly aware that someone else is there. Even if the baby is only the size of a raisin, its existence has a profound effect on how both parents view sex. (I know that many men have fantasized about a ménage à trois, but I am certain this is not what they had in mind.) This little "observer" might make you or your husband feel inhibited in sexual expression in the beginning. If it does inhibit you, don't worry—pure horniness will probably help you get over it quickly. If it doesn't, relax and know that you are not the first two people to have your sex life destroyed by parenthood. By the way, just wait until you have two or three kids running in and out of your bedroom! If you feel too self-conscious now to talk dirty and moan because of the presence of a fetus, just wait until you have a six-year-old who has hidden his tape recorder under your bed with the tape running. Now we're talking inhibition!)

Sex Like Mom and Dad Used to Have

All of the sudden, you and your husband have been transformed by this new pregnancy from two people with the spiritual inner life of teenagers into SOMEBODY'S PARENTS. The responsibilities of parenthood can be so frightening that this is often the breeding ground for some very profound sexual changes during pregnancy. The very same personality traits in each other that attracted you in the first place may seem completely unattractive behavior in a potential parent. My Girlfriend Dina's husband, who couldn't resist her habit of walking around the house in a short nightgown with no panties on before she got pregnant, immediately insisted that she start wearing pajamas with tops *and* bottoms after she got pregnant. He found the sexual advertising that had so delighted him before to be completely inappropriate for the mother of his child.

My Girlfriend Tory, married to a musician, had frequent and lusty sex with him before pregnancy, then found his late nights out and his partying with the boys a real drag when she got pregnant. It wasn't long before his tattooed body stopped turning her on and she found herself yearning to be with any heterosexual man featured in the J. Crew catalog, or better still, Ward Cleaver.

One of the most difficult emotional conflicts that couples encounter in their pregnant sex life is the SEX LIKE MOM AND DAD USED TO HAVE category, in that we all secretly harbor the belief that our parents never really "*did* it," or at least are loath to imagine the particulars if they did. If your husband begins to have the same expectations about you that he has about his own mother, you may find yourself with little more to do at night before you go to sleep than count sheep. You have all heard of the madonna/whore complex, where the husband only wants sex with "whores" but will only accept a "madonna" for the mother of his child. Rumor has it that Elvis would never touch Priscilla again after she got pregnant with Lisa Marie. (Or at least that is what Priscilla maintained to explain how she ended up sleeping with her karate teacher.) Psychoanalysts have mined this territory of the emotional life of men for years, and I certainly cannot add anything to their work. The only advice that the Girlfriends have come up with is, if you think you are married to a potential Elvis, play against type. If your mate thinks of you as Donna Reed now that you are pregnant, throw away all of your Laura Ashley dresses immediately and look for something in black with lots of cleavage. Do whatever you can to constantly remind him that you are still the same sexy thing who was so irresistible that he knocked you up in the first place.

"There Is Only Room for One of Us in There"

Another emotional issue that arises for many men is the popular worry that, by having intercourse with you, they will accidentally hurt the baby. From what I can gather in my conversations with prospective fathers, they seem to worry that the poor little baby is in the path of a big, strong battering ram. Isn't it just like a man to overestimate both the size and penetrative powers of his penis in this way? I have even heard some men suggest that they could *feel* the pregnancy with the tip of their penises during rigorous sex. You know, I just have to marvel at the confidence (or folly) that such a comment displays. After all, it would take a VERY long penis with extraordinary sensitivity to accomplish what these men are fretting about. Wow, wouldn't you like to meet *that* guy? All kidding aside, I have heard of a lot of men who were so freaked out by this battering-ram concept that they stopped having intercourse for the entire pregnancy. Now, between us Girlfriends, this is not usually such a big sacrifice on the husband's part but is the source of more work for the wife, because the husband's traditional suggestion of a substitute for intercourse over the nine (ten) months of pregnancy is oral sex. To my way of thinking, that just adds up to one more chore for the mommy.

As self-deluding as this battering-ram fear generally is, there can sometimes be some truth in it. Several of my Girlfriends say that they didn't really enjoy intercourse when they were pregnant because their terrifically virile husbands did penetrate farther than was comfortable. If you have a special reason to fear miscarriage, you might want to cut out the intercourse for however long your doctor (or your instinct) prescribes, because semen does contain a chemical that can help bring on the dilation of the cervix. While this property is not usually effective until the very end of pregnancy, it is a consideration for what are known as "high risk" pregnancies (ask your doctor if you fall into that ambiguous category).

The Genie Is Out of the Bottle

One pleasant emotional benefit of pregnant sex is that there is no longer any need to worry about getting pregnant. I know that sounds ridiculous, but even if you were really intending to get pregnant, you could still have been feeling some ambivalence about your decision. Once conception has occurred, however, if you have learned your "surrender" lesson, you will relax and stop second-guessing yourself. After fifteen years of worrying about my birth control failing me, it was such a relief not to have to give it a thought. Finally, my fear had come to pass, and it was absolutely fine. The barn door had been left open, the cow had escaped and now I could leave the door open and just have a fine time swinging on it. If you relied on gooky birth control methods like foams, caps, condoms, jellies and other slippery stuff, you are really in for a good time.

Just because everyone marches to the beat of his or her own drummer, I feel obligated to mention the group of people who say that they find the absence of the fear of pregnancy to have a *dampening* effect. These are the thrill-seekers, generally men, who only enjoy a sport when there is the danger of physical harm or death involved. For these daredevils, the fact that the parachute finally failed to open has made the prospect of further skydiving rather uninteresting. In other words, they were turned on by wondering each time if they had escaped making a baby, and now that they have finally failed, their attention goes to other, riskier sports.

I know of several people, generally women, who think of the conception of a baby as the only reason in the world to have sex in the first place. When they discover they are pregnant, they find any sexual overtures from their husbands to be inconvenient and, well, redundant. To them, pregnancy means nine months of not having to shave their legs. I call this the "Precious Vessel" approach to pregnancy; these women do not want to be messed with in any physical way until they have finished gestating. And they are probably married to the men who feel that their wife's pregnancy is just as good a time as any to start an affair. If you are fine with that, then everyone is getting their needs met. If you have a problem with extramarital affairs, then perhaps you should capitulate and dust off those faking-orgasm skills.

The Potent Seed and the Fertile Soil

Another positive emotional reaction to the news that you are pregnant can be a renewed sense of potency and fertility. Rare is the man who fails to puff up his chest with pride when told that he has impregnated his woman. Men just love to know that not only is the howitzer in good working order, but it is also shooting live ammo. As long as pregnancy has been around, and as ordinary as it can seem, when your husband and you succeed in making a baby, you feel like the patent holders on the process. One of my favorite television characters was Dr. Lilith Crane from *Cheers*. Remember how earthy and sexy she became when she found out she was pregnant with Frasier's child? She was so delighted with herself for fulfilling her biological destiny successfully that she turned herself on. She and Frasier were so aroused by their reproductive skills that they just couldn't wait to plow that fertile soil again and again.

Sybil

The thing that my Girlfriends and I found about the emotional life of a pregnant woman, especially where sex was concerned, was the *intensity* of all the emotions that you feel and the *rapidity* with which they will change. You may spend the entire day fantasizing about wild animal sex with your husband, to the point where you impatiently chew off all your fingernails waiting for him to get home.

Then he finally gets home, and he starts to go through the mail instead of studying the ultrasound Polaroids of the baby that you have taped to the refrigerator door, and you start screaming about how this is just one more sign that he is indifferent to you and your baby. By the time you have calmed down and might be able to think about sex again, you have fallen asleep in the bathtub.

It's as if your emotional engine has gotten stuck in fourth gear; you don't build up to a feeling so much as arrive at it at seventy miles an hour. Worse yet, your brakes don't work. You don't feel just *a little bit* hungry, you are not just *mildly* interested in sex and you don't get just *a tad* impatient at your husband's inability to predict and understand your moods.

For pregnant women, according to my survey of *Girlfriends*, the split is about sixty-forty between those who become more sexual and those who become almost completely uninterested. My Girlfriend Tracy, for example, felt like she was in a constant state of arousal, and the father of her child was thrilled to oblige her appetites. My Girlfriend Sondra was completely distracted by her pregnancy, and probably didn't much notice whether she had sex or not, but her husband was very turned on by her pregnant state, so they kept pretty busy despite her indifference. And Maryann is constantly stalking her husband in an attempt to get him to have sex with her (now that she is no longer throwing up), and he is looking distinctly fearful now that she really looks pregnant.

"Mr. Sandman, Bring Me a Dream. . . ."

By the second trimester of my own pregnancy, I thought about sex almost constantly. And when I wasn't thinking of it, I was dreaming about it. Let me tell you: These dreams were absolutely fantastic. The erotic fantasy life of some pregnant women suggests to me that progesterone is a great hallucinogenic, and my favorite aspect of its effect was the nightlife. I am not just talking about your ordinary sex dream where Tom Cruise and you are riding on a train together. I am talking about lifelike dreams about the actual sex act, and not just with movie idols or even your husband, but with just about any man you have happened to run into during the day. For me, that could mean the meter reader, the man next door, even my husband's friends. Taste and propriety were thrown completely out the window. (I did start to worry, though, when my minister showed up in my dream one night. Ever since then, I have felt a bit more intimate with him than I want to feel about a man in a robe and a clerical collar.) My Girlfriend Janis told me that the most frequent sex partner in her dreams was David Letterman. She figures that since she watched his show every night before she went to sleep, he was the last guy on her mind. (I wonder what that means for *Nightline* viewers?)

While the dreams in themselves are delicious, I still haven't told you the best part: IT IS COMMON FOR PREGNANT WOMEN TO EXPERIENCE AN ACTUAL *ORGASM* DURING ONE OF THESE SEX DREAMS! The first time it ever happened to me, I woke up thinking that there had been an earthquake (after all, I live in California), it was such a jolt. What a shock to realize that I had just had a very fulfilling sexual experience without anybody touching me. Let me make sure you understand exactly what I am telling you here: You do not *dream* that you have an orgasm, you actually *have* an orgasm! The thrill of these dreams used to incite me to shake my sleeping husband awake—to help keep the dream alive, as it were.

Ready, Willing and Able

Those women who are not put completely off sex while pregnant will probably find that they are not just *as* interested in sex as they were before, but *more* interested—more interested, in fact, than they have been since high school make-out parties. One of the most logical explanations for a pregnant woman's increased interest in sex, is the subtle enlargement of her sexual organs. The organs get stimulated, and the owner of the organs follows their lead. When you are pregnant, your labia, like your nipples, not only become darker in color and more sensitive, they get slightly (or, toward the end of pregnancy, *very*) engorged with blood. You may have noticed this during sex or while bathing, but you really should get a mirror and take a look. This engorgement is similar to what happens when you are sexually aroused. Here's another good reason to consider walking as your choice of exercise during pregnancy.

The Titty Fairy

My Girlfriend Sondra's husband calls the rapid growth spurt of a pregnant woman's breasts the arrival of the Titty Fairy. At the time of your first missing period, your breasts may be slightly larger than usual, just like they always get premenstrually. But in about another month, you will find that they have really gotten bigger, to the point where your bras no longer fit and you have cleavage where you have never seen it before. We Girlfriends have all noticed that this change in size happens very rapidly, like in less than a week—a time span that, in the life of a distracted pregnant woman, can seem like a matter of minutes. Your breasts will continue to grow throughout your pregnancy, but they will be eventually outpaced by your belly, so the impact won't be as dramatic as in the beginning.

Early in the pregnancy, especially if this is your first, you will have two or three months when the rest of your body looks fairly normal, but your breasts are heavy and full, just like in those romance novels. I have yet to hear of a man who wasn't deeply appreciative of this development (no pun intended).

As we have discussed, your breasts will be particularly sensitive, especially in the first couple of months. You might want to point this biological fact out to your husband, since his enthusiastic enjoyment of your breasts might make you want to howl in pain. After your husband has been properly indoctrinated about the need for a light touch, you may actually find this breast sensitivity to be very erotic; some of my Girlfriends have reported being able to achieve orgasm through breast stimulation alone. But a word of warning is important here because, as you get near your delivery date, breast stimulation can bring on or intensify labor. Yes, it's true: Nipple twisting is an organic alternative to pitocin, the labor-inducing drug. (Although, like most organic things, its effect is far subtler than my impatient nature can appreciate.) Anyway, accept this cautionary advice or talk to your doctor about it if you have any concerns regarding premature labor. Or, conversely, if your due date has come and gone and you are impatiently awaiting your baby's arrival, stimulate your breasts to your heart's content. The side benefit of all this breast handling is that it serves to toughen up your nipples in preparation for nursing, should you be so inclined.

By the way, in case you are not reading this book in chapter order, I will take this opportunity again to tell you to enjoy your large, full breasts now, and perhaps even take commemorative photos of them, because after you have finished delivering and nursing, your breasts will be smaller and far less perky than they ever were before. If this is news to you, I am sorry, but if your Girlfriends won't tell you the truth, who will?

Oral Sex

Oral sex is always fun, and it should continue to be so during pregnancy. But there are a few physiological changes that you should know about so that you can prepare your husband. For example, the engorgement of your sexual organs and the change in color might not be noticeable to your husband during intercourse, but during oral sex, the changes are really in his face, so to speak. It would probably be a good idea to mention the changes before he notices them for himself, because surprise is not always an aphrodisiac.

You would be very considerate if you also prepared him for the change in your *flavor* down there, if he hasn't already tasted the difference himself. There is some scientific explanation for this having to do with the uterine lining going from alkaline to acidic (or was it acidic to alkaline?), and it is entirely normal. But that doesn't mean it won't be a shock to your generous and loving husband. My Girlfriend Susie, who has three kids, says that her husband could always tell she was pregnant even before she knew it herself by his discriminating taste.

And Bigger, and Bigger, and Bigger!

One thing that always seemed unfair to me was that, as I grew increasingly interested in sex, I also just plain grew. Loving as my husband is, I knew that there came a point when having sex with me was more a mercy mission than an act of passion. Look, everyone is different, but a significant number of men are not really turned on by a woman who weighs more than they do.

As I have already mentioned, when I was pregnant with my second child, I had some spotting in my third month. My doctor advised that I forgo intercourse for four to six weeks. Naturally, I opted to forgo it for seven weeks, just to be conservative. When I was first "benched," I was still reasonably trim and sexy-looking, but by the time we felt it was safe to have sex again, I had unwittingly begun to resemble a character from *Fantasia*. Naively, I parked our firstborn with my Girlfriend and began preparations in anticipation of the big reunion. I washed and curled my hair, put on tons of makeup and slipped on (or should I say "tugged" on?) a silk camisole and tap pants. Well, I might as well have opened a parasol and walked the highwire for how much I looked like the ballet-dancing hippos in the Disney film. My husband actually risked his life by laughing at me, but the humor was so deeply and genuinely felt, he was willing to die for it.

My experience is not universal, however; some men just love their women fat and sassy and are very aroused by their big, beautiful gals. My Girlfriend Shannon tells me that, as far as her husband was concerned, the bigger she was, the better she was. He would whoop and holler during sex with her, just like a broncobuster. The gigantic breasts and cushiony behind were as inviting as any living thing could be. He particularly liked talking nasty to her during sex, since it felt scandalous to him to talk that way to a mother.

No More Missionary Style

During the first few months of pregnancy, almost any sexual position works. The only real hazards are those very sensitive breasts we talked about; they often cannot bear the pressure of a man lying on them. Later, as the belly grows, having sex can be like playing Twister, it becomes so challenging to accommodate the bumps and curves. You will eventually discover two disagreeable things about the old man-on-top woman-on-her-back missionary style.

> First, lying flat on your back forces the baby to rest on one of your major arteries and thereby cuts off your circulation.

> Second, the full belly between you and your partner can make frontal penetration nearly impossible, unless your husband has a twenty-four-inch penis, in which case he should consider charging stud fees.

Sometime in the middle of the pregnancy, a lot of couples move on to the sexual position known quaintly as "doggy style," where the woman is on her hands and knees and the man behind her. Most of my Girlfriends agree that this position can allow for the husband to penetrate too deeply against the cervix, so if it is not practiced with restraint it can hurt the woman. One of my personal favorites and one that we Girlfriends can all recommend wholeheartedly is the position fetchingly called "spoons." In this position, the man and woman both lie on their sides, with the woman facing away from the man. It's cuddly, it's effective and you can hold your pillow at the same time if you want. (More about the pregnant woman's affection for pillows later in this *Guide*.)

Good Old Sexy Shannon shared with me a position that I thought was pure genius. It was so good, in fact, that I mentioned it to Maryann the other day. Shannon and her husband would have sex a lot in their bathroom. In fact, if legend is true, one of her children was conceived in that room. She would lean over the sink and he would come up behind her. They said that the positioning was just right, and they loved watching themselves in the mirror. There was the added bonus that the sink came to just the right height to hide her big belly and thighs but to show her bountiful breasts off to their full advantage.

The Big O

I have saved the best for last. Now we will talk about orgasm. Wouldn't you just know that a pregnant orgasm would be different from a nonpregnant one? Orgasm is such a hard thing to describe and measure, but I will endeavor to do my best. After hundreds of hours of discussion with my Girlfriends on this subject (one of our favorites), we generally agree on three major points. First, if you are at all interested in sex, you can get turned on more quickly than ever before. Second, even though you are easily aroused, it will probably take you longer than it used to to reach orgasm. And third, you should take all the extra time you need, because the pregnant orgasm is even more profound, and longer-lasting, than a nonpregnant one. In fact, even once the initial impact is over, you will probably continue to feel "aftershocks" (remember, I live in earthquake country) for up to an hour after the orgasm. Sometimes these aftershocks can be a little scary, because they cause the uterus to seriously contract. Talk to your doctor about it, but most agree that your pregnancy can take this kind of tossing and turning if you are not in particular danger of miscarrying.

10

Looking the Best You Can

MATERNITY FASHIONS

**A**fter four pregnancies, there is one thing I know for certain: NO ONE GETS PREGNANT JUST SO THAT SHE CAN WEAR ALL THOSE NEAT MATERNITY CLOTHES. Unless you live on a South Sea island and your native garb is a muumuu, or you live in a nudist colony, you will indeed be forced to adjust your wardrobe to accommodate your changing figure, and this can present a real challenge. The challenge is twofold. First, finding clothes that are comfortable, appropriate to your lifestyle and *fashionable* is hard enough. Then, putting together a maternity wardrobe without spending a fortune is nearly impossible. In this chapter, my Girlfriends and I will endeavor to give you tips and advice to make this trying time more manageable.

Until a few years ago, the driving philosophy behind maternity clothes seemed to be to hide the pregnancy and draw attention away from the belly and up to the pregnant woman's glowing face. Putting together most maternity outfits involved gathering yards and yards of fabric, invariably some sort of polyester, up around the poor pregnant woman's neck and letting it skirt out to a circumference of about twenty feet. As if this were not unattractive enough, the neck was usually accented with some sailor collar or huge, droopy bow. The only real recent modification of that tent look has been the insertion of shoulder pads into nearly every dress, blouse, T-shirt and jacket, and this has only made matters worse. This unnecessary padding, combined with the rounded cheeks and pudgy upper arms of most pregnant women, has only succeeded in making them look like linebackers or Cabbage Patch dolls.

Fashion magazines have always advised women to stand naked in front of a three-way mirror to evaluate their figure's assets and liabilities and then to plan their wardrobes accordingly. I know this may sound sadistic, but I think this advice is even more valuable to pregnant women. I hate to tell you, but you should do this appraisal not just once, but at least once a month, because your figure will change noticeably from week to week. The prospect of confronting your pregnant body in such a harsh and unforgiving way can be terrifying, but if it will help you, think of yourself as a sort of biology experiment. Your mantra should be, "This too shall pass, this too shall pass . . ."

Here are some general descriptions of the three traditional phases, or trimesters, of pregnancy, and specific fashion warnings and suggestions for each.

The First Three Months

First of all, if this is not your first baby, skip this segment and move right into the discussion of the second trimester. Generally, the stomach of a woman who has had a baby before will pooch out about five minutes after conception, and she will look obviously pregnant in those first three months. Most of us pregnant with our second or subsequent children have never failed to comment on how big we got immediately. It must have something to do with the stomach muscles not ever being as taut again after the first pregnancy has yanked them apart.

For those of you who are having your first child, the general rule is that, for the first trimester, you get to be you, only with bigger breasts. You may notice that you are somewhat bloated, much like you get right before your period starts, but since that is never perceptible to anyone besides you, it doesn't really count. Even if you are eating constantly, as any good Girlfriend would, you will not really begin to show those pounds for a few more weeks.

During this time, you can probably wear most of your regular, nonmaternity clothes, but you may find it is more comfortable not to button the top of your jeans or wear those skintight black leather pants. One funny pattern that we Girlfriends noticed was our tendency to start the day out feeling relatively slender and end the day feeling unmistakably pregnant. I used to drive to work with my slim little stirrup pants looking sleek and smart right up to my crisp, white, tucked-in blouse. By the drive home at the end of the day, I would have unbuttoned the pants, pulled out the shirt and slipped my feet out of the stirrups to accommodate the bloating that had engulfed me.

One other warning, especially if you are going to be pregnant during the summer: The increased water retention that causes the bloating that I have described can worsen the appearance of cellulite. Make sure that you take a cold, detached look in a rear-viewing mirror to see if it is a good idea to wear your thong bikini in public (assuming it was ever a good idea in the first place).

The Second Three Months

This is the sticky wicket of maternity dressing because, especially in the fourth and fifth months, you may be too small for the full-blown tummy pockets of maternity clothes and too large for nearly everything in your closet. As much as you may think it is a senseless waste of money, you may find that the only solution is buying regular clothes in bigger sizes than you normally wear. If it makes you feel any more economical, you can rest assured that you will wear these clothes again after the baby is born and before you are your pre-pregnancy weight again. I have everything from size fours to size tens in my closet chronicling my four trips up the pregnancy ladder and back down again. That means that most of my Girlfriends, no matter what size they wear, know that in a pinch they can find something to wear in my closet.

Another possible source of interim wear to bridge the gap from regular to maternity clothes is your husband's closet. I would probably ignore the three-piece suits (although the vests could be fun), but the jeans, sweatshirts, sweaters and dress shirts just might look good on you. Even the most finicky husbands really won't complain about this pilfering from their closets if you flash the price tags of a couple of maternity dresses before their eyes. The bad news is, no matter how big your husband is, you will eventually outgrow even his clothes. I still remember the days in each of my four pregnancies when I learned that I weighed more than my husband.

I found that the pregnancy appraisal test in the three-way mirror was particularly distressing during the middle trimester of pregnancy. At this time I seemed to be pregnant everywhere and nowhere at the same time. By this I mean my breasts were even bigger than they were a month ago, but my waistline had completely disappeared and my belly was starting to pop out enough to provide a resting place for my breasts. This is the period when no one is sure whether you are pregnant or just spending too much time at the dessert table, so they don't mention your appearance. However, you can be sure that they are talking about it behind your back. This is when you will be tempted to buy a T-shirt with the motto, "I'm Not Fat, I'm Just Pregnant," but don't. Let's agree on one thing right now: A pregnant belly is not like the side of a city bus and is never a good place for slogans or advertisements like "Baby on Board."

The forward bulge of your tummy is mirrored by the backward bulge of your rear end. This development is a very important one that many women miss because they are so distracted by what is going on in front of them. Anthropologists suggest that nature provided this fuller and more shelflike behind so that our apelike ancestors had a convenient place on which the monkey babies could ride while the mothers wandered on all fours through the forest. (Doesn't evolution seem to take an awful long time?) All I know is, that fanny of yours will prevent any knit dress or jacket from falling straight from the shoulder to the hemline as it should. The final indignity that results from failing to notice this growth and take it into consideration is that you continue to wear clothes that stopped being flattering weeks ago, and you don't even know it.

This trimester is also the beginning of the "thigh problem" for many women, as it was for me. As nature prepares the body to carry the heavy, low-slung load of a very pregnant belly, it reinforces the buttressing by thickening the legs; just as when you are going to put a second story on your house, you need an extra-strong foundation to hold it all up. If you are like me and most of my Girlfriends, you have generously helped nature in this task by consuming bowls of cereal during the middle of the night and chocolate chip cookies dunked in whole milk every afternoon, justifying it all the while as a way of ensuring that you are meeting your increased need for calcium.

At this stage, my own body was pregnant from my apple cheeks to my round ankles. Shaving my legs in the shower every morning was a daily reminder that the body I was sudsing was not mine and felt nothing like the one I used to have. I call this condition "Total Body Pregnancy"; it's when you realize that the baby has taken over not just your uterus, but your entire being. Total Body Pregnancy was the reason why I never embraced leggings as a staple of my maternity wardrobe. The effect of squeezing my tummy, hips, thighs and knees into Lycra casings and having it all end at my swollen ankles (which were invariably blue because the veins were protruding) made my legs look like those balloon dachshunds that clowns make at children's parties.

My husband has an ongoing little "joke" with me from my first pregnancy that he thinks is really funny (I don't, by the way) and he has repeated it for me every pregnancy, around the six-month point. After he has watched me frantically try on and discard a mountain of clothes in an attempt to find one single article that I can wear out of the house without looking ridiculous, he offers this suggestion: "Why don't you just wear a dress and belt it?" Then he collapses in hysteria as I look for any heavy object within reach with which to wound him. This is his cruel reference to a time in my first pregnancy when I wore a huge tent dress that was still far too pregnant for me. I attempted to control some of its volume by belting it, and the result was that I looked like a basketball closed up in a beach umbrella. In other words, I was still neither here nor there as far as fashion was concerned—too pregnant and yet not pregnant enough. If you have only learned this one lesson—not to belt anything when pregnant—you have more than gotten your money's worth from this book.

The Last Three (or Four) Months

The mistakes of the middle trimester are not usually made in the last trimester, because by this time you are definitely "pregnant enough." At times you may be tempted to refuse to leave your house out of the frustration of trying to find something presentable to wear day after day. But I really believe that if you buy a few key articles of clothing, which we will discuss momentarily, the third trimester can be fashion emancipation. First of all, your stomach is now so very round and far-reaching that your thighs probably look thin by comparison. Second, very few sighted people will have any doubt that you are pregnant, not just fat, no matter what you wear. Best of all, your fashion choices are now so limited that you almost *have* to dress appropriately, in spite of yourself. In the third trimester, those loose and formless dresses that made you look like you were drowning in a sea of fabric earlier in your pregnancy will now look much prettier. Think of your full belly like the pole in a pup tent and you will understand why these clothes work better on very pregnant women—they need something to give them form.

Keep in mind that just as in the second trimester the rear end has to be considered in all fashion decisions because it causes clothes to hitch up, in the last months of pregnancy the pregnant belly can push even maternity dresses to their breaking point. If you have been getting by with nonmaternity dresses and tops in larger-than-usual sizes, this will be particularly critical, since the belly starts to pull up the front hem and the back hem gets even longer than before because you are now leaning backward in that way many pregnant women do. A little of the uneven-hem effect can look avant garde, but when the back of your dress touches your knees and the front threatens to show off your maternity underwear in the slightest breeze, it is time to retire those clothes and surrender to a couple of maternity pieces (they are designed for this) or to wear only nonmaternity dresses that are mid-calf or longer.

Maternity Stores

There are two schools of thought on the clothes one can buy in a maternity store. Some women love them and couldn't live without them, and other women think that they are fashion suicide, pure and simple. Those who love them are often women who eagerly enter a maternity store for the first time in their lives as soon as their home pregnancy tests come up positive. They curiously explore the secrets of these exclusive little spaces, which are usually staffed by post-menopausal women and never, ever seem to have any men present. This ritual of visiting a maternity shop is so deeply female that pregnant women are frequently seen in the company of their mothers or other such spiritual guides to introduce them to the mysteries of gussets at the top of pants and blouses with nursing flaps. If you go, you and your Girlfriend can hide in the dressing rooms to play with the prosthetic tummies that you slip into clothes to see what you will look like in full bloom, even if you are only a bud right now. I guess the comparable rite of passage for young men used to be when their fathers would take them to prostitutes to lose their virginity. Here is yet another example of our society's essential gender unfairness.

For my money, one of the best parts of shopping in a maternity store is the abundance of congratulations and approval that is heaped on you the minute you walk in and announce that you are qualified to shop there because YOU ARE PREGNANT. The other shoppers and saleswomen will seem fascinated with your pregnancy. They will be eager to hear your due date, whether you are having a boy or a girl and whether you plan on nursing. Maternity stores are one of the few places on earth where you can reasonably expect to find people who are almost as interested in your pregnancy as you are. Hey, they work on commission.

The other school of thought regarding maternity stores is that the route to fashion disaster begins at their doors. The first and greatest complaint is about the crummy fabrics. All of the dresses seem extremely flammable, so high is their polyester content. Even the maternity T-shirts that are supposed to be comparable to a regular Fruit of the Loom crew neck have a synthetic consistency that makes water bead up on them rather than soak in. And the jeans are really a joke. (They would be more accurately labeled "denim-free, jeanlike pants.") They are lamely intended to make pregnant women feel hip and youthful during gestation. As far as the Girlfriends and I are concerned, these jeans are the Cheez Whiz of the clothing business.

Another big complaint about maternity stores is that they seem to ignore sex appeal as a fashion goal. All you have to do is flip through the racks and see all the pastels, tiny floral prints, clown collars and prison matron jackets to see what the problem is. And the maternity equivalent of the simple cocktail dress is usually a large tent-shaped thing with sequins on it. Those designers must have a vicious sense of humor.

I think that the biggest complaint about maternity stores is that they charge too much money for their clothes. It really is a classic seller's market, because in most towns there is usually only one maternity store per mall. This means that if you need maternity panty hose, you have no real choice but to get them at that maternity store. Department stores used to stock some maternity things, but I guess that in creating space for the breadmakers and espresso machines, they don't have room for the world's mothers anymore. It is bad enough when a mother-to-be is so desperate that she considers buying a chintz jumpsuit, but to pay over two hundred dollars for it is robbery on the part of the store and gestational insanity on the part of the woman.

My advice to you during this fashion crisis is not to limit your options. Maternity clothes *are* much better now (still there is plenty of room for improvement). But do not look to maternity stores as your only wardrobe supplier, because you can make great outfits with nonmaternity clothes. On the other hand, there is no reason to be impressed by a woman who brags to you that she has had two kids and *never* worn anything designed specifically for pregnant women in her life. I guess the parts of that statement that are intended to inspire awe are the implications that, first, she always maintained her grand tradition of chic, and, second, she never got so large that regular clothes didn't fit her. To both of those implications, I say, "What a crock!" Sure, they may be true, or then again, she may have looked ridiculous her entire last trimester. If the latter implication is true, then who needs her? If the former is true, what in the world makes her think that a thirty-five-year-old woman in a baby-doll dress is chic?

In my surveys, unscientific though they be, I have found that the items women most frequently buy in maternity stores are nursing bras, bathing suits, panties, panty hose and leggings. The nursing bras are an obvious call, because no other shop on earth would think to carry such contraptions, and you will need their engineered support to carry those boobies around by the seventh or eighth month. If you choose to nurse your baby, you will be grateful for the little flaps that open up to expose your nipple without your having to get completely undressed. The value of the other items is explained in the following section.

PREGNANCY WARDROBE ESSENTIALS

The Bathing Suit

Since pregnancy lasts over three-quarters of a year, odds are that you will be in some stage of your pregnancy during the warm summer months. That means you will need a bathing suit. If you are lucky enough to be five months pregnant or less during bathing-suit season, you might be able to get away with a larger version of the regular, nonpregnant tank suit that you may already wear. Or, if you are like Princess Di, have beanpole legs and are in your early twenties, you may even go for the bikini-with-the-belly-pooching-out effect. I've always dreamed of that look, but since my first indication of pregnancy has always been the appearance of cellulite from my waist to my knees, I have traditionally opted for the lift that comes with lots of spandex and suspenders.

After the five-month mark, the nonmaternity suit may not work anymore, even if you are not already forty pounds above your normal weight. The first place it may start to fail you is in an area you may not notice. Yes, I am talking about the rear end again. It's time for another visit to the three-way mirror because, as your belly hogs the fabric it needs to cover its growing self, your behind is left with precious little coverage. The rear view of a copious bottom with only a small triangle of fabric straining to cover the middle is not a great look, especially if your legs are getting a bit dimply. It also is not long before the growing belly pulls up the front of the bathing suit so much that the leg holes stretch halfway up to your waist—another alarming sight.

If you think trying on bathing suits at the beginning of summer when you are not even pregnant is traumatic, just wait until you have to sample maternity bathing suits. It's a scream! The designs run the gamut from coy little skirts to no-nonsense tenting and on to funny things with horizontal stripes that resemble bumblebee costumes. During a couple of my pregnancies, I threw in the towel at this point. I just could not take the degradation anymore, and I gave up swimming anywhere but in my bathtub. But during my third pregnancy I found myself in Orlando, Florida, in August, and my choices were swim or die. That's when I bought my first maternity bathing suit.

I have to tell you, it wasn't all that bad. Ugly, maybe, but there are some wonderful benefits a maternity bathing suit offers that a regular suit doesn't. For one, they almost always provide a sturdy built-in bra, which can be a relief to women who are tired of carrying those breasts unassisted after all those months. The maternity suits are also cut wider from hip to hip in the back, so that you don't have to sunburn that virgin bottom skin. And then, of course, there is the pouch in front for your pregnant belly. If this pouch fits you as well as mine did, you might be tempted to wear the bathing suit under *all* your clothes because the support feels so good.

It's best if you avoid all the flounces and skirts and look for a bathing suit that is cut along the lines of a leotard. A plunging neck-line would be a nice thing, because you should never miss the oppor-tunity to show off your voluptuous breasts. Besides, cleavage is a much more effective device for diverting attention away from your legs and belly than any little skirt or sailor collar. I usually wear black bathing suits when I am not pregnant, and I was tempted to do the same when I was pregnant, on the deeply scientific theory that since black doesn't reflect light, I would look smaller in that color. The truth is, cut, not color, is what will make you look bigger or smaller in your maternity bathing suit. So what I would recom-mend is that you avoid the boring tiny florals and go for a great jewel-tone suit, or maybe even an animal print, and have some fun. If you are courageous enough to put on a bathing suit when preg-nant—and I know that this can be as intimidating as labor itself—then go all the way and commit! Remember the valuable lesson I learned in Orlando: PREGNANT WOMEN DESERVE TO SWIM, AND WE VOW TO SIT ON ANYONE WHO LOOKS AT US SIDEWAYS! Or even more liberatingly, remind yourself that you look perfectly appropriate for someone who is growing a baby inside her and that the auditions for Playmate of the Month will have to wait a while. My Girlfriend Dona's favorite part of wearing a bathing suit while she was pregnant was that it was the first time in years that she didn't feel obligated to hold her stomach in.

Leggings

You know what leggings are, right? They are those stretchy things we wear on our legs that are thicker than stockings but thinner than slacks. Unless we are in an exercise class or as trim as Cindy Craw-ford, we wear long tops over them so that the bulges on our thighs and tummies don't show. If you are one of those women I see with-out long blouses or jackets, shame on you! Take it for granted that no one wants to see the elastic waistband of your leggings, *ever*! Pregnant or not!

All pregnant women in North America seem drawn to leggings. They like the elasticity. If you are feeling bloated one day, they fit, and if nausea has left you unable to eat in days, they still fit. You can get through a few months of pregnancy with any old leggings that you happen to buy, because their stretching properties make them pretty much one-size-fits-all. But toward the end of the pregnancy, the inevitable will occur: You will sneeze or bend over, and the elastic top will instantaneously roll down to just above where your pubic bone would be if you could still feel it. This is an alarming feeling. I have seen countless pregnant women frantically grab the top of their pants and try to yank them back into place, oblivious to the stares of everyone else around them. This roller blind effect is also common in panty hose, so you should heed my advice and just go ahead and buy a couple of pairs of maternity leggings and panty hose *before* you need them. I assure you that you will be much more comfortable in the maternity versions, and since you will end up buying them eventually, buy them early and get your money's worth out of them.

As you will recall, I am not a big fan of leggings (at least for myself) in the first place, especially when worn with flat shoes and no socks. I think that women often fail to notice that even their knees and ankles can look pregnant. But I will agree that few clothes are more comfortable and versatile, so leggings are probably here to stay.

I suggest that you consider wearing boots or high shoes when you wear leggings during pregnancy, because they balance out the weight of your upper body and cover up your ankles at the same time. But my real fashion secret in this area is this: stirrups. Wear pants with stirrups, because they come down lower on your leg, and that creates the illusion of your leg being thinner and longer. Best of all, the stirrups won't grab at your fat ankles.

Bras

Even if you look like Olive Oyl when you are not pregnant and you can go braless with no discernible sag, YOU MUST WEAR A BRA WHEN YOU ARE PREGNANT. In fact, as you get really big and pregnant, you might even consider wearing a bra to bed so that you don't have your heavy breasts rolling around all night with your every toss and turn. The increased fluid retention and fat will really put a strain on your chest muscles, and since pregnancy and nursing are traumatic enough for your breasts, the least you could do is provide a comfortable sling for them. Also, if your breasts are particularly tender, a good bra provides a sort of shield between them and the threatening outside world.

You will notice almost immediately that your old bras are too small for your pregnant breasts. At first, if you are not particularly buxom to begin with, a larger size in the bra style that you traditionally wear should be sufficient. There will come a point, however, when a maternity bra really will be better.

I know that there are thousands of you saying that you are just fine in your 36DD, and that there is no need to buy one of those hideous, overpriced bras they sell in maternity stores. Really, we must stop dismissing everything in maternity stores, because some things truly are better, more supportive and more practical when they are designed specifically for the pregnant woman. And a bra is one of these things. First, a maternity bra has a lot more rows of hooks on the back, so that it can expand to accommodate not just your growing breasts but your rib cage, which is spreading to allow for the baby's growth. If you don't buy a maternity bra, you will find yourself having to buy new bras pretty frequently to keep up with your widening circumference. Second, the bands and straps of a maternity bra are wider, to provide more support and to distribute the weight of your growing milk factory. As your breasts get heavier, regular bra straps can really dig into your shoulders. The wider band under your breasts offer more undersupport, like a cantilever bridge. Third, the cups of maternity bras are fuller, to cover up more of your breast. This design is not intended to diminish your sexy cleavage, but to try to minimize the pull on your chest muscles. Maternity bras, like most bras for fuller bustlines, generally come with underwire cups. If you, like me, do not like underwire, especially to sleep in, keep looking, because you will be able to find the wireless options in good maternity stores.

When you are about eight months pregnant, you should buy yourself two or three nursing bras, if you intend to nurse. Nursing bras differ from maternity bras only in that they open in the front to allow you to feed your baby without taking the bra off, so you can buy nursing bras early on instead. Sometimes the front of the cup snaps closed in the middle of the bra, and sometimes the cup can be slipped off the breast, because the fabric is not stitched down to the band. Pick carefully, because you will be surprised by how long and how often you will be wearing these bras. I don't know about the rest of the world, but I wore a soft nursing bra to bed for nearly the entire six months that I nursed my first baby (and for the progressively shorter nursing periods of each successive baby). I just felt that milk-making breasts were too heavy and uncomfortable to be left to their own support. Not only that, but I was able to constantly wear nursing pads in the bra, which was a good thing because it's just as easy to spring a leak in the middle of the night as it is in the daytime.

Don't automatically assume that maternity bras and nursing bras are big white cotton garments that look like something your grandmother used to wear. Not only can you find pretty lacy things, but at least one company I know of has even begun making *black* lacy maternity and nursing bras. There is no need to sacrifice a year of your sexual desirability for a good bra. (You will, however, be asked to make that sacrifice for comfortable panties, so get ready.)

If you are going to go ahead and take the time to get yourself maternity and nursing bras, you may as well take the time to make sure they fit properly. This is when those experienced women in maternity stores can really be helpful. They know how to measure you and how to help you plan for any future growth, so turn yourself over to them for half an hour. It will be worth it.

Panties

Maternity underwear is the subject of a continuing debate among pregnant women. But there is one aspect upon which everybody agrees: MATERNITY PANTIES ARE REALLY UGLY. You should know that going in so that you don't flip out in the maternity store. They look a lot like the underwear you used to wear when you were six years old, the kind that used to be called "spanky pants." They are made huge, so that they cover your belly. That means that their elastic top will come to rest somewhere right under your maternity bra.

Why, you may be asking yourself, would you want to wear such an item? The answer is twofold: comfort, and to avoid that roller blind effect I described in panty hose and leggings. Of course, comfort is a very subjective matter. A surprising (at least to me) number of my Girlfriends wore G-strings throughout their pregnancies. They found that the minimal coverage was just fine and that the elastic band at the top fit neatly underneath their bellies. Just the thought of having something that far up between my legs while I was pregnant would have made me feel like I had a "wedgie," but I am not in a clear majority here. No matter which type of underwear you choose, however, you really should wear *some* kind of panties.

The reason is because you will have an increase in your vaginal discharge during pregnancy, and it is so easy to simply drop the panties in the wash at the end of the day.

Unlike with a maternity bra, the key to buying maternity underwear is to buy cheap and in quantity. They usually come in packs of two or three, and you should go for the cheapest you can find, as long as they have a cotton crotch. This wardrobe item only needs to last until you have had the baby and you no longer are bleeding (or, to be more precise, discharging lochia—leftover blood, mucus and tissue from your uterus). Unfortunately, they will still sort of fit immediately after you deliver, especially after you help fill them out with extrasuper sanitary napkins to deal with the torrential yuck that will be coming out of you. The idea is to use the huge panties throughout your pregnancy and then for as long as your recovery requires. If they get stained after delivery, you can just throw them away. Trust me—you will never be so happy to say good-bye to an article of clothing.

The "Core Outfit" Theory

Maternity clothes are unevenly stylish and consistently expensive. Concrete evidence of how difficult it is for pregnant women to dress well consistently is offered by the tabloids every week when they show pictures of glamorous models and actresses looking pregnant and unattractive. I mean, if a so-called supermodel can look dumpy, then why should *I* beat myself up over some of *my* fashion selections? The best advice we Girlfriends can offer you is to pick the look that is most flattering, comfortable and versatile for you and to stick with it though your entire pregnancy and recovery. This theory of discovering your "core outfit" will serve you well because experimentation can be the curse of the pregnant woman. If you look good in one outfit, just repeat it; it costs less money overall to have a wardrobe of interchangeable separates, it takes less time to get dressed when you wear pretty much the same thing every day and it will save you from showing up for work one day in tie-dyed overalls that you swear looked adorable in the store. Besides, nobody will give you fashion grief if you look pretty much the same every day when you are pregnant. (Since I started writing this book, I have heard from one of my East Coast Girlfriends that she has seen a maternity store that has actually taken *my* "core outfit" suggestion and sells a box of four or five essentials for a pregnant woman's attire.)

The "Going to the Office" Core Outfits

Women who work in offices or other businesses that require a professional and polished appearance can be stymied by their pregnant bodies. A lot of the mainstays of a pregnant woman's wardrobe, such as empire-waist dresses and flowing frocks, are frivolous-looking in an office. Stretch leggings and big shirts can look too informal and sloppy, and traditional maternity dresses are so straight and conventional-looking that you resemble a flight attendant.

Since dressing to be perceived as a competent professional person has often involved copying traditional men's fashions to a certain extent, we suggest once again that you borrow some clothes from your husband's closet. Some particular treasures that you might find in there are wool trousers, white dress shirts and vests. The general advice is to leave the jackets—much as you could use the coverage—because the broader shoulders will make you look huge. My Girlfriend Maryann recently showed up at a birthday luncheon in a pair of her husband's trousers over a bodysuit, held in place with suspenders. It really was a cute look and it showed off both her belly and her breasts to tremendous advantage. Another great look, which my Girlfriend Maria used to employ, was her husband's French-cuffed dress shirt untucked over his jeans and topped off with his vest. This vest idea is good, because you can buy several inexpensive vests and just alternate them over a basic "core outfit" of dark pants or leggings and a big white dress shirt. Keep in mind that the whole idea behind this particular fashion approach is to look like a girl who is wearing her father's clothes. Therefore, if the clothes from your husband's closet fit you snugly in any place besides the waist, they are useless, not to mention depressing.

If you don't already have one in your office wardrobe, you should get a long blazer. It is a terrific item, because it covers so much while still making you look nice and neat. If you buy the right size, it will not cling to your hips or bottom, and it can look good with your belly barely peeking through or buttoned up tight. The most critical matter in selecting a jacket is to find one that is long enough. It should come well down the thigh to make sure that it covers everything you need it to cover. Also, it should not have shoulders that are too broad or you will look like a pinhead.

If you feel more comfortable in skirts and dresses, I have just one suggestion. Wear opaque stockings. If you have the legs of a filly, you might be able to get away with regular sheers, but if you are like most of us, who get varicose veins, little red dots on our skin and cellulite down to our ankles, then some durable support weave panty hose in dark shades will look best. Once again, I hope you will at least give maternity panty hose a try; you really will be more comfortable.

Some "Core Outfits" to Consider

Four times I have been pregnant and four times I have had different maternity styles. I didn't create any of the styles alone, but rather copied or personalized styles created by my Girlfriends. Therefore, I call the various styles the "Sondra," the "Shannon," the "Corki" and the "Mindy."

The "Sondra" was basically a Laura Ashley look. It consisted of dresses made of velvets and corduroys, with high necks and long hems. It was a very English look, prim and romantic with the faint suggestion that, in spite of all evidence to the contrary, I was still a virgin. I was particularly fond of topping off the look with wide-brimmed straw hats. The look was a real crowd pleaser, and I was frequently told that I looked "just the way a pregnant woman should look." I actually think that people liked the asexuality of these clothes because it suggested that I was already taking this mommy business seriously. I liked the clothes because they were large and comfy and made of natural fabrics, which is virtually unheard of in other maternity clothes. Parents and in-laws nearly weep at a sight of a pregnant woman in Edwardian dress, especially around the holidays. Husbands, on the other hand, unanimously hate the style. They would no sooner want to have sex with a woman in a red, white and blue sailor dress than with Opie's Aunt Bee. The important secret here, which sexy Sondra intuitively knew, is to wear short skirts and high heels if your husband is taking you out. But sit down whenever possible. It's your only hope of getting lucky later on.

My second pregnancy was my "Shannon" period. It was based on styles from the fifties like Lucille Ball wore when she was pregnant with Little Ricky. Shannon introduced me to trapeze-style tops in bright colors or with loud patterns like polka dots. The tops were particularly good if they had boat necks or were off the shoulder, and a particular favorite was one that resembled an artist's smock. Shannon wore them over capri-length pants that were really just leggings that came to mid-calf. The perfect shoe for such a look was a mule or something like Peg Bundy would wear, but white canvas Keds were equally authentic and much more comfortable.

The "Corki" look was my third pregnancy. It consisted of hippie dresses with empire bodices and made of sheer rayons. Very "Woodstockish." It was much like wearing your nightgown all day, but in California that sort of thing is tolerated. The empire-bodice idea was good because it showed off my bustline and cut down on the volume of fabric that draped over my belly, so it was actually somewhat slimming. As pretty, and sexy, as these clothes were, however, they weren't really *me*. I felt more comfortable when I had more supportive and restrictive clothing. I guess I'm just not a hang loose kind of gal.

Most of these clothes were also totally inappropriate for an office job. So, during a period when I was working in an office, I discovered I was pregnant and turned to my Girlfriend Mindy for advice, and wardrobe tip #4, her key was to wear long jackets, dark stockings and livable heels. Mindy is an attorney, and she managed to look sexy and professional while pregnant, so she was a good person to emulate. Of course, she is famous from coast to coast for her great legs, so she did set an unreal standard for the rest of us. She wore maternity skirts and dresses with nonmaternity jackets. But no one noticed because she always wore high heels (by the way, did I mention her legs?).

I had a couple of businesswomen's maternity dresses, but I would start to hate them by lunchtime and by the end of the workday I couldn't wait to take them off and throw them on my floor. They were so boring and ill-fitting, and they always seemed to wrinkle worse than wax paper. My favorite article of clothing from this professional era was a black velour catsuit with a turtleneck, long sleeves and, best of all, stirrups. It was like wearing support hose for my entire body, and I loved it. I wore different jackets and long vests or sweaters over it to change the look a little, but it was the "core outfit." It was so popular that I passed it on to Amy, then she passed it back to me, and now Maryann is wearing it. We finally had to replace the zipper from overuse.

This leads to a very good bit of advice for all pregnant women. YOU SHOULD BORROW AS MUCH OF YOUR MATERNITY WARDROBE AS YOU POSSIBLY CAN. It is rarely an imposition on your Girlfriends to ask them to lend you a few things, because it is very rare for a nonpregnant woman to wear clothes she wore when she was pregnant. Even something like the catsuit I described, which is technically not a maternity article and really quite pretty on a slim body, will never be worn by any of us when we are not pregnant. By the way, that is sort of a universal truth: Once you are back to your old figure, you will be emotionally unable to ever wear an article of clothing that you wore when you were pregnant. After four pregnancies, I accumulated so many maternity clothes that I have a sort of "lending library" for my Girlfriends to borrow from. I actually have an inventory of all the clothes entered on my computer so that I know where everything is—not that I plan to use any of them ever again. Knock wood.

Accessories

I hate to accessorize because it makes me feel goofy (not to mention that I am really bad at it). Accessories can, however, really help break up the monotony of "core outfit" dressing without costing you too much money. I have admired how some of my Girlfriends, like Lili, can glob on ropes of fake pearls and look terrific, or how my Girlfriend Carol Lee could actually pull off the scarf look. The only personal advice I can offer in this area is this one, learned from my own mistakes: After about the sixth month of pregnancy, when your belly really starts to stick out, long necklaces and scarves will no longer hang straight. They will fall to one side of the bump or the other, or worse, they will end up lassoing a breast. Not a great look.

The "Clean Underwear" Theory

When getting dressed always ask yourself, "If I go into labor today, will my clothing embarrass me at the hospital?" This is a variation on the reason your mother always gave you for wearing clean underwear every day—because you never know if someone might see it. All pregnant women who are honest about it will admit to taking fashion shortcuts that they think they can get away with as long as they don't bend over or take off their jacket. How many of us have worn pants that no longer close at the top that we hold together with a rubber band running through the buttonhole, across the belly and around the button on the other side? (By the way, feel free to use this trick yourself in the early weeks of pregnancy, but get bigger pants as soon as possible.) My Girlfriends and I all plead guilty. How about those panty hose that are now so low in the crotch they make you walk like a penguin? Then there is the blouse that is way too short to cover the pregnant belly and that sits like a crop top above the gusset of your maternity pants, or worse, above the rubber band holding your old pants together. The long blazer can indeed hide these little cheats, but what if there is a strong wind? What if you spill coffee on the blazer? What if there is an unexpected heat wave and you just have to take off your blazer? Then what do you do, just sit there in misery? Go all the way home and change? No, you give up your too-small clothes, and earlier rather than later. So, in a nutshell, here is *The Girlfriends' Guide* to maternity fashion:

1   Don't Be a Snob; Buy Your Clothes From Any Kind of Store That Has What You Need.

2   At the Very Least, Buy a Bra, Panty Hose, Leggings, Jeans and a Bathing Suit From a Maternity Store.

3   Pick a Style and Stick With It Religiously. This Is Not a Time to Experiment.

4   Always Move Into Bigger Clothes Earlier Rather Than Later; You Will Save Yourself a Lot of Discomfort and, Possibly, Some Embarrassment.

5   Borrow Anything You Can.

6 Never Justify Buying an Expensive Outfit by Telling Yourself You Can Still Wear It After the Baby Is Born. If You Ever Wear That Outfit Again After You Have Gotten Your Figure Back, I Volunteer to *Eat* It.

11

Husbands of Pregnant Women

There is tremendous temptation for a pregnant woman to get so involved with her own emotions, thoughts and worries that she has little time or interest in acknowledging how her husband is coping with the pregnancy. This is completely understandable, in my estimation; after all, we are the ones inhabited by an alien, we are the ones with hormones splashing around like Niagara Falls and we are the ones who will have to somehow deliver the goods. All the husbands have to deal with is us—but therein lies the problem. Dealing with us can be a very demanding and frightening task, judging by what my Girlfriends' husbands have told me. In fact, one of them suggested that I subtitle this chapter, WHO ARE YOU AND WHAT HAVE YOU DONE WITH MY WIFE?

Gone is the woman he married. Not only doesn't she look the same, she doesn't act anything like her old self. And to many a husband, this is not a good thing. Even if he wasn't (God forbid) that crazy about his wife before, at least she was familiar. Now she is a pod, a person who looks like his wife used to look, but who is acting very differently. I can't speak for all couples, but to my husband it is a very simple matter: same = good; different = bad. He really didn't like not knowing who would be greeting him at the end of the day, the business-as-usual wife who required very little emotional maintenance or the hypersensitive, agenda-carrying pregnant woman who had moved into his home. Many were the days that he came home to find me poised to land on his head like a tiger crouching in a tree. Perhaps I wanted him to help me assemble the crib, *right then, before he went to the bathroom.* Other times I wanted him to get right back into his car and go out to buy me frozen yogurt. But the times he really dreaded the most were conversations that began: "You have no idea what it is like to be pregnant. You don't know what I am going through. . . ." He agreed with the premise, but he loathed the conversation, because he knew that I wouldn't feel satisfied until I made him sit and listen to all of my current concerns and dissatisfactions—he wasn't reading the pregnancy books I bought for him, he never told me I looked sexy anymore, I was worried that I was too selfish to be a good mother and needed him to tell me I was really the most generous and caring person he had ever known, and so on and so on. . . . One way or another, by gosh, he *would* know what I was going through, or I would kill both of us trying to explain it.

Normally, when an otherwise happily married couple is going through a bumpy time, sitting down and talking out the problem can be quite helpful. This is not true, however, when the better half of the couple is pregnant. If you believe the premise that women are from Venus and men are from Mars, then during pregnancy, women are scissors and men are either paper or stone. Simple biology will preclude the man and woman from having any clue as to what the other is feeling or thinking, and by the end of the nine (ten) months, neither of you will be honestly able to say that you care that much. But don't worry too much about this communication gap, because it will disappear after the baby is born and you are both physically and emotionally recovered. Parenting, unlike pregnancy, is usually a much more collaborative effort, and the two of you will be more in sync with your worries and your joys. You will be equal partners in the "How in the World Do We Raise a Child?" quandary.

You may, one desperate day, find yourself asking your husband point-blank if he thinks you are acting crazy. *This is an utter waste of time.* His response is absolutely meaningless, because a husband with any sort of survival instinct has learned early on to tell you only what you seem to want to hear. In other words, *he will lie.* I know that men lie about these things, because I have interviewed them with their wives *and* alone or with other husbands. When they are with their wives, they applaud what troupers the women have been during this ordeal, how beautiful and motherly they are be-coming and how much they admire them. Take the wives out of earshot (and throwing distance), however, and boy oh boy does the tune change. Then, especially when they are egged on by other hus-bands of pregnant women, these put-upon fellows let fly. Their wives are schizophrenic, they are constantly whimpering over some imagined slight, they sleep all the time, they eat all the time, they are bitchy. And finally these venting husbands really drive their point home with this boneheaded remark: "I don't know what the big deal is anyway. My mother had five kids and no car, let alone a cleaning lady, and she didn't lose *her* mind." I know, these are fight-ing words—but *don't* rise to the occasion.

Pregnancy, to many husbands, is just not a big enough deal to create such emotional chaos. They simply do not get it. My Girl-friend Maryann's husband, for example, is a trained medical man and might be expected to know better, but he devoutly believes that his wife has suffered a nervous breakdown that just coincidentally occurred during the first five months of her pregnancy. There is nothing anyone can say to convince him that her behavior is simply a reaction to the physical and emotional changes that she is going through. The fact that she happens to be pregnant could not *possibly* be significant enough to explain her emotional fragility or her vora-cious appetites for everything from food to sex. No mere pregnancy could cause those abberations, he maintains; it must be a brain tu-mor or mental illness.

All of these fellows have horror stories. One tells about a wife who stayed in bed in her pajamas all day. Another describes how his wife threatened a waiter's life when he told her that they were out of popovers at her favorite restaurant. Then there is always some story about a wife who comes home sobbing because the gas station attendant failed to clean her windshield or another driver pulled ahead of her in her lane, or somebody at the office smoked a ciga-rette near her. (This last bit is a recurring theme: Pregnant women are deeply wounded by people who do not acknowledge their spe-cial status by treating them gingerly. They don't ask to be relieved of their regular obligations and responsibilities; they just want a lit-tle respect while they are performing them pregnant.)

Naturally, there are exceptions to this description of pregnant husbands. For every ten men I give you who feel that the defensive position is the best one to take throughout their wife's pregnancy, you will give me one who has never felt more closely bound to his wife than during her pregnancy. We have all heard the myth about the exceptional man who says that his wife's pregnancy is *their* pregnancy, and that he wants to share as much of it with her as he can. This is the fellow who not only accompanies his wife on her monthly doctor's visit, but also brings a video camera to the checkup. Personally, I have to wonder about these guys. Does it seem to you that maybe they have too much time on their hands? I don't know, I'm just asking.

A drawback, though relatively unimportant, of having such an empathetic husband is that he might tend to *physically* experience your pregnancy in addition to identifying with your emotional experience. This can lead to something strange called the "Couvade Syndrome," which is just a pretentious way of saying that the husband gets fat, emotional and nauseous along with the pregnant wife. The reason that I find this loathsome is that if your husband is developing symptoms of his own, then before you know it, you will be called on to cater to *him*. Just as when you and your husband both have colds he always manages to be sicker than you are, now he can be more pregnant than you are. Tell him to go to work and mind his own business.

My husband is a bad comparison, because he hated nearly all the activities associated with pregnancy and having babies. (He just liked being a father, and if our babies could have come by Federal Express, he would have been deeply grateful.) First of all, as a general rule, he gets resentful if anyone in the house is in need of more care than he is. So, if I was nauseous, he had food poisoning. If I had bleeding during pregnancy, he was convinced he was developing an ulcer or a heart condition. Second of all, he is terrified of nearly everything having to do with bodily functions. It still offends him, after fifteen years of togetherness, when I try to pee and carry on a conversation with him at the same time. This being the case, you can imagine how he felt about coming with me to a vaginal exam.

He also used to be timid about the baby's and my well-being during pregnancy. He used to get frightened when I would put his hand on my stomach to feel the baby do somersaults toward the end of my pregnancy, when the flips were particularly dramatic. He was convinced that someone was going to get hurt, and that it was my job as the mother to stop all this roughhousing. When I went into labor, he invariably fell asleep (or more accurately, he went unconscious), no matter what time of day or night, because the stress of watching me in any sort of discomfort made him miserable. The only thing that he hated more than cutting the umbilical cord was coming with me to shop for the baby's clothes or furniture. Strolling through a baby store and comparing the musical tunes on various mobiles was like being stuck in a circle of Hades, as far as he was concerned. (Then again, shopping was overwhelming to most parents-to-be I talked to; who in the world knows whether a changing table should be its own piece of furniture or if it should come as part of the bureau?) But once those kids were here and I had survived, my husband became Superdad. So don't worry if your husband's paternal instinct isn't evident yet; it will come.

Husbands as Birth Coaches

Almost every couple expecting their first child will enroll in some sort of childbirth preparedness course. They are motivated by two things:

Everybody else has done it, and;

Their obstetrician told them to do it.

Most women who are pregnant with their first baby truly hope that a class such as Lamaze or Bradley will help them to forgo drugs during labor and delivery, or at least help them through the part before they get the drugs. Their husbands generally just acquiesce, because they long ago gave up challenging or disagreeing with anything their pregnant wives wanted. Almost 90 percent of the husbands I have talked to believed that childbirth preparedness courses were mandatory, and they generally didn't once consider shirking this commitment, until about fifteen minutes into the first class. In fact, initially they looked on this training as some way to finally participate in this experience that heretofore their wives had been hogging.

When asked, in retrospect, what they thought of their childbirth classes, my Girlfriends' husbands almost unanimously rolled their eyes. Sure, they learned many things they didn't know before, and yeah, the classes might have been a little helpful. But did they *like* them? No. First of all, men in Lamaze classes don't bond like women do. They don't feel particularly close to these strangers simply because they have pregnancy in common, even if their wives have memorized one another's phone numbers and pregnancy histories after the first class. The movies of actual births either scared them or sickened them, and they didn't particularly enjoy seeing a room of fat women, their wives included, lying on their sides and spreading their legs apart in pretend pushing exercises. They even hated walking from the parking lot to the classroom with a bed pillow under their arm like they were on their way to a slumber party.

Cruel as it may seem, the most universal complaints about childbirth classes were about the *teachers*. I don't know what it is about these women, and I certainly don't want to indict an entire profession, but some *are* a bit strange. I myself took childbirth preparedness courses with two of my pregnancies, and neither of my instructors was even married, let alone a mother. My first teacher was particularly reverential about this birthing business, and she described labor as a sort of touchy-feely lovefest that my husband and I would share. I think she envisioned us both naked and sweaty, with my husband massaging and soothing me through the difficult times. If she had ever given birth herself, she would have known that a husband who touches his wife while she is laboring risks getting his hand bitten—possibly off.

Our second course was a private one taught in our home over a few evenings toward the end of my pregnancy. By the second evening, my husband was so openly hostile to the flower-child instructor that he would get up in the middle of her lecture, order Chinese food over the phone and then eat the whole meal in front of her, without offering her so much as a fortune cookie. When she would suggest we watch some videos of other births, he would glare at her for trying to ruin his appetite. He actually offered to pay her double her class fee if she would agree to sign our "graduation" certificate and not come again.

I am going to go out on a limb here, but here goes: I think that the current fashionable thinking about husbands seeing their pregnant wives through the ordeal of delivering a baby is unnecessarily strict and limiting. Don't get me wrong; I think any man who is willing should be there for the labor and delivery—especially the delivery, because it is one of life's undisputed miracles. I also think that all delivering women should consider inviting along another *woman*; one who has had a baby herself is preferable, but any empathetic Girlfriend will do. You might be very fortunate and find that your labor and delivery nurse at the hospital fulfills your emotional needs; these women are truly great and can become instant Girl-friends in one's time of need.

With larger birthing rooms becoming all the rage these days, there is usually plenty of room for you, your husband, your doctor, your nurse and a friend or two. Especially if your labor lasts more than three or four hours—which I can practically guarantee it will—you will find that the companionship of someone other than the guy who got you into all this trouble in the first place will be very wel-come. Not only will *you* appreciate the companionship of a Girl-friend, but your husband will probably be secretly grateful for the chance to sit down outside somewhere and take a break.

Husbands Have Fears of Their Own

Not that I am suggesting that it is your job to do anything about it, but it might be nice to occasionally remind yourself that you are not the only one who is turning into a parent in the foreseeable future. You are not the only one in your house with worries and concerns. Husbands have fears of their own, and what follows is a list of most of them, in no particular order:

1 If He Becomes a Father, He Cannot Be the Baby Anymore.

A lot of us are married to men who require a certain amount of mothering to keep them happy. They like being nurtured and coddled, and they worry, with good reason, that you will have less time to do this for them if you are doing it for the baby. As my husband so succinctly put, "You are like a pie. Every time you get pregnant, my piece of the pie gets smaller."

2 A Baby Is So Expensive That the Family Will Go Broke.

Even if you don't go bankrupt immediately, at the very least your husband won't be able to get that jukebox he has al-ways wanted. This money worry is often at the top of the charts for husbands, probably because they are traditionally

expected to provide for the baby, at least while you are inca-
pacitated, and they don't know if they are up to the job. Even
if you are a two-income family and you intend to return to
work shortly after delivering, the truth remains, babies *are*
expensive, and they only get more expensive as they get
older. Most of us, however, have already decided that the
financial sacrifices are worth it, or else we wouldn't have gotten pregnant in the first place.

 ## 3 His Wife Will Get Ugly.

Well, maybe that is stated too harshly. Perhaps it is more
accurate to suggest that he is just afraid of not feeling as
sexually aroused by the new and enlarged version of his wife.
Or maybe he pictures women who don't get out of their
bathrobes or wash their hair often enough when they get
pregnant, and he worries that you will be like them.

4 His Wife Will Never Go Back to Her Old Self.

Remember, your husband fell in love with a woman who
looked a certain way, and pregnancy is most certainly going
to change that look dramatically. Even those men who think
that their pregnant wives are sexy, or cute, occasionally have
to wonder whether they will do what it takes to get their old
figures back, more or less, or if they will be forever altered.
Look at Grace Kelly, Elizabeth Taylor or other such former
beauties. They never again looked like they did in *Father of
the Bride* or *Rear Window* after having birthed a few children.
(We should all look so bad, right?) So, it can clearly happen
to the best of us.

5 The Rational, Stable Wife He Used to Have Will Be Permanently Replaced by This Sobbing, Sleepy, Impatient, Ravenous, Baby-Obsessed Person Who Has Gas.

No matter how much he wants to believe that this whole
matter of pregnancy-induced insanity is a temporary state of

affairs, he will worry that the old, fun you will never come back. It is so hard for men to imagine the emotional effect pregnancy has on a woman, never having experienced pregnancy or even PMS themselves, that they secretly suspect that this moodiness is not simply baby-related, but clear evidence of psychosis. If their friends with kids have told them anything about postpartum depression, then they worry that you will continue to be crazy even after the baby is born.

6 He Will Panic When His Wife Goes Into Labor and Be Unable to Find His Way to the Hospital.

Just as we have nightmares in which we misplace our babies, husbands have all sorts of nightmares about how they will mess up at the Big Moment. Every time they drive you to the hospital, whether for a tour, Lamaze classes or because you are making them practice, they will imagine trying to make the drive when their brains are rendered useless by terror. But don't *you* worry about your husband forgetting how to get to the hospital, because *you* will remember, and you will be yelling directions at him the whole way.

7 He Will Have to Deliver the Baby Himself.

He imagines the car breaking down or a blizzard or some other disaster occurring at the moment you most need to get to a hospital, and singlehandedly having to deliver the baby. That fear is not totally outside the realm of rationality, because nearly all of us have heard at least one story of a couple's encountering a hazard that almost prevented them from getting to the hospital. My brother-in-law was backing the car out of the garage during a January snowstorm in New York to take my sister-in-law to the hospital to have her baby. He had the driver's door open so that he could see clearly as he reversed down the slippery driveway. The door caught on a snowdrift and ripped right off the car. Do you think that stopped them from getting to the hospital on time? Not on your life. People are capable of amazing feats when they panic, and driving with no door was not going to get in the way of this delivery occurring in a professional setting.

8 | He Will Faint During Delivery (or Worse Yet, He Will Stay Conscious and Have to Watch the Whole Thing).

I think most men imagine fainting in the delivery room because it is one of those clichés from television and movies. Labor and delivery are not rapid, catch-you-off-guard occurrences, but rather slow and deliberate progressions. Therefore, they are not the kinds of things that make people faint. Vomit, perhaps, but not faint.

9 | The Doctor Will Insist That He Cut the Umbilical Cord.

Now this, on the other hand, does have some fainting elements to it. For one thing, the cord looks unquestionably like a part of the human biology, and therefore not like something that most people are inclined to want to damage in any way. Second, when you cut it, *stuff*, like blood, can come squirting out. If he doesn't know that in advance, your husband just may have his fainting fear come true. My Girlfriend Dona absolutely forbade her husband to cut her daughter's umbilical cord. Given his mechanical ability, it didn't seem like a very good idea. It wasn't all that high on his wish list, either, so he was only too happy to leave the task to professionals.

10 | Labor and Delivery Will Hurt His Wife, and He Won't Be Able to Make It Better.

This is a very common and very sweet concern among husbands. Most of my Girlfriends have told me that the hardest part of having a baby for their husbands was having to watch the women they love suffer. They don't know what to do to make it better, and they may feel faintly guilty at the passive role they must play. (And if they don't, most laboring wives will see to it that they do.) My own husband used to beg me to ask for an epidural the minute I changed out of my clothes and into a hospital gown. His thinking was, "We know this is going to hurt eventually, so do us both a favor and take the drugs now."

11 | He Will Never Be Able to Have Sex With His Wife Again.

A substantial number of men like to think of breasts and vaginas as being designed for one thing: THEM. Intellectually, they know that these organs will have to be shared with the new baby, but sexually, they don't want to know about it. Many husbands have wondered if they would ever want to have intercourse with their wives again if they were to see a bowling ball come out of her down there. My Girlfriend Patti never discussed this possibility with her husband; she simply headed the whole thing off at the pass by forbidding him to stand anywhere but at her head during delivery. If her doctor were to have offered to move a mirror down there so that both of them could see the baby crowning, she would have risked the seven years' bad luck and broken it over his head.

12 | His Wife Will Die and Leave Him With Some Strange Baby.

Both men and women admit to having irrational fears about the wife dying in childbirth; the wife is concerned for obvious reasons, and the husband fears that, in addition to losing someone he is rather fond of, he will be on his own with the baby. With rare exception, men think of tending to newborn babies as woman's work, and they have a hard time imagining doing all of the caring and nurturing involved in raising a child without the mother as the primary caretaker. Since this baby is still a stranger to him, and his wife is his family, he also worries that he would resent the baby if it were to hurt his wife in any way. By the way, because you are probably a mite sensitive at this time in your life, let me remind you of what you already know: It is almost unheard of in this day and age for women to die in childbirth.

13 | He Is Bound to This Woman Forever.

When you are married without children, the thought of breaking up can be heartbreaking, but you figure you can make the split somehow and eventually get on with your lives. Once the two of you have children together, however, you are in each other's life in a very real way for decades, whether you want to be or not. They are a joint, ongoing project that you will have in common no matter who else you may fall in love with or how much un-in-love the two of you may someday grow to be. The good news is, children keep you so busy and distracted that you may not even notice if your marriage has gone to pot.

14 | He Won't Be as Good a Father as His Father Was.

A good father is the stuff from which heroes are created. (A mother, no matter how good or bad, becomes the motivation for psychiatric therapy later in her children's lives.) If a man admired and loved his own father, there is sometimes the fear that he could never do the job as well himself. After all, *he* is merely a thirteen-year-old in a man's body, and *his father* was, well, a FATHER. The truth is, once he has a child of his own, your husband will come to see his father for the human being that he was, as uncertain about but as devoted to the job of child rearing as he himself is now.

15 | He Will Be as Good a Father as His Father Was.

This is the real world, and a lot of men grew up with less-than-ideal fathers, or even with no fathers at all. If your husband was not all that enamored of his own father's parenting abilities, he may be intimidated about becoming a father himself. There are no books or classes that teach you how to parent properly. If you are lucky, you learn it through emulation of your own parents. That sometimes leaves the people with no role models pretty much up in the air. Or worse, they develop unrealistic expectations for parenthood based on their own childish fantasies of what a *good* daddy would have been like, fantasies that are themselves based on fairy tales and television sitcom fathers.

For new fathers, as well as new mothers, the *Guide*'s advice is to trust your instincts; you will be fine at this parenting business. The biggest part of the job is showing up and loving this baby. If you are present, you can learn the rest along the way. The Girlfriends and I think that this worrying business is the greatest burden of pregnancy. So, daddies-to-be, you can think of us Girlfriends as *your* support group, too. We won't cure you of your worrying, but we will keep you company (and probably make fun of you a little) while you do it.

12

Coming Into the Homestretch

I can honestly say that I have never met a woman who within a month of her due date wasn't ready to have an end to this maternity marathon. (With the exception of my Girlfriend Mindy, but she was undergoing house repairs as part of her nesting instinct, and wasn't sure if there would be a floor to walk on by her due date.) No matter how chipper and enthusiastic they might have been for the preceding eight (nine) months, even the best of them get cranky and impatient. And who can blame them? They can hardly breathe anymore, they have grown too large for all but their biggest clothes, they aren't sleeping very well, they have chronic heartburn and indigestion and they are keenly aware that somehow, someway, that baby is going to have to come out of their bodies, *soon*! They usually have also come to realize that it is easier to care for a baby that is inside you than one that is outside.

There isn't really much to do at this point. Presumably, you will have had your baby shower. You will also have completed your childbirth preparedness classes. And, aside from putting your shower gifts away, your baby's room is probably pretty much organized, or purchased and awaiting delivery. If you have been working outside the home, chances are you have already begun your maternity leave or will be doing so soon. You may find that you have the unfamiliar sensation of having time on your hands, time that you fill with alternating bouts of boredom, excitement and fear.

As if all this anticipation weren't enough to keep you agitated, you will be increasingly irritated by the well-intentioned comments of nearly every person you brush by. They will say things like, "Wow! You're *huge*! When is that baby going to be born?" Or every week when you go to get a manicure or to do your grocery shopping, the clerk will say, "You mean you *still* haven't had that baby yet?" Your mother and mother-in-law will call you every single day on the pretense of just calling to chat, but really to see if you are in labor and have neglected to tell them. Talk about the watched pot never boiling. . . . In this chapter we will offer a sort of laundry list of the physical and emotional adjustments that are required to survive the last month of pregnancy. This may seem like the longest yard, but if you want to be reminded that you are almost finished, look ahead to the next chapter: It's about going to the hospital.

"I Can't Breathe!"

If you are under five feet nine inches and have a normal-sized baby growing inside you, just the act of filling your lungs will become difficult, if not impossible. The placenta—the space bubble that your baby is living in—grows upward and eventually pushes against your diaphragm and your lungs. At this point, most babies are head down in the blastoff position, so it is their bottoms and feet that are doing much of the encroaching. Call me crazy, but I found this difficulty in breathing sort of alarming. I tend to be a bit claustrophobic anyway, and this gentle suffocating sensation really used to bug me. I would stand as tall as I could, fold my arms under my breasts and pull up, as if I could create more space in there for the baby and me.

The best thing you can do at this stage of your pregnancy is to get on the floor on your hands and knees. This allows gravity to pull the baby forward and away from your spine and organs. It feels so good that you will wish you could crawl through the rest of your pregnancy. By the way, this is also a good position to try during labor, for a change of pace. Another reason why you will find yourself huffing and puffing more than The Little Engine That Could at the end of your pregnancy is from the sheer physical exertion of carrying around thirty or forty extra pounds.

An additional pregnancy condition that can add to your breathing problems is a condition called "pregnancy rhinitis," which is easily described as a chronic stuffy nose. Because the inside of your nose is lined with the same soft membrane that lines your vagina, it tends to succumb to the swelling that your vagina experiences. While full vaginal walls and labia can be sexually arousing, full sinus passages are merely heavy breathing without the fun. The miracle about this irritating condition is that it disappears almost the instant the baby is born. Until then, there isn't much you can do about it but sniffle.

"I Can't Eat Any More!"

This in itself is not much of a problem, but worth mentioning. Just as the growing baby has crowded your lungs and diaphragm out of the way, your stomach gets smashed flat like a pancake. You can no longer eat very much at one sitting because there isn't room in there for more than a few bites. You might think that this is welcome news, but don't get too excited, because it doesn't translate into any measurable weight loss. This is probably because you eat less at each meal, but you eat a lot more meals. By this point, what else is there to do? Some of the Girlfriends have reported that they have lost a couple of pounds right at the very end of their pregnancy (as in right before labor), but not usually over the entire last month.

Another physical condition that may lessen your enthusiasm for those hearty meals that characterized your middle trimester is indigestion. Those less fortunate of us may have experienced heartburn and rumbling tummies for much of our pregnancy, but at the end this condition can become much more pronounced. By this time, your baby's behind is so vigorously pressing against your diaphragm that your esophagus is stressing out and not keeping your food down in your stomach, where it belongs. You may be back to eating the comfort foods of early pregnancy, unless, of course, you are gambling that the wives' tales are true, and that spicy foods do indeed help bring on labor. No matter what you eat, antacids are the perfect dessert.

"I Can't Sleep!"

Being unable to go to sleep and stay asleep were my greatest challenges at the end of my pregnancy. Being tired was no guarantee that I was going to snooze when I went to bed each night. Some Stepford Wives cheerfully told me that this was nature's way of preparing me for the sleepless nights that I would experience as a new mother. That is like saying dieting will prepare you for starvation, if you should be asked to endure it. As far as I was concerned, no nature that was capable of giving chameleons the gift of disguise would be stupid enough to think that the cure for no sleep was more no sleep.

No, you can't sleep for two major reasons. First, the baby is pulling or sitting on every part of your body but your face and your feet (and those are swollen from water retention). Second, you are so preoccupied with what lies ahead; labor, delivery, *motherhood*, that you have a hard time turning your brain off at night. (Which is kind of ironic, because you will swear that you haven't been able to turn your brain *on* most days lately.)

Now is the time for a reappraisal of your relationship with your bed pillows. They will grow to become your best friends, not only the one or two that you have always known and loved, but all the new pillows you will buy (or steal from your husband) to help them in their duties. The Girlfriends and I agree that you will need at least three pillows by this point; one between your knees to keep you hips supported (I will explain why that works later), one propped slightly under your pregnant belly and one under your head and shoulders. Even better, you should consider buying one of those full-length body pillows that are sold in a million catalogs these days. I bought one, and after I got over the shock of how very big it was, I gamely brought it into bed. It felt magnificent, but it created a barrier between my husband and me in the bed that would have required helium to ascend. My husband referred to my giant pillow as my "Boyfriend," and I actually named it "Phil." Fortunately, or unfortunately, depending on my mood, my husband wasn't finding me particularly irresistible, so he never complained about the line of demarcation between us. If you ask me, I think he might have been grateful.

The one difficulty about my relationship with "Phil" was the difficulty "we" had when I wanted to turn over. First I would hurl myself from one side to the other, then I would grab Phil with both arms and both legs and flip it over with me, much like an alligator wrestler might do. It invariably shook the bed so violently that my husband nearly fell out and the comforter would land somewhere halfway across the room.

I am afraid we don't have nearly as good or specific advice to give you to help you make your brain comfortable enough to sleep. Your doctor may put me on *America's Most Wanted* for saying this, but I think that women who are coming to the end of a healthy and uneventful pregnancy deserve an occasional glass of wine before bed. A little toddy, along with a hot bath (not too hot, of course), can work wonders on the anxious insomniacs that most mothers-to-be become.

One of the biggest culprits in the pregnancy insomnia crisis is the pregnant woman's tendency to get leg cramps. I have no idea why they get them, but I do know that they are incredibly common. One minute you are clinging to your body pillow and dreaming about sex with some stranger and the next you are doubled over in a frantic attempt to massage out a muscle that has contracted like a snapped rubber band. I found that stretching my lower legs and flexing my feet could make my calf muscle spasm so violently that I thought my Achilles tendon was being removed without anesthesia. My only advice is to walk it off; there is really nothing else to be done.

"I Can't Walk!"

Everybody knows that you can recognize a pregnant woman from behind whether you can see her big belly or not. The first giveaway is usually her choice of shoes; they are large and roomy and definitely flat. In fact, they may even be scuffs or house slippers if the woman is really beyond caring anymore. The poor dear's extremities may be retaining so much water at this point that nothing else fits. Her feet, in these big shapeless shoes, drag and shuffle into position between steps, creating a locomotive sound. These feet are generally not within shouting distance of each other, with one supporting one hipbone and the other about three feet away, supporting the other. Topping this all off is the traditional maternal swayback of the very pregnant woman, where she looks as though she is pushing her belly ahead of her in a wheelbarrow.

Before I ever got pregnant, I looked contemptuously upon these slouching, scuffling women, wondering how low their self-esteem had to be to allow them to present themselves to the world in this condition. The least they could do, I thought with indignation, was to keep their legs together when they sat down. My mother, she who weighed all of 120 pounds at her most pregnant, would "tsk, tsk" behind these struggling souls and whisper to me that if I ever let myself go like that when I got pregnant, she wouldn't be seen in public with me.

Well, I did let myself go, to a certain extent, and by that time I didn't care or notice *who* was seen in public with me. If my mother thought I was going to struggle to look good for her when I didn't even do it for my own husband, she had another think coming. At this point, the only person I could still pull myself together for was my obstetrician. For him, I looked like Miss Maternity U.S.A. when I went in for my checkups: legs and pits freshly shaved, perfume, high-heeled shoes, clean hair (curled, even) and a tasteful amount of makeup. I felt that if I couldn't pull it together for at least one hour a month, all self-respect was truly lost. After the appointment, I would hurry home to change into something huge and stretchy and pig out.

One of the reasons I was able to look decent in the doctor's office was because he never had to see me walk very far. If he had, he would have seen that I could no longer bring my knees together and that my hip joints were so loose that I felt as though my thigh bones would pop out of the sockets with every step. Imagine that your bones are held in their proper positions by wrapping elastic bands around them. In pregnancy, the elasticity of these bands releases to allow your bones to spread apart to accommodate the pregnancy and eventual birth. As I mentioned earlier, your rib cage actually widens to allow for the pregnancy to spread up into that region. And I am sure you will be happy to hear that your pelvis spreads apart too to allow for the little watermelon to make its way out. So I guess you could call this ligament loosening a good thing. But it is also a troublesome thing if you jump out of bed in the middle of the night to pee and fall immediately to the floor because your legs slipped out of the standing/walking position. I remember feeling like I had stepped into a hole, so awkward was my balance and so asymmetrically did my legs settle in their hip joints. If you have dreamed of doing splits again for the first time since your cheerleader days, this may be your chance, because you will be pretty flexible. The only problem now is, once you get all the way down there, who is going to lift you back up? If left to your own devices, you would stay in the split until the baby crowned and knocked you off-balance.

So far, I have described reasons why walking is nearly impossible. Even if you were not pregnant, these biological changes would nearly cripple you. Let's add the fact that you are now housing a full-term baby in your belly, and all the water and placental yuck that comes with the package. And, if this is your first baby, it either already has or will soon drop lower into the pelvis in preparation for birth. This dropping—or "lightening," as it is sometimes called—does wonders for your breathing, because it moves the baby away from your diaphragm, but it makes walking an even crueler joke. Do you remember those childhood contests where you held a balloon between your knees and raced across a field? Being nine months pregnant with a baby that has dropped can feel something like that. Except now they're *water* balloons.

Speaking of a baby dangling between your thighs, my Girlfriend Colleen has coined the quaint term "vagina farts" for the squishy noises that sometimes emanate from between your legs when your baby is low and pressing hard on your cervix and the surrounding area. You can sometimes sound like a poopoo cushion when you walk.

Returning to your weight gain for a second, the last factor to consider in your inability to stride or slink in your former way is the thirty to forty pounds of fat, water and baby that upholster your body. Any overweight person waddles a bit, even without their ligaments being fully released and without a baby's head threatening to protrude between their legs. You don't run to catch the phone anymore, you couldn't jump for a million dollars and you lose your balance just getting out of the car. I cannot tell you how very many of my Girlfriends have reported falling flat on their faces during the last few weeks of pregnancy. The good news is, the babies are never any worse for the trauma.

"My Back Hurts!"

If there is any way to treat yourself to a massage toward the end of your pregnancy, please do so. Ask around of other mothers, nurses or childbirth preparedness instructors, because they might know of a masseuse who is familiar with the aches and pains of a very pregnant woman. There are even massage tables with pop-out centers so that you can lie on your stomach and have your baby comfortably nestled in a sort of pouch. I thought that this was the most wonderful thing, because I really started to yearn to sleep on my stomach after about six months of being on my side. One last thing: There are certain delicacies about the very pregnant body that only another woman can understand, so no matter how liberal and open-minded you might be about getting massages from men when you are not pregnant, when you are pregnant, insist upon a woman.

By the way, all of the pregnancy books that I read over the years suggested that the husbands learn massage and counterpressure techniques to help their wives get through pregnancy and delivery. It always looked so intimate and sweet in the books, but I don't know of one single Girlfriend who was ever cosseted through maternity in this way. One night when I was desperate, I begged my husband to massage my lower spine. He was so unimaginative in his massaging that he never moved his fingers from one single position, and I ended up with something resembling a rug burn on my back. My Girlfriends unanimously reported that when their husbands feebly tried to rub them during labor, they screamed at them, "Get your hands off of me!" (More about not wanting to be touched during labor in Chapter Fifteen.)

My Girlfriend Patti used to really suffer at the end of her pregnancies, from a pain that extended from her back, over her behind and down her leg. This particular condition, sciatica, is fairly common in pregnancy. It is easy to see why women get all sorts of aches and pains in their spines. The weight of your belly is concentrated within an area that is only about a foot long, and this can seriously pull your spine forward, thereby forcing you to hold your upper back unnaturally far back to compensate for the forward drag. Also, if your breasts are particularly heavy, they can pull on your shoulders and upper back. The best relief that we can suggest is to rest for a while on your left side with a pillow between your legs and under your head and shoulders. (The left side is the medically recommended side, because it allows for the most unimpeded flow of blood from your heart to your legs and baby.) You can also try the hands and knees back stretches I described earlier. Or you can sit cross-legged on the floor (what we used to call Indian style in elementary school). This cross-legged sit lets your belly rest on your calves and off your spine. And, if all of this fails to bring you any relief, call your doctor and ask if you can take an over-the-counter pain reliever.

"I Am Getting So Big That I Might Explode!"

By about the eighth (ninth) month of pregnancy, most first-timers mistakenly believe that their bellies cannot possibly get much bigger. They are as round as if they had swallowed basketballs, their skin is stretched and all the clothes in the maternity stores fit them perfectly. And then come the last four weeks. . . .

The pregnant belly of a woman who is about to give birth is not a graceful, rounded belly, but rather a thin covering of skin stretched over a child's elbows, knees and bony bottom. I always say that you can tell a woman is finishing her pregnancy when her stomach develops "corners." The baby is now so big and strong that at times its body parts are most definitely recognizable to your touch and seemingly recognizable to your eye. If your tummy isn't oddly shaped and threatening to rupture your belly button, your baby probably isn't cooked enough yet. Think of yourself as a Butterball turkey—when your belly button pops out, you're about done.

"My Doctor Says I Could Go Into Labor at Any Minute!"

As you come into the homestretch of pregnancy, you will begin to see your obstetrician more frequently, first every two weeks, then every week for the last three or four weeks. You may have noticed earlier in your pregnancy that your doctor seldom, if ever, performed a vaginal exam once the pregnancy was established. Now, however, he or she will start peeking up inside you again to look for some of the signs that birth is imminent. Your doctor will begin to give you reports like, "You are fifty percent effaced and one centimeter dilated." (Effacement and dilation refer to the cervix getting ready to let the baby out. More about these phenomena in Chapters Fifteen and Sixteen.) You will leave the office filled with anxiety, certain that you are going into labor that night, if you even make it through dinner. You will call your friends and relatives and put them on red alert in preparation for the call that you are in labor. When the baby still hasn't come three days later, you start looking forward to your next doctor's visit to hear more about effacement and dilation. I don't know why, but we all grasp onto this information as if it meant something, and it really doesn't mean much at all. The world is filled with women who live for weeks 70 percent effaced and three centimeters dilated. There are just as many women who go home after being told by their doctors that they are still closed tight as a drum, only to have their water break during dinner and their babies born before breakfast.

I could spend the next twenty pages telling you not to set too much store by these measurements, and you would still ignore me. Just as earlier in this *Guide* I warned you not to count on your due date as any exact indication of when to expect your baby, and you ignored me, you will wish me wrong on this matter. I know, because I did the same thing.

"I Can't Take One More Day of This!"

There will come a time, when you have about forty weeks under your belt (literally), that you start listening to folk wisdom about how to bring on labor and get this show on the road. I am treading on thin ice here, but I would be foolish if I pretended that you haven't heard about any of these things and haven't considered trying them. You know what I'm talking about: going on a long walk, having vigorous sex, eating hot, spicy food, drinking cod-liver oil and giving yourself an enema are all "home remedies" for "curing" a never-ending pregnancy. There was even a Hollywood restaurant which served a garden salad that was rumored to bring on labor. For a couple of weeks it became a story on the local news programs. Doctors and scientists studied the piles of lettuce and other grassy ingredients, only to give varying reports as to which was the magic potion. Some thought that it could be the cilantro (an herb used in a lot of Mexican and Chinese food). Others suggested that the exotic balsamic vinegar used to make the dressing was causing all the contractions. Either way, on any given day you could go for lunch at this restaurant and find several ripely pregnant women eating salad with gusto.

Of all the ways to encourage your labor to step it up a bit, walking is the most popular among doctors and fitness fanatics. I myself found an intravenous drip of pitocin to be slightly more effective, but you already know about my desire to cut to the chase in these matters. I did commit to a walking regimen with three of my pregnancies, because I was willing to try anything to get things moving along. I walked in deep sand on the beach, I race-walked through shopping malls (I must have looked like a clipper ship at full sail) and I insisted on taking stairs instead of elevators whenever possible. Sad to say, not once did any of my babies take the hint and consider moving out. Things were different after my water broke, however, and that walking business was suddenly a lot more effective. In fact, I had just enough time to stroll around the block a couple of times before I had contractions measurable enough to get the hospital to give me a labor room.

I must seriously tell you that once your water has broken, the baby will be born within a matter of a few hours, or else risk of infection develops as its pristine little bubble becomes exposed. *Always* call your doctor if you think that you have sprung a leak or that you are urinating uncontrollably. In fact, if your due date, myth though it may be, comes and goes without event, your doctor may consider moving things along by breaking your water for you. By the time the due date for my fourth baby arrived, I think I would have tried to pop my own bag of waters, if my arm had been long enough to reach all the way around my huge belly and anywhere near my vagina. But as they say on TV, "Do not attempt this stunt at home. It should only be performed by trained professionals."

My Girlfriend Caroline swears that vigorous sex at the end of pregnancy will bring on labor. From what I have read there is actually some science to support this notion, something about semen having a chemical like pitocin. I also think that "massaging" the cervix with penetration of your husband's you-know-what helps wake it up after nine (ten) months of sleeping and prepares it to stretch open. Then again, Caroline is well-known for her insatiable lust, so maybe this was just her ploy to get her husband to consent to an act of merciful intercourse when he would have preferred to watch the second half of *Monday Night Football*.

There is a technique that used to be called "stripping the membrane," but is now more euphemistically called "performing a vigorous internal examination." It is, of course, done by your doctor, and only after he or she is fully satisfied that the baby is completely baked and ready to pop out of the oven. I guess this technique works along the same lines as vigorous sex, but without the fun, in giving a wake-up call to your cervix. If you and your doctor agree to do this, be prepared for it to hurt like bad menstrual cramps and to be accompanied by as much blood as the beginning of your period. This "vigorous exam" may accomplish absolutely nothing (it never got my contractions to start), but I am told you stand a better chance of going into labor if the cramping sensation persists for a few hours rather than just calming down and going away as mine did. My Girlfriend Amy had great success with the one-two combination of a "vigorous internal examination" by her doctor and then an enema that she gave herself at home later that evening. By about four in the morning, she was pushing the baby out. (Funny, isn't it? I don't mind the thought of someone putting a twelve-inch stainless-steel hook up inside me to break my water, but the thought of an enema makes me feel dizzy.)

Very pregnant women have varying levels of irrationality. I have just indicated to you that I tend to get pretty darned impatient in my desire to move from pregnancy to motherhood, a condition I have always preferred. You may be more restrained, which is an admirable trait in a soon-to-be mom. You will probably want the baby out as fervently as I did, but your common sense and spiritual tranquility may allow you to accept the unpredictability of the situation. In fact, there is something so sweet and sentimental to be said for the experience of being awakened in the middle of the night by unmistakable contractions, lovingly nudging your husband awake with the words "Honey, it's time!" and the two of you dashing out in the darkness to your waiting car for your exhilarating ride to the hospital. But, charming as the scenario can be, I always tried to talk my doctor into inducing my labor at a time that was mutually convenient for the baby, the doctor and me. That guaranteed that the baby would be cooked, my doctor would be fed, rested and in town, my hair would be clean, my legs would be shaved and my toenails would be painted. It would also ensure that we made the dash to the hospital in the daytime with plenty of daylight to help us find our way to a hospital. Which way is better? My way, of course. Just kidding!

13

What to Take to the Hospital

A SUITCASE FULL OF USEFUL THINGS

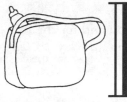

In addition to yourself, you will need to bring a suitcase to the hospital. Unless your baby comes very early, or you are still having trouble accepting the fact that you are, indeed, pregnant, you will have a bag packed and ready long before you go into labor. If, however, you need to go to the hospital and your bag isn't packed, JUST GO. Do not worry, because there is nothing you will really need until *after* the baby is born. In the relative calm after the baby is born, you can ask someone, preferably not your husband, to pack a bag for you and bring it to the hospital. If it absolutely must be your husband who packs your bag, give him a written list specifically itemizing every single article you want. If you just give him general instructions like, "Bring me something to wear home from the hospital and some things for a shower," there is a very good chance that you will be given a cocktail dress, tennis shoes, a shaver and shaving cream.

Make it easy on your husband and the hospital staff by bringing only one small (O.K., medium) bag. You will probably be moved at least once during your hospital stay, and someone is going to have to move your bag along with you. If you don't have several things with you, you will run less risk of losing something in the move. Don't worry that one reasonable-sized (meaning smaller than a steamer trunk) bag won't hold everything you will need in the hospital, because you really only need something for you and the baby to wear home and a few toiletries.

Your Going-Home Outfit

Obviously, I can't know in advance if you are going to have your baby during a heat wave or a blizzard, so I can't pick your outfit for you (much as I would love to). I can, however, offer some general suggestions.

1   Wear something that is big, no matter how much you long to wear your old jeans and have your svelte figure back. *You will still be fat*, and you will probably still look pregnant for several days (or weeks) after the baby is born. Maternity clothes are the obvious, though loathsome, choice. Much as this may depress you in the anticipation, it really won't be a very big deal when it happens, because at least *someone* will be wearing new clothes in small sizes: the baby. From now on and for the foreseeable future, no one will be looking at you anyway, at least not when the baby is in the same room.

2   Wear flat shoes. You will be a little groggy and off-balance after giving birth and lying in bed for twelve hours. The last thing you need is to try to safely carry your baby into your house while you are wobbling on a pair of stilettos. Also, you might still be retaining water at this point, and you won't want to be sausaged into anything too tight.

3   Wear a blouse or dress that "breathes" and is absorbent. The processes of checking out of the hospital, putting the baby into a car seat and heading home all conspire to make you perspire like crazy. And there is always a good chance that the baby will spit up on you at least once before you get home.

Also, if you intend to nurse, make sure that the blouse or dress you choose opens far enough down the front for you to get your breast out without too much trouble. You will have your breasts in and out of your clothes so often in the next few weeks that you will be beyond modesty. You will nurse in the middle of a monster truck competition and answer the door for the FedEx man (bearing yet another gift for baby) with your breast looking him right in the eye. Most shocking of all, you will soon think nothing of whipping your breast out and nursing your baby in front of your own *father*. Yikes! You probably don't believe me now, but just wait until you have been hiding in your bedroom nursing for an hour while the family reunion has been taking place, without you, in the living room; you'll come running out like some escapee from *National Geographic*.

4 Look somewhat attractive. You don't need to kill yourself getting all dolled up—as I mentioned, you probably won't be the center of everyone's attention—but keep in mind that your picture will be taken several dozen times between your leaving the hospital bed and your entering your home. Go for a little makeup and do your hair, and don't fret one more minute; but do brush your teeth, for the baby's sake. Then hold the baby up in front of your face like a shield and, if all else fails, threaten to open the camera of anyone caught taking a close-up of you.

Do Not Bring a Nightgown (Unless You Don't Mind Ruining It)

The Girlfriends' advice is to leave the pretty nightgowns and matching robes at home. Childbirth and its aftermath are very bloody, and if you wear your lovely things from home, you will be soaking them in Woolite for the next several weeks. Just wear the hospital gown they give you when you are admitted. Don't worry, you won't be wearing it long, because nowadays new mothers are sent home from the hospital so quickly that they barely have time to do anything more than brush their teeth and take a shower.

Bring Your Own Shampoos, Soaps and Lotions

After you have given birth, there are no greater delights on earth than taking a shower and brushing your teeth. It will probably have been hours since you have done either, and the effect of feeling clean will be almost as good as losing fifteen pounds. The toiletries that the hospital provides, assuming it provides anything, are industrial and in microscopic containers (à la "the food is lousy and the portions are too small"). Indulge yourself by packing some nice shampoo, shower foam or soap and lotion. Keep in mind, however, that your new baby has a virgin nose. The little thing could sneeze its head off if you have the whole room smelling like Giorgio. Select mild scents and skip the perfume and cologne altogether. Also, if you are planning to nurse your baby, avoid putting anything on your breasts, be it lotion or powder. After all, how would you feel if someone sprinkled White Shoulders dusting powder on *your* meal?

Leave Your Jewelry at Home

If your wedding band still fits without cutting off circulation in your ring finger, you can wear it to the hospital. Other than that, all jewelry should stay at home, where it won't get lost in the shuffle. You won't even need a watch, because your ever-ready birth coach will have one, and, failing that, every maternity room I have ever seen has a huge wall clock like the ones we had in school. Who knows, you may look so naked without your earrings and pendant that your mate might actually be inspired to go out and buy you a little bauble as a reward for your valor in the delivery room.

Bring a Pillow, or Two

We have already discussed the ever-deepening love you will have for your pillows during pregnancy. You sleep with them between your legs, you hug them against your chest, you even take them in the car with you for your ride to the hospital to deliver. As loving and supportive as they have been to you up to now, they have never been more worthy of your devotion than when you rest gently on them in your hospital bed. I don't know what hospital standard-issue pillows are made of, but I am tempted to say sawdust or crumbled plaster. Your own pillows will not only help you sleep comfortably (which you most certainly deserve to do at this point), but they will also help bolster you and the baby at feeding time. Best of all, they smell like home. (Just remember to leave your best white pillowcases at home, for obvious reasons.)

Leave this page open on your husband's pillow or pasted over his toilet:

ATTENTION, HUSBANDS:

THE GIRLFRIENDS' GUIDE HEARTILY
RECOMMENDS THAT YOU SHOW UP WITH A
GIFT OF SOME SORT SHORTLY AFTER THE
BABY IS BORN. YOU WILL ALMOST NEVER GO
WRONG WITH JEWELRY, SINCE IT WILL FIT
EVEN BEFORE YOUR WIFE HAS LOST HER
BABY FAT. IT INDICATES AN APPRECIATION OF
THE VALUE OF THE CHORE SHE HAS JUST
PERFORMED. IF PEOPLE GET GENEROUS
REWARDS SIMPLY FOR FINDING LOST DOGS,
YOUR WIFE IS NOW ENTITLED TO THE HOPE
DIAMOND FOR THE SERVICE SHE HAS
JUST RENDERED.

Bring Bedroom Slippers

I know that hospitals are supposed to be all sterile and such, but I have my doubts, especially where the carpets are concerned. When you are just resting in your room, you may find a thick pair of socks sufficient to keep your feet warm and cootie-free, but if you are prodded into strolling around the whole wing to help get your intestines working again, you will want to have some slippers that are flat and comfy and not too ugly. It is definitely best to skip the little mules with the feathers, because your balance may not be too good. Or worse, your legs might actually look good enough to arouse your husband and give him a hankering for sex. YIKES!

Bring Lots of Socks

My Girlfriends and I recommend that you bring thick socks, and lots of them. You will wear your first pair during labor, a time when lots of women get cold hands and feet, literally and figuratively. Your doctor will probably let you continue wearing your socks during delivery, but you will want to throw them away as soon as your consciousness returns, because they will probably be pretty bloody.

The other pairs are for you to wear in bed in the hospital so that when you get up to use the toilet, your little tootsies won't get cold or contaminated. Chances are you will end up tossing a couple of these pairs, too, because you will inevitably sense too late that your diaper has runneth over, and as you streak to the bathroom, there will be blood and watery stuff running down your legs and into your socks. (Don't spend too much time trying to visualize this; just take my word for it and move on.)

Bring Maternity Underwear

Unlike the socks, you will not need your underwear during labor and delivery, since most doctors agree that they tend to be a hindrance. You will, however, need three or four pairs, at least, for your hospital stay, no matter how brief. After the baby is born and all the other pregnancy stuff has come out of you, a nurse will put a couple of sanitary pads on you and you will lie in bed on disposable square mats. For the first few hours, you might skip underwear, because this is usually when the nurse will bring you ice packs for your swollen peepee. Plus, she will want to look at how you're doing "down there" every few hours.

After the ice pack period has passed, you will want your own underwear, both for modesty's sake and also to keep those sanitary pads where they belong. For this, we recommend maternity underwear, even if you were a G-string devotee during your pregnancy. No G-string is going to offer a whit of support for the pads you will need down there to soak up all the liquids that pour out of you for days after birth. And besides, after a vaginal birth and a couple of stitches, you will look upon your favorite "thong" as a vicious instrument of torture. No, what you need are big, soft spanky pants that feel soft and cushy and cheap.

Bring Lip Balm

Something about childbirth, even for those of us who did our Lamaze breathing only for the time it took to yell for the anesthesiologist, dries out the lips. Certainly you are being dehydrated by losing so much water during the birth, but in addition you won't be given anything to drink during labor and delivery, for fear that it will make you nauseous. If you don't think ahead to bring something for your lips, you will probably end up all chapped and cracked. You can't prevent that from happening to your nipples, but a good lip cream will help your mouth.

Bring a Pen

At first I was going to suggest that you bring paper, too, but then I was reminded by my Girlfriends that between learning to feed your baby, welcoming all your visitors, sleeping and trying to relax enough to go to the bathroom, you will have no time for composition. If you are deeply committed to your journal, then go ahead and bring it if it makes you feel better, but keep all the thank-you notes and birth-announcement envelopes at home.

(My Girlfriend Dorothea suggests, after just giving birth to her second child, that all baby-announcement envelopes, or at least labels, should be addressed and stamped during those last boring weeks of pregnancy. Then, when the baby is born, all you have to do is phone in the essential information to the stationers, and later beg your mother or Girlfriends to stuff the envelopes and drop them at the mailbox for you.)

Getting back to the pen, you will be asked to fill out several forms for such things as birth certificates, baby photos and breakfast menus during your hospital stay. The nurse will, after an hour of searching, generally find a three-inch pencil with no eraser for you to use. Not only will your hand cramp up, but the lead will wear down before you even get to your dinner request. While bringing a pen is by no means essential, you'll find it's the little things that often mean the most.

Bring Something to Eat

My Girlfriend Dona actually had the temerity to tell me that the hospital where she delivered had a *hospitality buffet* set up several hours a day for the maternity patients and their husbands! She even suspects that strangers from other wards frequently came in and helped themselves. *Do not expect to find the same setup at your own hospital.* In fact, getting anyone to bring you juice or a snack when it is not a scheduled meal time is the dictionary example for the word "futile."

After a task as arduous as delivering a baby, you will be starved. Contributing to this hunger is the fact that your body is getting ready to go into milk production. You will be tempted to accept your husband's sweet offer to dash down to the cafeteria and bring you back something to eat. Keep in mind, however, that you will not see the man again for nearly an hour, because he will tuck into a four-course meal for himself while he is waiting for your tuna sandwich to be wrapped to go. Remember, labor and delivery have taken their toll on him, too.

You will be so grateful to yourself if you have planned ahead and stashed some bottled water, boxed juice and nonperishable snacks such as granola bars or dried fruit or crackers in your suitcase. Try to avoid the candy bars and cookies at this time. Much as you may love chocolate, your body is sapped and needs more nutritious replenishment. Besides, a lot of babies can't digest the milk of a mother who has been eating Milk Duds all night, so hold off on the junk.

Bring Something to Read

Most hospital rooms have televisions, but if you have time on your hands, you might want to read. Personal experience has shown me that linear thinking is almost totally absent in new mothers, so don't bring anything that requires concentration or memory, because you will have neither. A magazine or two will be quite intellectually challenging, especially if they have complicated things like the *Cosmo* tests about whether your sex life is as good as it should be or *Glamour* "do's and don'ts."

Bring Your Own Sanitary Pads

Things may vary from hospital to hospital, but when I had my kids I was given the kind of sanitary pads that needed a belt to hook them to or safety pins to keep them in place. Jeez, I hadn't seen one of those things since I'd read the book *Growing Up and Liking It*.

What a relic! What you need are the maxi-est pads manufactured, with the adhesive strips on the backs. Bring the jumbo box, because you will really use them fast, often two at a time, for the first couple of days, *even if you have had a cesarean section.* If you're lucky the hospital will provide them and you'll never use yours, but better safe than sorry.

Bring a Nursing Bra

If you know that you want to breast-feed your baby, or if you are uncertain but might give it a try, you should bring a nursing bra to the hospital with you. (You will appreciate the support and protection even if you don't intend to nurse, and you should continue wearing your industrial-strength maternity bras, because you will still experience the filling of your breasts.)

Even though babies want to and should nurse right after they are born, they are not getting mother's milk yet. I am sure you have read all about colostrum, the yellowish fluid that the baby sucks from your breasts preceding the manufacturing of milk. You have a wonderful window of opportunity to learn to nurse during this colostrum stage, because the baby isn't starving to death and your breasts aren't too big to maneuver. The day your milk comes in, however, all hell breaks loose. I swear, in a matter of a couple of hours, my breasts went from soft and full to the size and firmness of a regulation NFL football. I think that the only reason my baby wasn't petrified by these breasts, which were far bigger than his head, was that he was so hungry. That was when I first realized how much I was going to love my nursing bra. I wore one day and night for months, because sleeping with breasts that are full of milk can be very uncomfortable. Legend has it that French women go to bed wearing "sleeping bras" in the belief that breasts deserve to be supported at all times. Now that I have seen how hard a woman's breasts have to work, I think they not only deserve a pretty bra, but a paid vacation for two to the Caribbean.

While we are on the subject of nursing bras, you should also bring nursing breast pads, which are disposable, absorbent circles that catch minor leaks. You slip them into your bra between your nipple and the nursing flap of the bra. They keep your bra clean longer, and the last thing you will be needing when you get home from the hospital is extra laundry.

You might also want to check out a newer contraption called a "breast shield." These are cups made out of latex or plastic, and they fit right over your nipples. They not only catch more leakage than the pads, but they keep your bra from chafing against your chewed-on nipples by creating an airspace around them.

Bring a Book on Nursing

Getting a baby to drink from your breasts can prove to be more difficult than learning to use a Cuisinart. I know that it is the most natural act in the world, but I have seen women sobbing over their failure to get the baby to "latch on" properly to the nipple so that the milk comes out. Here is the first news flash of novices: The milk does not just come out a hole at the tip of your nipple, as I had always imagined. It comes out of several little holes all over the nipple, and it only comes out when the baby has it in a vicelike grip, with the entire brown part of your breast against the roof of its mouth.

Before you panic, let me assure you that almost every hospital will have someone on staff who can teach you to nurse your baby. Some people are so qualified at it that they are called "lactation specialists." This is also where a good book with illustrations can be very handy. While your baby is resting and you are still relatively calm, you can study the book, and then when the baby awakes crying and hungry, perhaps you will have a faint idea of what you are supposed to do. Trust me, if you don't seem to have the technique perfected immediately, some nurse is guaranteed to grab your breast in one hand and the baby's head in the other and manipulate them until she gets them both to do what she wants. Your job at this point is to sit there as quietly as possible and watch yourself being manhandled by a total stranger.

Bring a Camera and Film

This is going to be the most incredible experience of your entire existence, and you must commemorate it with lots of pictures. For the rest of your life, you will love sentimentally going over the pictures of the day your baby was born. Nowadays, video cameras are even more popular at birthing parties than still cameras. And we all know people who cherish their videotaped recollections of *every single detail* of the baby's birth. My personal rule is that no camera, still or video, is allowed below my waist, but that is really because I don't trust those guys who work in the one-hour photo labs. What if I get famous someday and one of those guys has held on to a few of my negatives? Or worse, what if my six-year-old finds the videotape and mistakes it for his *Lion King* tape?

Remember, labor and delivery almost always last far longer than you will plan for (or can imagine). Therefore, unless you carefully plan ahead, your husband could find himself out of film or with a dead battery just as the baby is coming down the pike. If he is videotaping the event, suggest to him that he try to save the battery by using the AC plug or, to be on the safe side, by having two or three batteries charged for this occasion.

There seems to be a touch of the artist in many medical people, and they are often quite willing to take pictures for you if your husband feels too faint or if he wants to keep his hands free to hold his new baby. My son's pediatrician was a terrific photographer. He not only shot pictures during the birth, but he followed the baby into the nursery and then out to meet the grandparents, clicking all the while. Being dressed in doctor's scrubs worked rather like a press pass; he went anywhere and shot anything he wanted without anyone kicking him out.

Bring Your Telephone List

As you can well imagine, there are several people who are going to want to know when the baby is born. In fact, I can think of a few who will not speak to you or have Thanksgiving dinner with you if you fail to call them as soon as the little tyke has been whisked off to the nursery. Chances are, the job of telecommunicating will fall to your husband, since you will be either too tired or too blissed out to handle something as complicated as a phone. Don't forget—your husband, too, has just had his universe changed, and he may only remember to call the person he was supposed to meet for breakfast the next morning, or might even be unable to recall anyone's phone number.

Your job, in the boring days before your labor begins, is to put together a call list with names and numbers *ranked in order of importance*. For example, first on the list should be *your* parents, since you are the hero here. Then his parents, then grandparents, best friends, and neighbors (if you haven't already called them when you were in labor). If the calls are ranked, your husband may tire of this chore and not finish the list, but at least he will have hit the most critical calls before falling asleep in the leatherette chair beside your hospital bed or going off in search of food.

One last thing about telephoning people with the news that you two have become parents. If the birth has occurred in the middle of the night or after 10:00 P.M. or before 8:00 A.M., the only people who will want to hear from you *immediately* will be your parents, siblings and friends who have kids of their own. Friends who have never personally experienced this miracle will see this call only as an interruption of their slumber, and would prefer hearing your glorious news after they have had some coffee.

Bring a Girlfriend

Even though she won't fit into a small overnight bag, do seriously consider bringing a Girlfriend to the hospital with you when you go in to have your baby. Any warm, loving Girlfriend will do, but she would be particularly spectacular if she herself had at some time given birth. As I have been saying since I started this book, having babies is woman's work, and having other women around to reassure you, gossip with you and encourage you is invaluable. If you are really, really lucky, you might have a Girlfriend like Amy, who massaged my feet whenever I had a contraction. I will never forget her calm and tireless presence.

Perhaps you are thinking to yourself that labor and delivery are a private time, for only a husband and wife to share. You worry that you will break the mystical spell by having anyone other than the co-creator of this baby in the room with you. *News flash!* First, your room will be anything but private, even if you have a so-called private room. Before your obstetrician arrives, you will probably have several complete strangers with their hands up inside you. The anesthesiologist will come and go, a nurse or two will be there and then, at the end of their shift, they will be replaced by other nurses. Second, labor goes on and on and on, wearing out even the most dedicated spouses. About five hours into it, your husband will probably be down the hall chatting with his newfound friends in the waiting room and you will be watching *Wheel of Fortune* in between your contractions. Rather than rage at your husband for tiring of this tedium and mentioning for the third time that he is hungry, give the guy a break and have a Girlfriend come in and sit with you. If you want to preserve a sacred moment, clear everyone but your husband (who is probably having a donut and coffee at this point) out of the room when your doctor tells you it is time to push. Then the two of you can share becoming the three of you.

What to Bring for the Baby

Isn't that a mind-bender—packing things for a person you haven't even met yet? Not that the baby is left naked until you bring it something to wear from home. You see, the hospital will immediately dress him or her in a T-shirt and a diaper, wrap him or her up really snugly in a hospital-issue receiving blanket (which I stole and put in my babies' keepsake boxes, for some sentimental reason that I can't exactly recall right now) and sometimes stick a knit stocking cap on that tiny little head to keep him or her toasty warm.

YOU MUST HAVE A CAR SEAT!

Now that I think about it, the only thing that you absolutely, positively, no negotiating must bring to the hospital in which to take the baby home is a proper car seat. In fact, hospitals in most states are prohibited by law from letting a baby be discharged until they have been assured that it will be put into a car seat that meets safety regulations, and that the parents know how to use it properly.

There are a million car seats on the market, and they can range in price from about forty to over a hundred dollars. Some of them are designed so that they can accommodate baby sizes from newborn to toddler, through the adjustment of the harness straps and the way the seat is buckled into your seat belts. Really spend some time on this, because a good car seat can be your darling baby's barrier against all the things we are too frightened to even imagine. Ask your Girlfriends, read *Consumer Reports*, browse through the stores until you find one that you are happy with.

Many of my Girlfriends ended up buying two car seats for their babies. The first one, which was useful for about six months, was the sort of bucket-shaped model that is only intended for newborns. This shape is appropriate because newborns have no spine or neck control at this point and are comfortable in a sort of curled-up position. You will be astonished at how tiny your new baby will look in a car seat of any kind, and if you buy one of the big ones now, you will feel obliged to sit beside the baby in the backseat and steady its wobbly head with your hands.

Remember, the big difference in car seats for newborns and car seats for older babies is this: NEWBORN BABIES' CAR SEATS FACE BACKWARD IN THE CAR. This is because studies have shown that this puts them less at risk for whiplash in a sudden stop.

We Girlfriends all opted for the infant car seats that look like plastic buckets and that latch onto a base that remains buckled into the seat belt of the car. The bucket part where the baby nestles can be released from the base and carried out of the car by a handle so that you don't have to wake the baby up to get it out of the car. This way it doubles as a baby seat for use inside the house. Some of these seats also have sunshades; get one of those if you can, because you will spend the next several months worrying about the sun beating down on your baby's face, both for fear of sunburn and because it makes them so cranky.

One reason to consider buying a brand-new car seat (as opposed to borrowing one that your Girlfriend's child has outgrown) is because there are often safety improvements with each newer model. In fact, some of the really old models of seven to ten years ago might not even meet current safety requirements.

I want to say one last thing about car seats, and then I will get on to the fun stuff: Recent studies have shown that thousands of otherwise intelligent parents are using or installing the car seats incorrectly. READ THE MANUAL! If it says that the seat belt has to be cinched with the "enclosed metal clip," don't throw the metal clip away—use it! If is says that the seat belt has to be inserted through a series of tunnels underneath the car seat, then go through every single one, not just the big one in the middle. Also, don't assume that all car seats work alike. You have to read the manual every time you get a new one. I know it can be irritating to figure out those silly diagrams, but keep reminding yourself that there is a baby at stake. So, for once in your life, *read the instructions*. And then, when you are sure you know how the thing works, practice installing it and releasing it several times. Take advantage of your relatively calm state of mind before the baby comes to master this technology.

The Going Home Outfit, Continued

Picking this outfit is so much fun. The only warnings I have are to pick something that doesn't have too many buttons or need to be pulled over the baby's head, because dressing your newborn for the first time is traumatic (for you, not for the baby). And select clothing that has legs instead of a gown, because the seat belt needs to latch between the baby's legs.

A T-SHIRT

Working from the inside out, the first essential is a T-shirt. This shirt should have already been laundered at home (as should all baby clothes, at least for the first three months) with one of the mild baby detergents sold in any grocery store. Some infant T-shirts pull over the baby's head, but for a new mother, the shirts that tie or snap closed on the side like a kimono are far less frightening. For the first few days, pulling anything over your new baby's head will convince you that you are at risk of suffocating it or breaking its neck. Since logic will have little effect on you at this point, I won't bother to reassure you about how very resilient your baby is. Instead, I suggest clothing that will allow you to avoid the situation entirely.

In your shopping excursions for the baby's layette, you will encounter T-shirts that pull over the baby's head and snap between its legs. These articles are traditionally called "onesies." We Girlfriends think they are great, but not for the brand-new baby. First of all, they involve that neck-breaking suffocation thing. Second, they make it difficult to get to the baby's belly button to clean it with alcohol until the umbilical stump falls off. And third, the crotch snaps hold the shirt against the belly button, which can't be too comfortable while there is still a stump there.

THE DIAPER

The next article in the newborn's uniform is a diaper. I have absolutely no opinion whatsoever about whether you should choose cloth or disposable diapers. Living in Southern California, I can't decide whether it is worse to add to the landfills with disposables or to contribute to the drought and to the chemicals in our water supply by machine-washing the cloth ones. All I can really tell you about diapers is to change them regularly and to fold down the tops to allow that healing belly button to stay dry and free of chafing—and to remember that all babies need to wear them for at least the next couple of years.

FOOTSIES

You should put something on the baby's feet. For the first couple of days of life, these little creatures have a hard time regulating their body temperatures, and their head, hands and feet need to be kept cozy. You can either dress the baby in pajamas with the feet sewn on or you can put on the little stretch booties that are sold in all baby stores and drugstores. Whatever you do, don't plan to put shoes on your newborn. I know these little doll shoes may look cute in the store displays, but a real baby's feet are so tiny and rounded that the shoes are irritating to them. Besides, it's nearly impossible for you to put anything other than a sock on an infant's kicking foot; and even socks won't stay on for long.

THE STYLISH PART

What you choose to put over the core baby uniform is subject to your own taste (or sense of humor, since baby clothes can be very funny). One thing you should know, however, is that the vast majority of new babies sleep almost constantly for the first few days. For that reason, it makes sense to dress them in soft pajamas or rompers rather than miniature sailor suits or tiny dresses. It is also helpful to know that the current wisdom has babies sleeping on their sides or backs, so you might choose clothes that button or snap up the front or on the shoulder rather than up the back, where the baby would have to lie on them. And stay away from frills, buttons and bows for now.

TO CAP OR NOT TO CAP?

Until a couple of decades ago, it was unheard of to take a child outdoors without a hat or bonnet on. A capless baby was viewed by all the other mothers as a sorely neglected child who was certain to catch a cold. My mother-in-law, who lives in New York, would silently pray to St. Jude when she'd see me take her California grand-children out bareheaded. I know that if she had been my mother and not my mother-in-law she would have threatened to report me to the child welfare offices. But since she didn't want to interfere, she'd surreptitiously shield the baby and put her hands over its head when she thought I was not looking. She was right, I must admit, that babies *do* lose a lot of heat from their heads, so if there is a chill in the air a hat is a very good idea. Besides, I love my mother-in-law, so if a cap makes her happy, then why not? (At least when she is around to see.) You don't have to go out and buy tiny caps for your newborn if you can't find them small enough or if they are too expensive, because most hospitals supply a great little knit hat that looks like a longshoreman's cap. Even more preciously, they come in pink for girls and blue for boys, so they eliminate the tedium of constantly having strangers ask your baby's sex. There is no reason, however, to be overly protective and dress the baby like an Es-kimo—unless, of course, your baby *is* an Eskimo.

A PACIFIER

Regardless of your preconceived opinions about "binkies," do your-self a favor and buy a couple. (Your hospital may provide them, but why take anything for granted?) You may thank me for this advice when your husband is driving you home from the hospital, you are sitting in the backseat next to the baby and the baby starts to wail inconsolably. Traditionally, all new parents start to perspire and ex-perience shallow breathing at a time like this. You don't know whether you are supposed to speed up and get home as fast as you can, pull over to the side of the road and take the baby out of the car seat to feed it or, in desperation, take the baby out of the car seat and hold it in your lap for the rest of the ride. Whatever you do, **do not drive one inch with the baby out of its car seat**. Not only is it incredibly dangerous, but it is also illegal. A rule as a par-ent is not to let momentary desperation make you do stupid things. Otherwise you will be facing an entire future of doing stupid things.

Here is what you do: Put a pacifier in its mouth and gently tap its end until the baby calms down enough to suck on it. Then, if you have nightmares about your six-year-old going to school with a pacifier, you can add it to the ever-growing list of things to worry about later.

A BLANKET

You will want to wrap the baby in a blanket, even if the weather is mild. This is because being wrapped up nice and tight lets the baby relax and feel protected. When its arms and legs are moving around too freely, it feels like it is falling and its reflex is to jerk to attention. Even in a car seat, you can tuck the blanket around the baby, especially over its hands and feet.

AN "URP CLOTH"

My Girlfriend Sondra invented the fetching title of "urp cloths" for the blankets that mothers wear over their shoulders when they are burping their babies. Not only do they serve the obvious function of protecting your clothing from spit-up, but they also protect the baby's face from any irritating fabrics or detergent residues in your clothes. You will constantly use them, too, to wipe drool or some other such accumulated baby froth from the little one's face.

These urp cloths get better with laundering, since most cloth diapers start out a little stiff when you buy them. Even better than a diaper, in the Girlfriends' estimation, was the Carter's waffle-weave blanket that is sold in most baby stores. It is such an inexpensive blanket that you can buy several. I used them to wrap the baby in, to clean the baby's nose on, to lay over the car seat, and I always had one over my shoulder. They became such a familiar part of my wardrobe that I frequently left the house wearing them and not noticing. It was quite the fashion statement, especially if it was soiled.

THE NECK DONUT

A couple of years ago, I noticed a new product in one of the zillions of baby catalogs I receive. It was a small U-shaped ring made of cotton fabric and stuffed with batting. Its purpose was to support the sleeping infant's head in a car seat, baby swing or infant carrier. I wasn't sure at first whether this was a brilliant invention or just another useless gimmick to sell to naive mothers-to-be. After using it with two of my children, however, I have decided that it is, indeed, a stroke of genius. An infant's neck is so weak and its head is so heavy that a baby sleeping in a car seat looks like it is about to tumble forward at any moment. The neck donut gives the heavy head a place to rest and makes a new mother worry a little less about whiplash. And, as we all know, one less thing to worry about is a gift from God.

14

Baby "Stuff"

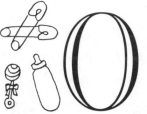

ne tiny (seven pounds on the average) baby requires tons of "stuff" for its care, maintenance and comfort. Take the diaper bag, for example; when filled with all the "stuff" required to take a baby out of the house, it is bigger and far heavier than the baby itself. If you are pregnant with your first baby (which I presume you are, since women who are pregnant and taking care of other children have no time to read anything), you will be clueless about what "stuff" is absolutely essential and what stuff is a complete waste of space and, more important, money. Whether you look forward to the prospect of shopping for your baby-to-be with great anticipation or with an overwhelming sense of ineptitude, you will ultimately have to purchase several things in preparation. If you like, you can while away some of the boredom at the end of your pregnancy by lining the baby's drawers and folding and refolding its undershirts. Or, if you are superstitious, you can pick out and pay for all your baby "stuff," and have the store keep it for you until the baby is born.

Whatever you do, do not just walk into a baby store and ask them to tell you what "stuff" you need for your baby. They know a sucker when they see one, and when you walk in with your big belly blazing the way, you may as well have the word "lollipop" tattooed on your head. Even the most scrupulous salesperson will be tempted to insist that you buy the matching ginger jar lamp just because it is trimmed in the same fabric as the crib bumpers. They probably don't mean to take advantage of your utter and complete ignorance in this area; it's just that they succumb to the enchantment of all baby things like the rest of us do. Sure, if you have a bedroom the size of a showroom to devote to one tiny baby and all the money in the world to spend on it, take the salesperson's word for it: You need everything, and you need it now. Otherwise, resist the temptations as best you can and confine your initial purchases to the essentials. Remember, there will be many months and years after the baby is born to accumulate the Winnie-the-Pooh matching bookends and the Beatrix Potter matching plate, cup and place mat. Besides, these are just the type of useless, adorable gifts your friends and relatives will delight in buying for you. Trust me, they won't be able to help but feel mildly depressed if you tell them all you really want is a car seat. If you are like most of us, you will be able to survive without such things as heating blankets to wrap around your baby-wipe boxes to keep the wipes from chilling your baby's bottom. Granted, it's a considerate little invention, because baby wipes really are cold, but you can scrunch them up in your hand to warm them if you want to take the chill out. This kind of item is just one of millions of products that you can be talked into buying when the combination of motherly guilt and total cluelessness are combining in your progesterone-addled psyche.

Relax and Take a Deep Breath

Just like it would be ridiculous to buy your baby's first ten-speed bicycle before it is even born, it is also ridiculous for you to run frantically from store to store collecting high chairs, playpens and walkers this early on. In fact, you really don't even have to buy a crib until the baby is about three months old. Sure, it's fun to have the little baby suite all set up and ready the day you come home from the hospital, but it's also fun to be able to pay your bills every month and not give your husband the slightest opportunity to start that crushingly boring routine about how having a baby is sending him to the poorhouse. Spread the expenditures out a little bit; it hurts less that way.

While we're on the subject of the poorhouse, the Girlfriends and

I would like to suggest that you sit down in a rare rational moment and really give yourself a budget of what you can afford to buy in preparation for the baby's arrival. Then double it. (Just kidding . . . sort of.) Then shop around. Baby things do go on sale, and their prices will vary greatly depending on the store you're in. Baby "stuff" is also sold in some fairly unlikely places, such as those membership discount warehouses. I once bought a baby swing in one of those places for less than half what the mall baby store was charging. It might even be a good idea to read an authoritative publication like *Consumer Reports* to find out what products are considered the best, most affordable and safest before you spend the big bucks on them. Better still, have your husband read it; it will give him something to do.

Another reason not to buy everything while you are still pregnant is that you don't really know your baby yet or what your particular mothering needs will be. If you have a colicky baby, you may feel that the most essential part of your arsenal is a front pouch to wear the baby in while you try to accomplish something involving your hands. You may not yet know if you are going to nurse exclusively or supplement with bottles, so buying a case of formula may be a bit premature. And that jogging stroller that looks so athletic and inspiring in the store may just piss you off after the baby is born because you don't have the time or energy to shower, let alone sprint through the neighborhood. Keep in mind that the people who manufacture baby "stuff" are very cunning indeed. They constantly modify and improve their products to encourage all of us to throw away last year's model and buy the new one. It is better to wait until you really need something before you buy it so that you have the most up-to-date version.

Beg, Borrow and Steal

Baby stuff, particularly furniture, is generally made to endure all sorts of infantile wear and tear. Babies usually outgrow their stuff rather than wear it out, which means that you should keep your eyes open for some used things with which to help set up your nursery. Cribs, changing tables, chests of drawers, hampers, mobiles, walkers, baby seats, rockers and strollers should all be able to service at least two babies, if not three or four. Ask around to see if your friends are ready to say good-bye to the baby years and give up the crib they have been storing in the garage. Perhaps they will agree to *lend* you some of their baby paraphernalia that is collecting dust in the garage or attic if you promise to give it back when the stork drops another baby down their chimney. Garage sales are also a great possibility. Some communities even have secondhand stores that exclusively sell used baby items.

If you decide to purchase most of your baby stuff new, expect to use it for at least two babies. In other words, resist buying a pink crib just because your first baby is a girl. Don't do what I did after my second baby had moved onto a "big-girl" bed and donate all your baby stuff to your church, because accidents can happen. Look at me—two "surprises" later, I have four children, and I had to buy everything all over again. I guess the general rule should be, don't part with your big-ticket baby stuff until you have reached menopause, had your tubes tied, had your husband fixed or, more realistically, run out of room.

While I do believe that you can make do with all sorts of non-baby stuff, I think it is important for me to praise products designed specifically for babies, for several reasons. In the case of furniture, it is safer for your baby than regular furniture, as it is finished and painted with nontoxic paints and stains and it has smooth, rounded corners and knobs that can't be easily removed and eaten. One of its very best features of a baby dresser is that the drawers are on safety runners so that they can't be pulled out by a curious crawling baby and land on its head or toes. You will be amazed at how much babies love drawers and everything in them. They can spend hours opening and closing them and pulling out every item of clothing inside. You will still have to worry about pinched fingers, even with baby furniture, but at least you won't have to worry about the dresser toppling over.

What follows is a list of baby stuff that we Girlfriends recommend you buy now, before the baby comes. These are the things we agree are really basic and essential to your baby's care and comfort, and, in some cases, to your sanity. We are not going to discuss all baby products; if you have fallen in love with a musical mobile with the Seven Dwarfs on it, who are we to deny you that pleasure? You will also be amazed at the variety of unique and occasionally wonderful things that people will give you at your baby shower or when the baby is born. This is the bare-bones list of what you will need to get through those first few weeks when you feel that you are having an out-of-body experience.

A Place for the Baby to Sleep

Especially if you are nursing, you will probably end up with the baby sleeping beside you in your bed much of the time. This is because the two of you will be so sleepy after a good meal that you simply burp and go unconscious (often in unison). If your husband is like mine, however, he will be petrified by the possibility that he might roll over onto the baby in his sleep and squish it. (To be perfectly candid, the fear will occur to you as well in the beginning.) Therefore, you will need some other place for the baby to sleep when your husband has the nerve to claim his place in the bed. For the first couple of months, my babies slept beside my side of the bed in a bassinet. I bought it for under forty dollars at a popular children's toy and furniture store. It looks like a white wicker basket on a stand, and you can buy a white eyelet skirt and bumper set in the same store to make it look all pretty and babyish. Some of my Girlfriends have used a cradle beside their bed, but I never found that the sideways rocking motion soothed my babies, and I was always afraid of my dogs brushing past and making the baby think it was experiencing its first earthquake.

If you (like nearly all of us) are not ready to put your baby in a crib in another room as soon as it comes home from the hospital, either because you can't hear it breathe that far away or because you are too exhausted to walk all the way down the hall to fetch the baby every time it wants to eat in the middle of the night or because you want the baby near you every minute, and if you think that buying a bassinet is a waste of money because it can only be used for two or three months, consider letting your baby sleep in a baby buggy. Relax—I am not talking about the strollers where the babies sit upright facing forward. I mean the big old buggies that in England are called prams. I received one of those fabulous vehicles at my first baby shower, and all four of my kids napped in it until they outgrew it. It was just so handy to be able to roll them around without waking them, and I could keep them near me as I moved around the house in search of a room that wasn't so messy that it made me feel guilty enough to think about cleaning it.

Eventually, unless you ascribe to the Family Bed philosophy (don't ask; it's way too organic for me to describe with a straight face), you will have to get a crib. In most cases, they do not automatically come with a mattress. (Wouldn't you just know it?) You will have to select from a variety of mattresses priced from nearly nothing to over a hundred dollars. My rule of thumb is to buy the cheapest one you can find that satisfies all fire-retardant regulations and looks sturdy enough to support a baby who may weigh as much as thirty pounds before he is ready to move to a bed. Then buy a couple of nice soft mattress pads to make it more cushy for the baby. Don't go overboard on the cushiness, however, because the baby's face shouldn't be able to sink into the fabric. Since most babies do not lie flat and stretched out like adults when they sleep, but rather creep around the perimeter of the crib in search of a cozy corner, I cannot justify paying premium price for a mattress with "extra back support" or any other such claim.

By the way, because of babies' propensity for creeping around in their sleep, you will need to buy padded crib bumpers to protect their soft little heads. Do not get seduced, however, into thinking that you need a matching pillow and comforter, because they are not only useless but potentially dangerous if the baby were to crawl under them. Most of my Girlfriends ended up using the baby comforters and pillows elsewhere in the baby's room, like thrown over the arm of the rocking chair.

Several years ago I spent the big bucks on a beautiful white crib that was touted as a particularly good investment because it converted into a "toddler bed" when the child was ready to get rid of the side rails. While the crib was great in many respects, I must admit that I have never once used the "toddler bed" feature, and in hindsight, I would not have paid extra for it. Of course, my children were born so close together that each toddler was hurried out of the crib and into a bed as soon as the subsequent baby had outgrown the bassinet and needed to move into the crib. (Hey, now that I think about it, I really did get my money's worth out of that thing, toddler bed or not.)

Even more important than the price and decorative style of the crib are the safety elements. First of all, never buy a crib that has posts in the corners or large decorative knobs or any other protrusion that could catch the baby's clothing in any way. Most manufacturers are no longer making cribs with this design, but this is particularly important if you are buying or inheriting a used crib.

If the crib you have selected has been repainted by the previous owner, make sure that it is lead-free or don't buy it. Or if you simply must buy it, have it stripped and painted with nontoxic paint intended for baby furniture. Babies love to chew on the side rails of their cribs when they are teething and able to pull into a standing position, and this is not a good way to introduce lead into their diets. (As if any way is a good way.) My daughter Jade has gnawed so ferociously on her crib that it looks like we have been using it for a beaver cage.

Pick a crib that requires only one hand to release the side rail. Otherwise you will be forever trying to hold the baby between your shoulder and your neck to free up two hands to simultaneously pull out two release buttons. If this gymnastic feat isn't irksome enough in itself, just wait until you have gotten a cranky, teething baby to sleep after two hours of rocking it, only to jar it awake as you struggle to get the crib side down to put it to bed (and restore circulation to your arms). When the baby is a newborn and still quite similar in activity level to a five-pound sack of rice, you will have the crib mattress on its highest rungs. During that stage, you won't have to raise or lower the crib sides, because you'll be able to easily reach over and set the baby down. As the baby gets older, though, and learns to pull into a standing position, the mattress will have to be moved down lower. That is when the side rails will have to be lowered, to enable you to put the sleeping baby into the crib without having it free-fall the last five inches to the mattress.

Drawers

Especially if you have a baby shower or get lots of gifts, it won't be long before your baby has a wardrobe far more extensive than yours. And after all, since you presumably no longer spit up after every meal, you don't need enough undershirts to allow for three or four changes a day, but your baby will. Even the teeniest, tiniest baby will need several drawers in which to store all the shirts, nighties, booties, blankets and "urp cloths" that you will wisely have acquired before going into labor. I suppose if you were really strapped for cash, you could put some of the baby's things in one of the drawers where you used to keep your own skinny clothes and belts before you got pregnant, but an investment in a chest of drawers will have to be made in the near future.

A Place to Change the Baby's Diaper

Right after they show you the lovely cribs, the baby furniture salespeople will direct you to the matching changing tables. If you love them and can afford them, then by all means, help yourself, but if you are a little short of space or money, ask them to show you the tray-shaped boards with pads in them that will fit on any decent-sized chest of drawers. As long as you can fit the changing tray onto your bureau securely and have enough leftover space to set diaper wipes, a couple of diapers and baby ointment for the baby's bottom, you are in great shape. You will probably find that your baby will outgrow the changing table by the time it is twelve months old, if not long before. By about nine months, babies get so squirmy and adroit at eluding your grasp that the only safe place to dress and change them will be a big bed, or better still, the floor, which is where they will probably end up eventually. By the way, it is essential to remind you that babies learn to roll or wiggle off changing tables or beds in an instant, usually with little or no warning, so you should NEVER TURN YOUR BACK ON THEM, even if it is just to toss the dirty diaper in the can.

Diaper Bin

I realize that if you are really trying to pinch pennies, you can live without a trash can devoted entirely to your baby, but as the baby gets older and the diapers get more toxic, you will not only be squeamish about tossing them into your kitchen trash can, but you will yearn for an airtight container to imprison the ever-more-offensive smells. (Something akin to what they store nuclear waste in might be appropriate.) Newborn diapers are bouquets of flowers compared with those of an eleven-month-old who is eating spaghetti, chicken, peas and anything he has swiped from the dog's bowl when you weren't looking. YOU MUST HAVE A DIAPER BIN, AND IT MUST HAVE AN AIRTIGHT LID. (And your *husband* must empty it regularly.)

Baby Bottles

Even if you intend to nurse your baby exclusively, you will want to have some baby bottles so that you can express some of your milk and store it for use at another time. And, of course, if your baby is taking formula as a supplement to breast milk or instead of breast milk, you will need several bottles. We recommend that you buy at least six in the beginning. You need this many because it is most economical and convenient to buy formula in the large cans or in powder form. When you open up a can, you should pour *all* of it into bottles or a plastic container rather than store the leftovers in a can in the refrigerator. Also, when you mix up a batch of formula from powder, you save a lot of time by mixing up at least a quart and filling several bottles and having them on hand for the rest of the day. I don't have any deeply held opinions about whether you should get the traditional plastic bottles, the ones with the disposable liners or the ones with the hole in the middle to form handles, so you're free to choose whatever you like without my interference.

I do have an opinion about the nipples, however, When I was pregnant, I bought several nipples and tried them all out myself, and I do mean myself. I sucked and chewed on every kind and color of nipple that I could find. The result of my survey was that clear nipples taste better than brown ones, especially after they have been in the dishwasher or sterilizer, at which point the brown ones taste like stale coffee. Also, I liked the idea of a nipple that was slightly flat-ended and curved to fit up against the roof of the baby's mouth like a mother's nipple fits during nursing. These are sold under several brand names such as Nuk and Mini-Mam. By the way, I subjected pacifiers to the same taste tests and reached the same conclusions. If you are willing to take my advice and buy at least a couple of pacifiers, *just in case,* then it is probably a good idea to buy them by the same manufacturer as the one that makes your bottle nipples to avoid any unnecessary infantile mouth confusion.

In the beginning, your baby will probably not drink more than two or three ounces of formula or breast milk at a feeding, so the little four-ounce bottles are the most convenient. But then again, you can go ahead and buy the eight-ounce bottles, which you will certainly need in a few months, and just fill them up halfway for your newborn. Once the baby has a more ferocious appetite (and after all the cheerful pictures have chipped off the four-ounce bottles), you will definitely want to buy eight-ounce bottles.

This talk of baby bottles brings up a related issue, and that is, do you need a bottle sterilizer? I am loath to admit to such risk-taking where my infants are concerned, but I did not use bottle sterilizers for three of my four babies. (I am not going to tell you which one received the more scrupulous care because it could fan the already-raging fires of sibling rivalry in this house.) It seemed sufficient to me to separate the nipples from the plastic rings (something you should always remember to do, by the way), wash all the bottle pieces in hot soapy water and then stick them in the dishwasher. There are wonderful little plastic baskets and racks that you can buy in baby specialty stores to hold the nipples and rings and bottles. This helps avoid the awful situation known as "Melting Nipple Syndrome," when the smaller parts fall to the bottom of the dishwasher and liquefy on the heating element.

I know that when I open my dishwasher just after its cycle is complete, I get enough steam in my face to open my pores, so I think it is safe to presume things get pretty hot in there. Nonetheless, your mother or mother-in-law may insist that no modern mother would consider *not* using a sterilizer. The thought of grown-up food particles possibly mixing with the baby's pristine bottles in the dishwasher makes some people positively queasy. Let me put it this way: If your mother wants to buy the contraption for you, let her, but I would never recommend wasting your own money on a sterilizer when the dishwasher seems completely up to the task of keeping your baby's bottles germ-free. Of course, I also happen to think it is safe to touch a newborn with normally washed hands, and yet my Girlfriend Corki made every visitor to her home scrub with Phisohex before they could approach the baby. Everyone's standards are different. After your first baby, you will discover that your standards of cleanliness will relax more with each subsequent baby. (And, no, it was not my *first* baby who was treated to sterilized bottles, so don't think you caught me!)

It goes something like this: If your *first* baby's pacifier falls on the floor, you put it in the sterilizer or boiling water before you give it back to her. If your *second* baby's pacifier falls on the floor, you wash it in hot water in the sink before giving it back to her. If your *third* baby's pacifier falls to the floor, you stick it in your own mouth to clean it, and then give it back to her. And you can't even imagine my *fourth* child and her pacifier! If she drops it to the floor, no one notices, and she has to pull it out of the dog's mouth and stick it back in her mouth herself.

Another standard that tends to relax with each subsequent baby is the strict separation of the baby's laundry from that of the rest of the family. Not only do we give our firstborns a whole washing machine to themselves, we buy special sensitive detergents for them. Third and fourth children are lucky if all their little socks and undershirts don't turn lavender because they were accidentally washed with their big brother's karate uniform belt. Anyway, getting back

194 THE GIRLFRIENDS' GUIDE TO PREGNANCY

to bottle sterilizers, I would put them on the list of optional purchases, but I am showing my deference to more fanatical mothers by mentioning them in this part of the list.

Baby Seats

Newborn babies cannot sit in strollers. They remain in the adorable little tucked lima bean position for several weeks, so if you want to carry them in something other than your arms, it will either have to be an infant seat, a baby sling or pouch that you wear on your chest or a baby carriage that allows them to lie on a flat surface. There is one other thing sold in most stylish baby stores, called a "Moses basket," that mothers are supposed to carry their babies in. It is really a woven basket with a canopy and lined with an adorable chintz fabric. Sorry, but I do not recommend that you buy one, irresistible as they may be (although odds are good that you will receive one at your baby shower from someone who has never had a baby of her own), because they are big, heavy and don't free up your hands. **And they can never be used to hold a sleeping infant in the car.**

The clear victor in the Best Thing to Carry Your Baby in Contest is the infant car seat that lifts out with a movement of the plastic handle on top to become a baby carrier and seat. It even has a little sun canopy, which you will grow to love since mothers are forever trying to shield their baby's eyes from glare. These pop-out car seats are terrific, because you don't have to bother the baby at all as you move it out of the car and into the house, the grocery store or the pediatrician's office (of course, it will eventually be in for a very rude awakening by the pediatrician, but I am getting ahead of myself). Most babies find it impossible to ride for more than five minutes in a car without falling asleep.

Let me take this moment to remind you of a very important tenet of motherhood: IF YOU CAN AVOID IT IN ANY WAY, NEVER WAKE A SLEEPING BABY. The routine of clamping the car seat into the base to put it in the car and releasing it to take it out will become automatic within weeks, but it is nearly impossible to accomplish on the first few tries. For that reason, we recommend that you practice the drill several times before the baby arrives to claim that seat of honor.

Look around for the newest addition to this pop-out car seat/

baby seat: the matching stroller frame. It is a collapsible stroller base that the car seat pops into just as it fits into its car seat base. It also has a nice big basket below the baby to hold the gigantic arsenal of stuff you will be toting with an infant in your care. I loved mine, and found it particularly useful on airplane trips, because I could stroll the baby right up to the door of the plane, pop out the carrier (with baby, of course,) and ask the flight attendant to stow the folded stroller frame for me or put it in the luggage compartment. Since the current wisdom about babies and airplane travel is that they should have their own seat and sit in a car seat on that seat, it has been a very convenient (albeit expensive, since I have to pay for an extra ticket) way to get the baby and its carrier onto the plane. Even if you opt to share your seat with the baby by holding it in your arms, you can take a rest by putting the car seat on the floor after takeoff and letting the baby rest there for a while. I should mention that my Girlfriend Dona thinks that this combination car seat/baby carriage is boxy and unattractive (and if truth be told so do I), but very occasionally practicality must prevail.

My Girlfriends and I are also big supporters of the baby pouches that you strap over your shoulders and tie around your waist to carry your baby on your chest. First of all, both of your arms are free, and what a feeling of sublime liberation that will be to a new mother. Second, all you have to do is gaze down to make sure that your baby is well and happy. And third—and to many of us most important of all—by having the baby in a pouch on your chest, you have make it nearly impossible for overly enthusiastic admirers with hands that have touched God-knows-what to kitchie-koo your little angel. Babies almost universally love living in these pouches, because they stay toasty warm, they can hear your heartbeat and your voice vibrate in your chest and they are constantly soothed by your movements, just like when they were in your womb. Later, when the baby can hold its head up securely—which coincides with the time it starts giving you a neck ache by dragging down your front— you can switch to a backpack baby holder (which you don't need to buy right away). A backpack allows the baby to see the world over your shoulder (or over your head, if it stands on the bar down by your waist belt). Taking long walks with my baby in a backpack was my secret weapon in regaining what fragments were left of my girlish figure.

Baby carriages, or prams, are good for the first several months, but they are not really the most practical contraptions on earth, for a couple of reasons. First, they are extraordinarily expensive (as in several hundred dollars). And second, by about halfway through the first year, most babies become impatient with looking only at the sky and birds (and the odd faces that occasionally peer in at them). They want to sit facing forward so that they can see the world and its wonders head-on. For this you will need a stroller. In the course of your shopping, you will probably see baby carriages that convert to strollers. This is the ideal solution, as far as I am concerned. They are ultimately economical, and they can be used for two to three years per child. Be careful, however, when choosing this vehicle, not to make your decision based solely on the flashy black enamel frame with the leopard-print fabric, hip as it may be. Here, again, is where a glance at *Consumer Reports* would be wise.

Insist that the salesperson not only demonstrate how the thing transforms itself, but also how it folds up and unfolds to fit into your car. *Then,* make him or her stand there and watch *you* try to master these skills. I drove around with my carriage in full upright position for four months before I figured out how to make it collapse. Fortunately, I drive a huge trucklike car so there was room for it. But I can save you this embarrassment (like when you lug the gigantic thing out at the car wash and the other mothers look at you like you've just pulled a full-sized elephant out of your car) and the inconvenience by recommending that you practice playing with your stroller several more times before the baby comes.

Whatever you do, do not buy an umbrella stroller—at least not yet. As attractive as these strollers may be, with their near weightlessness, their simple operation and their cheaper price, they are simply not for newborns. They don't recline, so the newborn would tumble forward in them, and they offer nothing to support the sides or head of the little critter. Remember, the first couple of months of motherhood will be devoted to helping your new baby manage its gigantic head, which seems to wobble and jerk alarmingly unless it is braced or cradled in some way.

Baby Bathing

Yeah, yeah, I know that you can keep a newborn clean enough with a thin little baby washcloth and some warm water, but I promise you that once the belly button scab falls off, you will have a primordial urge to put that little body into a bath. In the meantime, a newborn's bath time consists of a warm sponge bath, with each body part getting individual attention while the rest of the baby is wrapped up warmly in a towel. Then, some attention must be paid to its belly button scab, and if it is a circumcized boy, to its healing penis. For the belly button you will need to clean the area with alcohol, either on a cotton ball or, my favorite, a Q-Tip. The alcohol not only cleans the area, but helps the stump to dry and eventually fall off. The poor little penis will need a good, *but gentle,* cleaning, and then probably an application of an antibacterial cream and a protective gauze pad.

After the belly button and penis have healed, you are ready for the plunge. Unless you are a contortionist, or willing to get into the tub every time your baby does, the family bathtub will be utterly useless. What you need is a basin of some sort that you can set on a table or counter so that the baby is at your waist height. Trust me when I tell you that there is truly nothing more slippery than a wet newborn (except, perhaps, a raw egg, but you've already broken *its* shell). For about ten dollars you can buy a plastic baby bathtub that is lined in a spongy rubber to help keep the baby from sliding to the bottom. They are great, they are cheap, and you need one.

You may think that you simply put a tiny baby into the bath and soap it up with whatever bar or liquid soap that the rest of the family uses. *Wrong!* Their skin is so sensitive that almost any kind of alkaline-based soap can cause dryness, if not rashes. If truth be told, no soap is really necessary at all for bathing a tiny baby, because the only "dirt" it gets on it can be pretty successfully removed with warm water and a thorough, gentle scrub. If you feel deprived of the joy of sudsing your baby by this information, don't fret: I felt that way, too, and I found several gentle baby washes to satisfy my motherly urge to clean. Once you have selected your favorite baby wash, you will need to invest in several baby washcloths with which to apply it. No grown-up's washcloth is ever going to get that mysterious dark, linty stuff out from between the baby's toes without dislocating the toes in the process.

As all mothers know, there are few things more delicious and worthy of extra protection than a baby's bottom. Unfortunately, sitting in urine (or fouler excretions) for even a short time will irritate that precious area, and you will want to apply a cream or ointment to form a waterproof barrier between the baby and its debris. Discuss particular brands with your pediatrician-to-be and your mommy Girlfriends. One or two brands come up in every conversation and should do the job just fine.

More controversial in the baby-skin department is the use of baby powders. The popular wisdom is that any kind of talc is so fine that it could be inhaled by the baby and dust its itty bitty-lungs. You don't need that. The more politically correct baby powders are made with cornstarch instead of talc, and aren't as readily inhaled. Still, particularly where baby girls are concerned, a very good question needs to be asked: "Who needs more gunk to collect in all the tiny creases and crevices?" If you just cannot resist the enchanting smell of baby powder, then pat a little on the baby's back and tummy, and avoid the diaper area altogether.

You will also need several other little tools to help you experience the total joy of annoying a baby. One essential instrument of torture is the bulb nose aspirator, which is used to suck mucus out of a congested baby's nose. Each baby is issued one in the hospital, so don't forget to take yours home with you. A simple thing like the inability to blow its nose or clear its throat can make a baby suffer terribly, and you can save the day by siphoning off some of the offending fluids. Be advised: Babies universally loathe this experience, but they are invariably relieved by the results.

Even more frightening than the aspirator, at least for the mother, are the tiny fingernail clippers or scissors. I am sorry to force upon you this responsibility of cutting something that is paper-thin, less than an eighth of an inch in size and prone to move unexpectedly, but babies need their nails trimmed often or they will cut their faces or—horror of horrors—eyes with their razor-sharp nails. The best Girlfriend advice is for you to try to cut your baby's nails while it is sleeping. Even if you only get two or three clips done before it wakes up, if you approach the task every time the baby takes a nap, you will ultimately complete the manicure in about twenty-four hours.

As to whether you should buy the clippers or the scissors, I have no idea. I was equally inept with both, and I managed to take what looked like the top off my firstborn's thumb during our first trimming experience. I don't know who cried harder, him or me, but I do know that even now, seven years later, he still hates for me to cut his nails. Between you and me, I preferred *biting* my babies' nails off. I would chew on their fingers while I was feeding them, and they hardly noticed what I was doing.

The Baby's Bag

As I mentioned earlier, leaving the house with a newborn baby requires more planning and provisions than the landing on the beach at Normandy. You need diapers, changes of clothes, diaper wipes, bottles, blankets, a pad or cloth to change the baby on in case you have to lay the pure sweet thing down somewhere less hygienic than you might have chosen (like the counter in a public bathroom), pacifiers (or not), hats, creams, water for you (if you are nursing), snacks for you (if you are nursing or simply still eating like a pregnant woman), sunblock, rattles, favorite stuffed animals and, my personal essential since I live miles from civilization, baby Tylenol. All this stuff traditionally goes into a diaper bag, and you will probably want to continue that tradition. By my third child, however, I grew to hate diaper bags. I hated the way they looked, I hated how dirty they became almost immediately (nothing on this planet stains worse than baby formula or baby spit-up). Because no mother carries both a diaper bag *and* a purse (she just throws her keys and wallet into the baby's bag), the diaper bag becomes an unfortunate part of your fashion statement. For my third child, I branched out to backpacks from camping or hiking stores, with some success. By my fourth baby, I actually bought a black leather biker-chick shoulder bag as a sign of my coolness in the face of chronic maternity. I don't think anyone was fooled. The minimum you should be looking for is something that is washable or vinyl, that has compartments to separate the baby bottles from the dirty diapers and your wallet from both and, most important, something with a shoulder strap, because your hands will be full of baby, infant seat, stroller, etc. Keeping in mind that this metamorphosis from baby bag to shared bag *will* occur, perhaps you should forgo the black and white polka dot bag with the smiling giraffe on the sides.

Baby Medicines

On your first or second visit to the pediatrician you will be given a small complimentary bottle of some sort of baby acetaminophen (like Tylenol) to take the fever and sting out of the baby's first immunization. (Bring a bottle of the grown-up version for yourself, because this shot will be more painful for you than it will be for the

baby.) NEVER ADMINISTER ANY MEDICATIONS WITH-
OUT SPECIFIC DIRECTION FROM YOUR PEDIATRI-
CIAN. For convenience' sake, however, it wouldn't hurt to have
whatever he or she recommends for fever and pain in the house in
advance, in case you call in the middle of the night with a sick baby
and are told that a little Tylenol will make things all better. It beats
sending your husband out in his pajamas in search of an all-night
pharmacy.

Baby Thermometer

To be completely honest with you (like, when haven't I been?), I
never ever took any of my children's temperatures when they were
infants. No disease seemed so threatening that I was willing to go
probing with a rectal thermometer with a blob of petroleum jelly on
the end of it. It is pretty apparent when babies have a temperature—
not only do their foreheads and cheeks get hot, but so do their
hands, tummy and neck—so I relied on the "touch and guess"
method. Most of my other Girlfriends, however, were much more
intrepid than I and always knew their babies' temperatures to the
second decimal point. Baby rectal thermometers are inexpensive
and available everywhere (just make sure it says "rectal" on it), so
you should pick one up. Here's another Girlfriend tip: An equally
good use for a rectal thermometer is to help an infant make poopoo.
It's as much a reflex as hitting your knee with a hammer and kicking
your leg out. In goes the rectal thermometer and out comes the re-
calcitrant poop.

To my mind, the single greatest invention of our century was the
electronic ear thermometer. This amazing gizmo actually bounces a light
beam off the baby's eardrum and interprets it into body temperature
in about two seconds. You can even stick that thing in the baby's
ear while it is sound asleep! It costs about eighty dollars, but the
price seems to be dropping every year, just like what happened with
pocket calculators, so shop around. Better yet, you might hint that
a couple of your Girlfriends go together on it as a baby shower
gift for you. You will like it so much you will be taking your own
temperature, and your husband's, just for the fun of it.

Baby Light

Not until you have your baby in your home and are up changing its
diaper several times a night will you fully comprehend the value of

a light on a dimmer switch or a strong night-light. If you have to turn on regular lights to see the business at hand, you not only wake the baby completely but risk giving yourself a blinding headache. You are not performing surgery here (especially now that the days of diaper pins are long since gone), and you just need enough light to make sure you are diapering the right end of the baby and that you have thoroughly cleaned its tushy before putting on a new diaper. Forget about the forty-seven tiny snaps on the inside leg of the sleeper! Just snap three or four and the goal of keeping it around the baby's legs is achieved. Save perfection for when there are other people around to admire it.

A very dim light also sets a wonderfully soothing mood for both you and the baby when you are feeding it. There he lies in your arms, all warm, listening to your heart and feeling that womblike darkness. He might not be looking at you in his ecstatic comfort, but I guarantee you will be gazing at him as if you have seen a beauty so sublime it makes your heart and lungs contract.

Baby Surveillance

You will be tempted to have your baby in your arms, in your bed or propped in a baby seat right before your eyes at all times, but it won't be too long before you realize that a sleeping baby is a gift from heaven, intended to be used by you to do such exotic things as lie down, take a bath or put the week's dishes in the dishwasher. With a baby monitor, you can do these things and still obsess over your baby's every breath and coo. In its simplest and most functional form, a baby monitor consists of a speaker that you place near the baby and a receiver that you set next to you or even clip onto your belt as you move around. They are incredibly sensitive, picking up the sound of each inhalation if you turn them up loud enough. The most popular brands are sold for under fifty dollars (good gift item), and are made out of plastic and can be dropped on the floor repeatedly or knocked off the bureau into the diaper can without noticeable damage. I am monitoring my fourth child with the set I bought seven years ago for my first baby, and it appears capable of spying on my kids for me for years to come. (This is a good thing, because I have noticed that, as they get older, their secret lives become more dramatic and potentially dangerous; such as, "Hey, let's go into your mom's room and tie her sheets together and throw them over the window and swing down into the pool like Tarzan." If you put the baby monitor in a child's room from birth, he becomes oblivious to the monitor's existence and doesn't think to turn it off before hatching some diabolical scheme.)

Breast Pump

If you think that your physical changes reach their most outrageous by the end of nine (ten) months of pregnancy, you have another think coming. Just wait until you experience your breasts filling to capacity with milk. This near-explosion state is called "engorgement," and it is not only alarming, but very uncomfortable. If you are nursing, the only relief is to get some of the milk out, and I mean as quickly as you possibly can. Nonnursing mothers just have to endure this and wait until their bodies get the message that the milk factory is closed for business. Many doctors give injections to women who are certain they don't want to nurse to help get this message across sooner rather than later.

Generally, your baby will be happy to siphon off the extra milk for you, but sometimes he just isn't hungry or willing to wake up from his nap yet. Or your breasts and nipples can get so full and hard that the baby can't latch on properly and suck any milk out. For this reason, the Girlfriends heartily recommend that you get a breast pump to milk yourself (in the bovine sense of the word). It may sound distasteful now, but boy will you be grateful for it later. Not only can you relieve yourself or make your breasts more manageable for your hungry baby (my Girlfriend Amy used to make so much milk that she had to pump ounces of it off before feeding her babies or else she'd gag them), but you can make yourself more comfortable and stimulate your breasts to learn to make even more milk if you want them to. The reason that you will want them to increase production is the best part of all about having a breast pump at your disposal. You can fill baby bottles with breast milk and HAVE SOMEONE ELSE FEED YOUR BABY while you take a nap or shave your legs for the first time in a month. Stored breast milk is like liquid gold to a nursing mother; the more you have on hand, the more often you can find time for yourself.

Breast pumps range in types from very simple and inexpensive cylinders that look rather like giant syringes, to electric milking machines that can empty two breasts simultaneously in a matter of minutes. Since no one wants to fork out the hundreds of dollars required to buy a milking machine that will probably be used for fewer than twelve months, several nurses and lactation specialists have created a booming business by renting them to new mothers. If you can manage this, I really think you should, because as odd as it will be to watch your nipples get stretched about four inches long into suction cups, it is pretty much an idiot-proof invention. Those hand pumps never got a single drop out of this idiot, and I tried several of them. (The only difficult thing about electric breast pumps can be in assembling the hoses that connect the pump to the bottles, so ask the rental agency or pharmacy to put it all together for you before you blithely take it home.)

Diapers

Let's not hear any groaning out there! I realize that you *expected* to put diapers on your baby, I just figure you have no idea how *many* diapers you'll need in those first few days. Look at it this way: You will probably nurse every three to four hours around the clock in the beginning. Before each feeding, right after the baby has awakened from its nap, you will need to change its diaper. Chances are you will hear or feel some sensation *during the feeding* to lead you to believe that the diaper should be changed again immediately. There are also those odd times when the baby has been awake for a bit and you just feel the need to remove the diaper to make sure it's not wet. That's about ten to twelve diapers in just one day. Don't think for a minute that you will feel like dashing to the store to buy more diapers on your second or third day home with a new baby, so buy a small package of the smallest newborn size and the next size up. Whatever size fits, use it. Lucky for you, newborn diapers come with gender-general decorations and are usually all white. That isn't the case as the babies get bigger; little girls' diapers are pink with kittens or rainbows on them, and boys' diapers are blue with suitable masculine borders like dump trucks or trains. I guarantee that even if you were given a case of free diapers and they happened to be pink, you would use them for gift wrapping before you would put them on your firstborn *son!* It's an illness, I know, and we could all keep our therapists busy for weeks over this issue of gender stereotypes, but it's the truth. Oh yes, one last diaper matter: As we discussed earlier, it's your choice — cloth or disposable.

Clothes

What they don't need in *variety* of clothes, newborn babies make up for in their need for *volume*. In its first few weeks of life, a baby can live quite happily and securely in an undershirt, a diaper, socks or footsies and wrapped up tight in a receiving or waffle-weave blanket. I know you won't leave it at that; none of us since the beginning of time have been able to resist the desire to add the funny hat, the velour pajamas, the pretend running shoes, etc., but you really could get by with less.

Let's start, then, with the fundamentals. Since we have already mentioned that you should have mountains of diapers ready in preparation for the new baby, we can move right into T-shirts. As I said in the previous chapter, the Girlfriends recommend T-shirts that tie closed rather than having to be pulled over the baby's bobbly head. We also think that you should buy about six of them to begin with. That allows for three changes a day, plus a day to fail to get any laundry done. Since the undershirt is the "foundation garment" of a tiny baby, you will probably always have one on your little angel for the first few months. Spend enough money that the shirts are soft and absorbent, but don't spend so much that they have couture designers' names appliquéd on them, because you will be amazed at how quickly the baby will grow out of these things. Also, unlike other articles of baby clothing that can be passed on to friends' babies or saved for your future children, infant T-shirts almost always need to be thrown away after your baby has finished with them. (Remember what I told you about formula and baby spit-up having more staining power than grape juice mixed with india ink?)

Babies' feet look incredibly skinny and small when you first see them. It's hard to imagine any article of clothing fitting them and staying on, and the truth is, few do, but that doesn't stop us from putting socks on them, and then putting them on again and again every time they are kicked off. Buy three or four pairs to start. They don't get dirty very fast (except when your baby puts its foot in its poopy diaper while you are trying to change it), so you don't really have to change them as constantly as, say, the T-shirts. However, since they are only about three inches long, they tend to get lost constantly. A bit of useful advice here is to buy all your footsies in the same color so that you can always make a pair, no matter how many you have managed to lose.

The Girlfriends are unanimous in their praise of the drawstring nightgown for newborns. These little articles are terrific, because you tie them closed at the bottom and the baby can't wiggle its legs out and get cold at that rare moment when you're not looking. Most importantly it also captures socks that are trying to escape. They also make for any easy diaper change, which will be profoundly appreciated in the middle of the night. You don't have any snaps or buttons to deal with in your stupor, just untie the bag, pull it up over the baby's belly, change the diaper and tie it snugly back into place. Save the pajamas and sleepers with legs for later when the baby has outgrown the drawstring gowns and/or wants to move its legs more purposefully than the gown allows for.

I have saved the discussion of blankets for the clothing section, because they really are an article that the baby will wear constantly in the first couple of months. I think of blankets as being either one of two types: the swaddling type or the overblanket type. The swaddling types are usually the thin flannel or cotton waffle weaves that wrap firmly around the baby and make it feel snug and secure without making it break out in a sweat. These blankets are machine-washable and inexpensive, and they are changed nearly every time you change the baby. These are also the blankets that can be used as the "urp cloths" we mentioned in the previous chapter, you know, the ones you wear like capes to protect you and the baby from spit-up.

The overblanket type is usually a beautiful woven and fringed thing that looks like wool, even though it is usually a polyester blend. These items usually have decorations or satin borders on them and they tend to be heavier than the swaddling blankets. These are what I refer to as the "going out" blankets, because you only wrap your angel in them to impress people or to protect them from the air outside. They look particularly pretty draped over a baby in a carriage or in your arms at a family gathering. Otherwise, they tend to be itchy and hot.

All the Other Stuff

Baby stores will become fun destinations for you after the baby is born and the two of you feel like shopping again. These baby shopping excursions will definitely replace your pre-pregnancy shopping sprees, because you still won't be wearing your normal size, and you won't have the need for anything that can't be washed and worn without ironing. Once you have made the basic purchases we have just listed for you, you can improvise and overspend to your heart's content on every new miniature cowboy or ballerina outfit, solar system wall hanging, womb-sounds teddy bear and motorized baby hammock that strikes your fancy. Enjoy yourself and try it all if you want to (and can afford it). In the meantime, we Girlfriends have done our job of getting you prepared; you are on your own from here.

15

Labor Begins (Finally!)

here are two universal concerns about labor among pregnant women: "Will it hurt?" and "How will you know when it is happening?" The answer to the first concern, "Will it hurt?" can be simply answered for now by saying yes, it will hurt, but probably not too badly for the first few hours. Of more immediate importance is how to tell if you are about to go into labor—or if you are, indeed, already there.

My Girlfriends and I have amassed as many indications as we could think of that your baby is coming soon, and here they are:

The Nesting Instinct

A couple of days before you go into labor, you may feel an irresistible urge to clean your house or defrost your refrigerator or put all your CDs in alphabetical order or some other such anal task. I am not talking about the normal panicky cleaning fits some of us fall into when our mother calls and says she is stopping by unexpectedly, or the way you finally get around to putting the broken toilet paper dispenser back on the wall because your brother and his new wife are coming to stay for the weekend. No, I am talking about the kind of feverish cleaning where you use your husband's toothbrush to scour the pipe that goes from the back of your toilet into the wall. I'm talking about taking off every switchplate cover in the house and soaking them all in Pine Sol. This is the time when otherwise rational women truly believe that they cannot sleep for one more night in a house where the baseboards have not been freshly painted. This is nature's way of making sure that you will be ready for the new baby, and it is called "nesting."

A week after her due date (which was a purely fictional concept in the first place), my Girlfriend Mindy was discovered by her mother tottering at the top of a six-foot ladder, feverishly sponging down the shelves at the top of her closets. To indicate how out of character this was, I have to tell you that Mindy's "baby" is now seven years old, and that those shelves have never seen a sponge since. Mindy's alarmed mother tried speaking soothingly to her, much as one would talk to a person standing on a skyscraper ledge threatening to jump. "Are you sure that's such a good idea, dear?" she asked. "Why don't you come on down and let me do that for you?" But Mindy was powerless to stop and completely unable to see how bizarrely she was behaving.

My Girlfriend Sondra started cooking as she neared her delivery date. She calmly and rationally explained that she just wanted to have a few meals frozen so that her husband could microwave them when she was in the hospital and when she first got home. It made sense, until I saw Sondra's car in the grocery store parking lot at 7:00 A.M., waiting for it to open. She made so many casseroles that she filled her own freezer and soon spread out to her Girlfriend's across the street. When she tired of casseroles, she decided it was imperative that she provide some variety for her lucky husband, so she taught herself all the intricacies of Chinese cooking in the pre-dawn hours before the grocery store opened. Then she moved on to barbecuing everything she could get her hands on, even if it meant standing outside in the rain holding an umbrella over the gas grill. Let me cut to the chase: Sondra went into labor, went to the hospital, gave birth and came home before her husband had time to eat one single lasagna, and she celebrated the birth of her daughter by baking Belgian waffles for her parents and in-laws only about six hours after the baby was born. (O.K., so maybe Sondra's not such a good example.)

One morning at dawn near the end of her pregnancy, my Girlfriend Shirley's husband awoke to find her side of the bed empty.

Convinced that she was in labor or giving birth in some other room in the house, he leapt naked from the bed to find her. She didn't answer his calls, and he couldn't find her anywhere in the house, even though her car was still in the garage. Then he looked down the steep hill that many people in Los Angeles refer to as their "backyard." There was Shirley, pushing and pulling a wheelbarrow filled with fertilizer up and down the hill. Her baby was going to come home to a house with grass, by God, and Shirley had been working toward that end since hours before the sun came up. No mere gardener could be trusted with fertilizing *her* baby's lawn; no, it was *mother's* work.

Windowsills and shutters became my obsession during one pregnancy. I was determined to eliminate all dust from all rooms, and I bought several contraptions to brush it up, wipe it off or filter it out of the air completely. One night I awoke feeling as if I had been electrocuted—I had had the sudden realization that all that dust I had brushed off the sills and shutters must have landed in the carpet. My husband had to physically restrain me from ripping up all the carpet in the house.

My Girlfriend Jillian, who expresses her nesting instinct in ways more artistic than antiseptic (and who has a cleaning lady to help her with the more mundane scrubbing matters), started frantically putting all her loose photos in albums and desperately trying to bring up to date the baby books of the two children she already had when she was waiting to deliver her third. (By the way, this baby-book thing can be a real burden, especially after the first baby. Pretty soon the book becomes little more than a storage folder for all the clippings and doctor's reports and report cards that you can jam in it, everything out of order and unattached. You can take it from me: All mothers have deep-seated guilt about unfinished baby books. And if they don't, they have way too much time on their hands—or, better still, no baby books!)

Anyway, getting back to Jillian, there she was on the floor, surrounded by photographs and albums with a pregnancy the size of a world globe on her lap, trying to make some organization out of this memory chaos. Her understanding, or fearful, husband passed by this scene several times, but dared not suggest that maybe a nap would be more beneficial at this point. No, Jillian had a mission and would glue-gun anyone who thwarted her. Wouldn't you know, she slipped the very last photo into the very last album, then heard a little "pop" sound. Her water had broken, right on cue.

General Pissed-Offedness

Another indication that you are rounding the homestretch may be a persistent and increased crankiness. I know, I know—pregnant women are accused of being emotionally unpredictable frequently during the entire nine (ten) months of their pregnancies. But there are a lot of good reasons why you should be particularly cranky at this point: 1) You are not sleeping very much or very well; 2) You are bored with being a biology experiment; and 3) You feel oppressively aware that there is no backing out of this delivery thing now and you are beginning to suspect that the baby is much easier to deal with while it is inside you than it will be when it is on the outside.

But my Girlfriends and I think there is something even more unique about these last few weeks of crankiness; something that, to the experienced eye, indicates that *this woman is about to erupt*. Think of her as a volcano; she is a big old mountain of a thing, as she has been for a few months now, but from the outside you can't tell if she is dormant or filled with seething lava. Only a thin trickle of steam indicates that she is about to blow. I remember seeing my Girlfriend Maria at a children's birthday party right before the birth of her son. When I went up to say hello, she looked as if she couldn't quite place me, even though we had been friends for ten years. To the casual observer she must have looked calm to the point of being nearly unconscious, but to the other mothers in the crowd, she was clearly going to have that baby within hours. Her intuition was telling her that she was about to undergo the greatest challenge and transformation of her life, and she seemed to be hunkering down in preparation.

As they face the biggest task of their lives, many women begin a subtle kind of withdrawal from their everyday lives. They develop what I call the "Stranger in a Strange Land" Syndrome, where they go through the motions of their usual business, but feel distanced from and uninvolved in it. Things that they would normally find amusing become trivial or irritating. They are sick and tired of being pregnant. They want to get the ordeal of birth going so that they can stop dreading it, once and for all. This is a good time for friends and family, especially husbands, to stay out of the pregnant woman's way as much as possible, and to answer "yes" to anything she asks, because any confrontation now is bound to be messy.

My Girlfriend Julee, who is a manicurist, was the brightest, cheeriest pregnant person you have ever seen. Every week I would try to pry one single complaint out of her, and every week I was disappointed. As far as she was concerned, nausea was a minor inconvenience, heartburn was something to be endured with good humor and she still didn't know what hemorrhoids were. Then came her last three weeks. Overnight, the old Julee had been snatched away, and in her place was a woman who showed up for work and spent the day with her head down, looking at the hand in front of her. She filed and painted those nails with such fervor that you would think she believed each stroke was bringing her that much closer to the end of her pregnancy. She had begun the long march, and she was prepared to deck anyone who stood between her and her destination. All of the gossip and chatter that flew around her in the manicure salon just sailed right by her. She didn't seem to hear any of it, and if she did it must have seemed completely meaningless and trivial to a woman facing what she was facing.

The Baby Drops

That certainly sounds dangerous, doesn't it? But the change it is meant to describe is subtle and often barely noticeable. There will come a time at the end of your pregnancy when you might notice the baby sitting lower in your stomach than before. This is because it is starting to lock into the birth position, and it is being held in place by your uterus. This generally only happens with your first baby, because in subsequent pregnancies your weakened stomach muscles "drop" the baby the minute it gets heavy. Dropping is also referred to by some as "lightening" (for reasons that I will never understand, because absolutely nothing is getting "lighter" at this point).

Like so many things in pregnancy, dropping is a good news/bad news proposition. The good news is that you will find it easier to take a deep breath and fill out your traumatized lungs. The bad news is that in order for your lungs to be liberated, your stomach and bladder have to be sacrificed. From now on, you will get full long before you finish a serving of food. That is not such a bad thing, but what happens to your bladder is that you will constantly feel like you are about to wet your pants, and when you sit down to relieve yourself nothing more than a teaspoon or two will come out.

Diarrhea

Some of my Girlfriends have told me that their tummies felt crampy all day before they went into labor, and that their stools were all loose and watery. We concur that it can be hard to tell the difference between diarrhea cramps and early labor contractions. In fact, as we Girlfriends think back on it, we believe that they were probably the same thing. For this reason, it is wise to pay particular attention to a funky tummy in your third trimester. Just as you feel the need to clean everything before your baby is born, your intestines also seem to have a nesting instinct. Often, shortly before or during the early stages of labor, you may find your bowels wanting to clean out anything you may have eaten in the last twenty-four hours. If it happens to you, be grateful, because this evacuation means you are off and running, and because there will be less poopoo on the delivery table when you push. Until recently, it was traditional hospital procedure to give all delivering women enemas. Since then, the prevailing wisdom has been that a little poop never killed anyone.

Passing the Mucus Plug

The mucus plug is exactly what it sounds like; a kind of bloody, snotty thing that corks up your cervix so that no nasty germs get through to your uterus while the baby is in there growing. The thinning of the cervix and the beginning of its dilation can make it so that the plug is no longer big enough to fill the hole, and out your vagina it comes! I will never forget my Girlfriend Lorraine screaming for me from the bathroom when she was very very pregnant. "Look in there," she cried, pointing into the toilet and staring into the bowl bug-eyed. "What is *that?*" I, who had not yet had children myself and had never seen anything so disgusting floating in a bowl, just stood there dumbly and held tight to her arm, because I was certain at least one of us would faint.

There are two important things to know about passing your mucus plug. First, labor will begin soon, but not necessarily immediately. Many Girlfriends have passed their plugs and not really gone into labor for a couple more days. And second, this is only a good thing. It does not hurt, and since it usually happens while you are sitting on the toilet, it doesn't even make a mess. Oh yes, one last thing: Not everyone passes their mucus plug before active labor and delivery. I, for example, have never seen my mucus plug, and believe me, I have peered into many a toilet bowl hoping to find one.

Your Water Breaks

Everyone has heard this expression with regard to pregnancy, but very few of us know what to expect or recognize it when it happens to us. Of course, *water* doesn't really break, but the *membrane* that has been filled with water for your little baby to float around in for the last forty weeks does. This is the result of a uterine contraction or the baby's head pushing against it and popping it. Sometimes it pops like a water balloon, with a gush of water soaking you, your clothes and wherever you have been lying or standing. Other times the bag just springs a leak and you feel a constant trickle of water between your legs. Either way, the universal sensation is: "I am peeing, and I can't stop!"

My Girlfriend Jillian says that when it happened to her, she rushed to the toilet. She peed so much (or did what she thought was peeing—although she would never use that word for the function, because she hates it) that she reached behind herself and flushed the toilet halfway through, because she really worried that she would fill the bowl and it would overflow onto the bathroom floor. And this is a mother of *four*, so you know that this birthing business is just full of surprises. What contributes to the sensation that the water supply is unending is the fact that it is, indeed, unending. Your body replenishes the water (placental fluid) at an astonishing rate so that the baby doesn't get dry and pruney, or more important, so that infection doesn't set in, so you really can just dribble away for hours.

Since about half of all expectant mothers will have their water break at home before they go to the hospital, it is a very good idea for you to prepare for its happening to you. One particularly good idea is to put a mattress protector or a plastic sheet on your bed. (There is a big tendency for water to break in bed and really gush, because the baby is relaxing on your spine or side when you sleep.) Then, when you stand up, the flow will stop or slow down a lot, because the baby's head will go back down on your cervix and act like a drain plug. The other suggestion I would make is that you should always wear a sanitary napkin during your last few weeks.

One napkin, even a super-duper maxi, definitely won't be enough to soak up all the water, but it will give you running time to get out of the checkout line of the grocery store and into a bathroom.

There are two important things you should know about your water breaking:

It Does Not Hurt at All!

You Must Call Your Doctor and Get Ready to Go to the Hospital, Because This Event Will Only End With a Baby Coming Out. You Can Go for a Few Days Without Your Plug, but If You Are Near or Past Your Due Date, Your Doctor Will Probably Not Want You to Walk Around With Your Water Draining Out for More Than a Few Hours.

Dilation and Effacement

By the time you have delivered your baby, you will toss around these two words with great casualness, but for now, let me explain what they mean. Dilation, which we Girlfriends agree is the more important of the two, refers to the stretching open of the cervix, the short tunnel that connects your uterus to your vagina. Effacement describes the shortening of that tunnel in preparation for birth. By the time you are ready to push, the tunnel that is the cervix is so short that it's not so much a tunnel anymore as it is a sort of membrane between the uterus and the vagina. And in dilation, this membrane is stretched big enough for a baby's head to come out. Dilation is measured on a scale of one to ten. If you are one or two centimeters open or dilated, that baby isn't going anywhere. By the time your cervix is open ten centimeters wide, which theoretically means the doctor can stick all ten of his or her fingertips inside the opening, it's bombs away!

Unless you are a contortionist, you cannot determine for yourself if you are dilating or effacing. These are things your doctor will report to you during your last few office visits. For first-time mothers, there is tremendous satisfaction in calling your friends and family to announce that your doctor has just told you that you are two centimeters dilated and 25 percent effaced. With that kind of news, labor is certain to be right around the corner, right? Well, not necessarily. Millions of pregnant women are on the street right this very minute, walking around two and three centimeters dilated, and their babies may still not come for another week or two (or even three. Sorry!).

Other very pregnant women forlornly leave their doctor's office after being told that their cervix is closed up tight as a clam, only to go into active labor that very same night. So my advice is this: If you are effacing and dilating, go ahead and get excited, because the least it can do is relieve your boredom. And if you are not changing at all in there, do not worry one little bit, because it does not mean a thing. By my fourth pregnancy, I walked around for weeks so dilated that my vagina made little squeaking noises with every step and it felt like the baby's head was between my thighs. But did the baby come early? Not by one second!

Contractions

The confusing thing about contractions is that they come in all forms and intensities. I would estimate that about 99 percent of us go into labor having absolutely no idea what to expect. And when it begins, we all wonder, "Is this *really* it?" The Girlfriends' rule of thumb is this: If you think you might be in labor, stay calm. Rarely does a first baby slip out ten minutes after the first contraction, so there will probably be no need to call 911 at this point. It is important, however, that you don't be a Labor Martyr, either. If you feel unusual in any way, pick up the phone and call your doctor, even if you just saw him or her two hours ago. Believe me when I tell you that doctors *expect* you to rely on them to tell you if you are in labor or not. Call them; it makes them feel needed.

The Myth of False Labor

This is probably a good time to talk about false labor. The most reassuring thing I can tell you about false labor is that it is a myth.

That's right, hogwash. It's just one more thing to make you feel that you are ignorant and out of control when you are pregnant. All contractions are contractions, and all contractions are preparation for birth. Some just occur closer to the time of birth than others. Therefore, you are not a moron if you feel contractions, go to the hospital and then get sent home. It happens all of the time. It simply means that these contractions you are feeling are not *noticeably* dilating and effacing your cervix, and you might have a few more hours or days before things start opening up in there.

My Girlfriend Sondra had me drive her to the doctor when her second baby was due. We really flew down the freeway, because she was having contractions, and since she had already had one baby, she knew what labor felt like. Half an hour later, we were sent home empty-handed; no open sesame. A week later she felt contractions again, but this time they were stronger and more regular, so she skipped the doctor's office and met him directly at the hospital. Wouldn't you know, still no open sesame? But by this time Sondra had had enough of this torture, and she refused to leave the hospital. She informed her doctor, with a hint of hysteria in her voice, that she would not go home until she had a new baby to take with her.

In fact, your uterus has been contracting ever since your egg got fertilized, but you probably didn't really start noticing it until the middle or end of your pregnancy. The contractions that do not noticeably open up your cervix are called Braxton Hicks contractions. They are designed by God to get you in the mood for labor. Toward the end of your pregnancy, your uterus will frequently contract, with increasing intensity. Sometimes your belly gets so hard and rigid that you could bounce a dime off it. Most pregnancy books say that Braxton Hicks contractions do not hurt, and compared to productive contractions this may be true, but my Girlfriends who had a lot of them say they were by no means painless. While they may not feel like a knife stabbing you in the tummy, they can be serious enough to take your breath away and make you feel the need to sit down or lean against something. By the way, early labor can feel exactly the same way, so you can see why it's so easy to get confused.

Some women feel mild cramping contractions for a full day or two before their contractions get compelling enough for them to go to the hospital. My Girlfriends Janis and Tracy both felt kind of punk, as though they were getting the flu or their periods (remember those?), when they were in the early stages of labor. They called their doctors to check in, and then casually kept an eye on the clock to see if there was any regularity or pattern to their moments of crampiness. In the meantime, they called their families and hung around the house. My Girlfriend Patti had these mild contractions at first, too, but she had no intention of waiting all day in her house for something to happen. She and her husband went to a matinee movie, and then to the hospital.

My Girlfriend Amy never had time to buy a box of popcorn, let alone see an entire movie, because her labor always came out of the clear blue sky and with the intensity of a thunderstorm. With the first contraction, she knew it was time to go to the hospital, and by the time she got there she was already feeling the urge to push. Her description of trying to take off her cowboy boots in a tiny hospital bathroom while in hard labor is really very funny (cowboy boots are problematic even under the best of circumstances). A quick, efficient labor can be good and bad. It is good if you dread a long-drawn-out, tiring labor, but it is bad if you have your heart set on an epidural, because there really won't be time for one.

If you are feeling the flulike, periodlike symptoms (and your baby is due, of course), and you would like to try to move things along a bit, walking could be a good idea. If you don't feel like walking, however, don't worry one little bit, because sleep is equally valuable at this time, and a little nap might be the perfect thing. In fact, some women will have irregular and relatively manageable contractions for more than a day. The pains are not strong enough to make them rush to the hospital, but they are too strong for them to get any sleep. If this happens to you, your doctor might prescribe a sedative or sleep medication so that you can get some rest before the final rounds of labor begin.

You might want to eat something light, because once you get to the hospital it's ice chips and cotton swabs that taste like lemon until you get that baby out. Chances are you are so excited and nervous that food is the last thing on your mind, but a little soup or a milk shake couldn't hurt.

Scheduled C-Section

One other very persuasive indication that your baby is coming soon is a scheduled C-section. With a scheduled C-section, you and your doctor have agreed to a time at which you will enter the hospital in a fairly calm and leisurely fashion, and he or she will extract your baby through a small slit at the top of your pubic hair. There are a lot of reasons to schedule a cesarean section, such as medical conditions like placenta previa (don't ask), breech babies or twins or triplets. Other women elect to have a cesarean because they want to maintain the vaginal tone of a teenager, and their doctors find a medical explanation that will suit their insurance company. And then there are those women who temperamentally just cannot take the uncertainty and guessing that waiting for labor to begin entails. If they are lucky, their doctors, too, will help them contour their insurance policies to cover this planned delivery. Of course, I cannot have a clear conscience unless I remind you that it is actually better for the baby to be born vaginally, for many reasons: The squeezing involved helps force the fluid out of their lungs, you will need less anesthesia (if you consider this a *good* thing) and your recovery will be quicker. Still, C-sections are very safe for mother and child, and the recovery time is surprisingly short.

Yes, I read the papers, and I am aware of the outrage in some quarters about the number of unnecessary C-sections that are performed in the United States. Am I resentful or indignant? Not particularly. The temptation will be extraordinary for you at this point in your pregnancy to sincerely feel that you would rather have your fingernails pulled out by their roots than succumb to a C-section. You will be convinced that the big emotional payoff of pregnancy lies in the physical challenge of laboring and delivering the baby vaginally. Very gingerly, I suggest that you don't set these kinds of expectations for yourself. A significant number of women who have their hearts set on vaginal births will end up having C-sections, and there is absolutely no reason for this to be a source of disappointment.

As someone who has had babies both ways, I must admit that I don't really have a preference for one over the other. Having a healthy baby was all I really wanted, and I didn't care how I got it. In fact, by the fourth child, I was begging my doctor for a C-section, in the fear that if I had any more big noggins come through my vagina, my husband would be able to yodel and hear his echo down there. My doctor then gave me the disappointing information that it is the *first* vaginal birth that does most of the stretching, so I grudgingly agreed to let yet another one come through the tunnel (and made him promise to stitch me up very, very carefully afterward).

So Now That You Are in Labor, What Should You Do?

All of the popular books on pregnancy will tell you not to rush off to the hospital too early because they will hook you up to an IV and not give you anything to eat or drink. It is also suggested in these books that, once you get to the hospital, you will be forced to lie down. This is considered a bad thing, because lying down is one of the least productive postures for a woman in labor. I would just like to say that I was *never* asked to lie down when I was in labor, at least not until I went for the epidural, and then it was a tremendous relief to lie down. In fact, after the baby was born, a nurse was at my bedside within hours telling me I had to get up and walk around. But I digress. . . .

If you and your doctor agree that you are fine and comfortable laboring at home for the first few hours, that is wonderful. I, however, love maternity wards. I love all the new mothers, the pictures of babies on the walls, the nursery full of babies, the abundance of trained medical professionals. I cannot think of a place where I would rather be in labor, no matter how many hours lie ahead of me. You have a choice: You can walk around your own house to help your labor along or you can walk around the hospital. At least at the hospital, you won't feel compelled to make all the beds and unload the dishwasher while you walk. And you won't have to rush to get there.

16
Going to the Hospital

ll right, Girlfriend—here we go! You and your doctor have reason to believe that your baby is on its way and it is time to go to the hospital (or whatever other professional birthing center filled with competent and caring medical people you have selected). I swear, this time is so filled with excitement, fear and anticipation that no astronaut getting ready to enter a space capsule has ever felt more anxious. It isn't liftoff yet, but from now on everything leads to this ultimate conclusion. This is what you have been building up to and preparing for for nine (ten) months, but you still don't really know what to expect, even if you have already had kids.

A general suggestion for both astronauts and women about to have babies is to try to get a shower in before liftoff, because it will be quite a while before the opportunity will arise again. If you are not laboring so hard that you risk giving birth on your shower tiles, hop in for a quick shampoo and underarm shave before leaving for the hospital. The two rules in this area are:

Do Not Take a Shower If You Are Alone in the House, Because You May Decide Mid-Suds That It Wasn't Such a Good Idea After All and You Might Need Someone to Help You Out.

Do Not Take a Tub Bath If You Have Any Reason to Think That Your Water Has Broken, Because You May Introduce Bacteria Into Your Uterus. Besides, If You Think Getting Out of the *Shower* While Experiencing Contractions Is a Challenge, Wait Until You Try Hoisting Yourself Out of a Tub.

The Drive

I know that you have never even considered this, but it will make me feel better if I just say it: DO NOT TRY TO DRIVE YOURSELF TO THE HOSPITAL. Even if you think that the contractions are bearable and that you are perfectly fine to drive, don't get behind the wheel, because conditions in labor have been known to change very quickly. Also, women in labor are rather like people who have been drinking, they think they are acting normally and are in control, but they should not be allowed behind the steering wheel of a car under any circumstances. If your husband isn't home, call a Girlfriend, a neighbor, a cab or 911.

One revelation that almost all of my Girlfriends had was that the car ride to the hospital is a bigger deal than they had imagined it would be. In their meticulous planning and anticipating, they had pictured what they would do at home and what they would do at the hospital, but the car ride in between had been an inconsequential detail. Then, when they were actually in labor and in the car, they realized that this ride might be a challenge in itself. It can be as uncomfortable as a ride in a wagon on a plank bench with square wooden wheels.

First of all, sitting upright with a seat belt around you is not the most comfortable position in which to labor. If your front passenger seat reclines, put it back as far as it will go. If it doesn't, ride in the backseat, where you can sprawl. Do try to wear your seat belt, even if you are reclining or leaning in the back. Your driver will be particularly nervous and prone to slamming on the brakes unexpectedly, so being strapped to your seat will help you cope. Besides, you haven't come through the last nine (ten) months in pure and perfect health only to get injured in the car ride to deliver the baby.

Like the princess with the pea under her mattress, you will feel every pothole and piece of gravel in the road during this ride. You will also be feeling a tad irritable in your condition, so you will probably curse the Department of Public Works the whole way (when you are not silently cursing your darling husband for turning so sharply, stopping so abruptly and getting you pregnant in the first place). One good way to counter this is to bring your bed pillows from home, as many as you can carry. (You will not only love their familiar comfort during the car ride, but you will continue to appreciate them in your hospital bed, where they traditionally top the bed with some polyurethane wafer-shaped thing that they have slipped into a pillowcase.) Put one pillow under your head and one between your legs, and try to rest on your side in the car. (Once again, the left side is the politically correct one, but at a time like this, embrace any side that works for you.)

Try turning on the radio. Its familiar music or mundane chatter might be reassuring and might distract you from whatever discomfort you may be feeling. It will also help relieve you of the obligation of keeping up a conversation with your husband, who will be as nervous as you are. An old doctors' rule of thumb is that if you are experiencing a "productive" contraction, you will be unable to speak during it, or at most only be able to make strained, high-pitched noises. As soon as the contraction passes, you will return to your garrulous, or complaining, self. So if you are in active labor during the car ride, your conversation will be punctuated by contractions. If the radio is irritating you, ask your husband to turn it off, even if it's your husband's favorite song. Be creative in your endeavors to be comfortable. Try silence, try asking your husband to tell you a story or a joke, try singing "A Hundred Bottles of Beer on the Wall." Heck, you could even try out those Lamaze skills and see if you think they are going to get you through this ordeal. (Why waste valuable time at the hospital when you could be getting your epidural?)

Bring a bottle of water (room temperature is best, because you will be less inclined to get stomach cramps from it) in the car with you to sip along the way. Once you are checked into the hospital, you won't be given another taste of that glorious liquid until the baby is on its way to the nursery to be measured and weighed. (Even then, it will be a challenge to flag down a nurse or orderly to get you something to drink, because the doctor and nurses seem to magically disappear along with the baby.) Don't drink too much or too fast, however, because you might get nauseous, and the only thing worse than having contractions in a moving car is vomiting at the same time.

Checking Into the Hospital

Please don't hold me to the details because every hospital has its own routines and policies, but what follows is a general description of what happens once you get to the hospital.

Under ideal circumstances, you have preregistered and handled all your paperwork and insurance stuff weeks ago. Also ideally, labor is progressing at a manageable pace, and you have had time to call your doctor and he has told the hospital you are coming. Under these conditions, you will go to whichever admissions desk handles maternity patients, a bit of information you will have learned beforehand. Within seconds you will find yourself seated in a wheelchair, whether you want one or not. Don't start arguing or making a scene about the wheelchair, because it's required by the hospital's insurance policy. Besides, if you start out complaining and arguing, you may piss off someone upon whose mercy you will have to rely later. Shut up, sit back and enjoy the ride.

If you have not been preadmitted to the hospital, you may have to check in via the emergency room. Don't worry—they move visibly pregnant women right to the head of the line here, no matter how many broken legs are ahead of you. After a quick check-in, you might be taken to an area called "triage." This is usually a larger room with several nurses and several beds (divided by curtains, if you are lucky). In triage, you are examined and put on a monitor to see if you are having productive contractions. If you are, then your doctor is called and you are sent to a labor room. If you are not, you will be told to get dressed and go home. If this happens to you, please do not be too discouraged, and don't be in the least bit embarrassed. The reason I can describe triage to you is because I have been there a couple of times myself and have been sent home, even though I had already given birth to two children and you might have thought I would know better.

My husband hates triage, and he wants me to warn you about it. The reason he hates it is because every time we have been there, there has been some woman in the bed next to me moaning and crying in labor, and basically scaring him to death. If that happens to you, just mind your own business and repeat to yourself, "I am just fine. The woman next to me is no indication of how my own labor will go." Trust me—these words are true, and there is no sense in letting someone else's fear contaminate you. You will be just fine. And by the way, so will she.

The trend in consumer-pleasing hospitals is to make the labor and delivery rooms more homelike and less surgical. Often, uncomplicated deliveries take place in the same room where you have labored. Do not take this new development for granted; in the not-too-distant past, right when you least wanted to move (like when your contractions were coming one on top of the next), you were taken from a labor room to a bright and sterile surgical room to deliver, with stirrups and everything. I had my last two babies in rooms with televisions, telephones, a stereo and even lights that could be dimmed.

Once you are admitted either to triage or to your labor room, you will be given a big plastic bag and directed to a bathroom to change into a hospital gown. The plastic bag is for you to put your own clothes and shoes in. Yes, you must take off everything, including bras, panties and watches. You may, however, keep your socks on, and you will be grateful for this small comfort.

At this time you will meet someone who will become a very important figure in your life, your labor and delivery nurse. This person—more than your doctor, more than your husband and certainly more than any book on pregnancy—will help get you through this ordeal. Trust her advice; she has been through this birthing business hundreds of times and knows what she is talking about. If the angels are smiling on you, she will be a Girlfriend by the time this ordeal is over. On the slim chance, however, that you discover immediately that you can't stand the nurse who has been assigned to you, beg your husband to see if you can trade her in for another model. Don't make it about *her* being mean or insensitive or having bad breath. Now is the time for you to be humble; say that it is *you* who is hard to get along with and you are so sorry to be so irrational, but you simply can't help yourself. The Girlfriends believe that you should do your best to avoid offending anyone who might be called on later to save your life. Trust us—later on, when you are about to push, the chances are good that you will offend or insult several people. Just make sure that your nurse is someone you can rely on and trust, you know, like the Ultimate Girlfriend.

Soon after you have changed into hospital garb, you will have a fetal monitor strapped around your belly like a belt. This is fun, because it communicates your contractions to a machine beside your bed and shows the baby's heartbeat. Please be warned that changing positions, either yours or the baby's, can interfere with the monitor's ability to detect the heartbeat. *This does not mean that anything is wrong with the baby.* It just means that the belt has to be adjusted.

You will probably have an IV needle placed in the back of your hand or forearm and connected to a bottle of saline solution. The rationale is that the saline keeps you from becoming dehydrated and that if you need any other medications quickly, the doctors already have a tap in place. How you will feel about this is hard for me to predict. Some of my Girlfriends made a real fuss over the IV, as if only a sadist would add to a laboring woman's discomfort by sticking her with a big needle. Others, like myself found the experience of labor and impending birth so overwhelming that I barely noticed it.

Hurry Up and Wait

After the initial excitement of settling in and hooking up, you will probably not have much to do. Especially with first babies, labor tends to go on for hours, punctuated by a doctor or your new best friend (your nurse) occasionally reaching inside you to report how dilated you are, or are not, getting. If you are not too uncomfortable, try to rest, because pushing a baby out is a surprisingly athletic feat and you will need your strength.

Now is a good time for your Girlfriends to drop by or to phone them, because you might be a little bored (at least when you are not having a contraction). Nearly every one of my Girlfriends was shocked by how long and how hard the contractions have to be to get your cervix dilated enough for a baby to come out, a diameter of ten centimeters. It is so common for a Girlfriend to labor for six hours and endure contractions that make her see stars and then be told she is only four centimeters dilated. It feels like you are running a race where they keep moving back the finish line, and this can really rock a woman's ability to cope. You may also be stricken by the fear that you are not physically strong or athletic enough to give birth after all. Keep in mind what I told you earlier: This is not a fitness test, and you will manage to get that baby out, even if someone has to sit on your stomach to help you push.

You might think to yourself, "I could take this pain if someone would promise me it would all be over in two hours." That's the problem—no one will know how much longer your labor will last, and that will be disheartening. Try not to focus on the labor at this point, but on the prize at the end of the race: a precious baby placed in your trembling arms. Remember, to paraphrase *Annie*, the sun and the baby will come out tomorrow, at the very latest.

How Much Does Labor Hurt?

Early labor is most easily compared with the worst case of menstrual cramps you can imagine, but with more total body involvement. A good contraction is so overwhelming that you will be unable to do anything else but contract. Not only will you not be able to talk, but you will not be that crazy about listening, either. Several of my laboring Girlfriends have yelled "Shut up" to their husbands and other visitors because their conversation irritated them during a contraction.

As labor progresses, it can take on a variety of personalities. You may have heard of someone's traumatic "back labor," for example, when the baby presented itself in such a way that it pressed against the mother's spine. Other women describe contractions that came so close together they didn't have time to prepare for the next one. Generally, however, when women talk about the pain of labor, they are referring as much to the marathon of pain as its intensity. One hour of hitting yourself with a hammer may hurt a lot, but fifteen hours of it will certainly make you delirious. We all agree that the hardest part is not having any idea how long you will have to bear up. The fear that the pain might continue indefinitely is what usually brings down even the strongest of us. We would give anything if only someone could guarantee that there were only seventy minutes left (you know, like on the StairMaster).

The other thing that can break down a laboring woman's control is nausea. I bet no one ever told you about that, right? Well, Girlfriends, it is extremely common for laboring women, especially as they near that final part of labor called "transition," to feel sick and throw up. Think of this as one more way that nature has of cleaning you out in preparation for birth. Do not think of it as abnormal or an imposition on anyone (except you, that is). Simply tell the nurse or nearest person that you are sick, and you will be stunned at how quickly they will get a basin or a towel under your chin. Think of vomiting as a respite of sorts, an interruption of our regular programming that will leave you feeling lighter and better.

Pushing

I have a Girlfriend, a professional woman of intellect and experience, who actually told me she didn't realize that you have to push to get a baby out. She thought that the contractions would be hard enough to move the baby down the birth canal, without any extra work on her part. Boy, was she surprised. Pushing is real physical work, and it can take anywhere from a few minutes to several hours. Once you are dilated and fully effaced, a nurse will stand at your head and a doctor will stand in the catcher's position, and they will coach you through this athletic feat.

On each contraction, you will grab your knees or thighs with your hands in an effort to fold up tight and make as little room for the baby in your lap as possible. On the assumption that this won't be enough to give him the hint, you will also push down with every muscle between your chest and your knees. The sensation that will immediately come to mind is making a bowel movement. Congratulations—you are doing it right! You can be really sure of your technique if your face is squeezed so tight that you feel like you are giving yourself crow's-feet all the way to the back of your scalp. Don't worry for one second if you feel like the baby is coming out of the wrong hole; at a time like this any hole will do. (Besides, he or she probably has a better sense of direction than you think.)

If you don't take any pain relief, either because you don't want it or because your doctor has determined that the baby is coming too fast for it to be of much use, the most terrifying moment of your life comes when you are told it is time to push. As much as nature is already making you feel like bearing down, you are way too smart to think that moving that baby out of your vagina isn't going to hurt. Imagine a burning sensation involving your entire crotch area, combined with stretching that makes you think your hips will break or you will break in half—or better yet, don't.

Now catch your breath, because I am going to tell you the one and only way to make this pain subside: PUSH RIGHT THROUGH THE PAIN AS HARD AS YOU CAN. That's right—do the opposite of what your mind is telling you to do, which is to lie still and whimper. This will take a tremendous amount of courage on your part, but I promise that it will help. Either it will activate a pain-numbing mechanism that nature provides when the baby's head pushes through the cervix, or it will simply get the whole ordeal over with sooner rather than later. One thing I can tell you for certain: Lying there and repeating "I changed my mind, I changed my mind—I don't want a baby!" will provide absolutely no relief.

Now is finally the time when your husband can really join in and help. He can push you into a sitting position with each contraction to help you bear down, or he can help you and the nurse hold your legs in the up-and-ready position (you'll resemble a frog, by the way). Then again, helping you may interfere with his camera duties, so you'll have to carefully delegate the various responsibilities.

The Epidural

The most common method of pain relief for a laboring woman is the epidural, a combination of drugs released into the fluid surrounding your spinal cord through a needle in your lower back. As you are reading this description, you are probably so alarmed that you are convinced you would rather go through labor sober than to have anybody sticking needles into your spine. After a few good hours of hard labor, however, you would probably welcome an epidural even if it was administered through your eyeballs.

An anesthesiologist must administer an epidural. The good part about this is that no amateurs will be puncturing your spine and crippling you for life. The bad part is that not all hospitals have anesthesiologists on duty twenty-four hours a day, so there may not be one around when you want one. My Girlfriend Chris decided at the last minute that she didn't want to do an unmedicated delivery of her third child. She had gone the frontier-woman route with her previous two babies, and she had nothing left to prove to anyone. She asked her doctor to call an anesthesiologist to give her an epidural. Unfortunately, he was at home asleep, and by the time he got to the hospital, Chris was holding Baby #3 in her exhausted arms. The lesson here is if there is even a remote chance that you will want an epidural, tell your doctor several times during your pregnancy, and remind him or her when you call announcing that you are in labor. Then say it again, over and over to anyone in a white uniform, from the minute you arrive in the hospital until you feel that tap in your back.

When given an epidural, you will either roll over on your side or sit on the side of your bed with a nurse bracing you for support. The doctor will then have you curl up in a ball as best you can under the circumstances; this separates your spine so that they can get to the magic spot. Chances are you will have a contraction sometime during the procedure, but they will be very patient and wait until you can lie completely still. Then you will be given a shot of Novocain in your back. Moments later, the doctor will put a thin shunt into your back and tape it in place. You may be surprised to learn that an epidural is like an IV in that it remains in place in your back during the rest of labor and delivery. That way, the anesthesiologist can monitor your pain level and administer more or less of the drug accordingly. You can lie on the shunt and roll around, and you won't feel or disturb it.

You will probably feel the sensation of an electrical shock running through your legs when the epidural is first activated. Don't let this frighten you. It is momentary and completely normal, and in retrospect will not even register on your pain-o-meter. After the zap has passed, the relief is almost immediate. You will be infinitely grateful and astonished when you see another contraction registering on the graph paper from the monitor beside your bed while you feel nothing more than pressure. This is generally when pregnant women get their personalities back. They become nice and loving to their husbands, and chatty with their nurses and Girlfriends. Even better, many of them are able to take a nap.

Wonderful as an epidural can be, it has a couple of little drawbacks. The most immediate one is that it tends to slow down productive labor. The other is that you may be so numb from the waist down that you cannot push hard enough to get the baby out. For this second reason, the anesthesiologist might turn down the epidural when it is time to push so that you can be of some assistance at this critical juncture. Or you can try what my Girlfriend Janis did. She swore on the life of her husband that she would find a way to push without feeling if they would just promise not to turn down her epidural. The doctor agreed to give it a try, and Janis *willed* that little girl out, through sheer terror.

Pitocin

You might be dilating at a centimeter an hour, get an epidural and then fail to dilate any more for quite some time. This is when the drug, pitocin, might be administered. Pitocin is dripped into your system through the IV in your hand, so no new puncturing is required. The drug is also used to induce labor when doctors and mothers mutually decide that the baby has overstayed its welcome. It usually brings on contractions that are hard and constant—so hard and constant that women who have been laboring bravely without pain medication scream for the epidural if they have been given pitocin to encourage a sluggish labor. Any notions of "hee-hee" Lamaze breathing through these contractions will usually result in hyperventilation and tremendous frustration, but, hey, you can take my word for it or decide for yourself when the occasion presents itself.

An Alternate Route

All the pitocin and laboring in the world just may not result in your cervix's opening up enough for the baby to come out. You are probably a dishrag at this point, and even your baby may be showing signs of fatigue. Then comes the suggestion that you have dreaded for nine (ten) months: "Maybe we should consider a C-section." This suggestion is almost universally met with great disappointment and alarm, usually manifested in a sobbing fit. Suddenly your dreams of childbirth are shattered. Your hopes of meeting the physical challenge and emerging victorious don't apply. This disappointment and feeling of failure is almost always more upsetting to women than the prospect of having their stomachs cut open with a knife. In fact, I have Girlfriends who, years after their C-sections, still feel robbed of one of life's great experiences, who still think that if they had been allowed to labor "just a little longer" the baby would have been born vaginally.

Please don't start restricting yourself now with expectations and rules about what denotes a "successful" delivery and what denotes a "failure." A delivery that results in a healthy mother and baby is a gift from God, no matter how that delivery was achieved. Period. Childbirth is not like a visit to a spa: It is not designed for your personal enjoyment and fulfillment. It is not an opportunity to demonstrate your abilities or fitness. It is designed to perpetuate the species, and nothing more. I think this feeling of being "gypped" by a birth experience that doesn't match our expectations is one more example of that yuppie self-centeredness that is one of our least attractive characteristics.

If you and the doctor determine that you are going to have a C-section, the first thing that will happen is that your epidural will be turned up. If you don't have an epidural in place, you will be given one immediately, or, if time is critical, you will be put to sleep with a general anesthesia or given a spinal block. I have had a C-section with an epidural, and the sensation I remember most was all the jostling about. I felt no pain, but I did feel like I was being moved around, inside and out. And I was surprised at how long it took to get the baby out. I am sure they can do it faster if they have to, but a leisurely C-section consists of methodical incisions through each individual layer between the outside world and your baby, not one deep cut right to the baby. Once the baby is delivered and its umbilical cord clamped off, you will probably be given some long-lasting painkiller like morphine. The rest is euphoria, at least until the morphine wears off.

Birth

Since I am a "mature" mother (read "older"), I have always had genetic tests that revealed, among other things, the sex of my baby. Some women choose not to have their doctors tell them this information, because they want to be surprised at birth. I, however, still find everything about giving birth surprising or shocking, and I don't need to add one more thing. Besides, I like to start decorating the nursery as early as possible, so I have always known whether I was having a boy or a girl. You might not know, however, and here it is your big moment. With that last exhausted push comes the announcement "It's a boy!" or "It's a girl!" Make sure that you hear the definitive statement from a medical person, because fathers are notorious for seeing the umbilical cord and mistaking it for a penis.

Only trust those people who have their anatomy knowledge certified by a medical degree.

There are no words for me to adequately describe the feeling of seeing your baby the moment it emerges from your body. Even if you are exhausted and disoriented from labor and medication, looking at the creature who has been living inside of you for all this time will be the closest thing to seeing God that life can provide without the help of a burning bush or a parting sea. In all your imaginings, this is probably where your movie ended, with your baby being put into your arms, you and your husband gazing lovingly into each other's eyes, the music swelling and the credits starting to roll. Sorry to be the one to tell you, but that is not exactly how it goes in real life. . . .

If you have had a vaginal birth, the baby might be placed on your belly for warmth while the doctor clamps the umbilical cord and someone (perhaps your husband) cuts it. Then you still have some pushing to do, because the placenta has to come out, too. If you have had a C-section, they take the placenta out for you, so lie back and relax. After you have pushed out the placenta (and a lot of other bloody, gooky stuff that can look alarming but is perfectly normal), the doctor will reach inside you to see if there is anything left up inside you that might cause infection. This part is not fun, and it usually comes as a surprise to a new mother who wants to be left in peace after what she has just endured. Breathe deeply for this part, or ask the doctor to turn up the epidural.

Then comes the stitching. Chances are, if you had a vaginal birth and it is your first, your doctor performed an episiotomy before the baby emerged. That means he or she made a slit in your stretching skin to make more room for the baby to come out. The justification for this is that if the cut weren't made, the baby would tear you anyway, and it's theoretically easier to stitch up a slit than a tear, or something like that. My experience was that I ended up with episiotomies *and* tears, so I had more stitches than Frankenstein's monster. The stitching part usually does not hurt, but it does take a while, so while your husband and the nurse are having fun with your baby, you are lying with your knees wide open and your precious parts being sewn back together.

Love at First Sight?

You may take one look at your new baby and sob with the depth of love and devotion you immediately feel. Or, you may take a look to make sure it is whole and healthy, and then secretly hope that some professionally trained person takes it away somewhere. This does not mean that you will not love your baby as much as the next mother does or that you have the character of a slug, so take it easy on yourself. Birth is traumatic, even under the best of circumstances, and you may need a while to allow your emotions to catch up with your new identity. Think of it this way: Even your dearest friend may have taken a while to work her way into your heart, and she didn't give you stretch marks, so why should you feel obliged to fall in love with this little stranger the minute you lay eyes on it? Just know that it will happen, and you will grow to feel a love so fervent that your insides hurt and you can't take a deep breath without it catching.

Now What?

Your doctor and nurse will leave once they finish putting you back together as best they can. Your baby will be taken to the nursery to be given an injection of vitamin K, weighed and measured, foot- and hand-printed and having other such bureaucratic stuff done to it. It will also be evaluated for its alertness, reflexes, strength and, in our family, sense of humor. The result of this evaluation is called your baby's Apgar score. But I don't want to say much more about it, because tests and evaluations give me performance anxiety.

You will be moved from the birthing room to a regular hospital room. During your stay, your time will be spent putting ice packs on your swollen privates, resting as much as possible, learning to nurse and change diapers and receiving visitors. You won't realize it for quite some time, but this enchanted period ends much too soon. In fact, in about three months, you will long to check back into the hospital, where your meals (albeit tasteless) are prepared for you, your sheets are cleaned every day, and your baby is taken away by capable professionals whenever you get tired. The Girl-friends advise that you stay in the hospital as long as your insurance allows you to. Even if it's just one more day, that is twenty-four hours of postponing the inevitable: a lifetime of work and responsibility.

17

Postpartum Dementia

It really is shocking, but the hospital or birthing center is eventually going to turn over to your care a helpless, fragile and needful human being. So, counting you and your husband, that makes three of you. With less training than you got when you learned to insert your diaphragm, you are expected to go home and raise this baby to adulthood. (If you are not frightened at this prospect, then you certainly don't have a very vivid imagination.)

As alone as you may feel at this moment, most of your fears have been experienced by Girlfriends since the beginning of the ability of the human animal to be neurotic. And if their words aren't enough to get you started worrying, all you have to do is watch daytime television, because every talk show and news broadcast on every channel will be about some child-related disaster. What follows is a list of some of the most common paranoias about mothering:

"I'll Break Its Neck!"

We have heard so many times that newborns have no ability to support their own heads that we live in fear of their little noggins jerking out of our careful grasp, snapping off their necks and rolling onto the floor. So far, in all my research, I have never heard of a mother accidentally injuring her baby by letting go of its head. It is true, however, that you should hold the baby with two hands, because they frequently jerk their heads unexpectedly and can fall backward out of your grip if you aren't paying attention. The most anxious moments (truly terrifying in the beginning) are when you are dressing or bathing the baby, because a newborn's head feels at least as heavy as the rest of its body parts combined.

The companion worry to "I'll Break Its Neck!" is "I'll Squish Its Head!" The entire top of a newborn's head is soft, because the bones of the skull haven't joined together over the top. You will have no problem being gentle with this area, but every one of your Girl-friends' little children or your own older kids are guaranteed to pat on it hard with their grimy mitts—or more likely, with a wooden block. Don't wait for the Girlfriends to notice and stop their dar-lings; just grab away the offending hand and sweetly say "No, No" through your clenched teeth.

"As Soon as We Stop Watching the Baby, It Will Stop Breathing!"

Just wait until you see how many times you'll stand beside your sleeping baby and stare at it as if its lungs are only working through the sheer force of your will and concentration. New mothers are terrified of something dreadful happening to their babies while they aren't on watch. If the mother happens to have enjoyed a particu-larly restful snooze of three straight hours, she will fly to the baby in morbid dread that it must have died to allow her to sleep so long. Heaven forbid that the baby is sleeping quietly, because the frantic mother will have to pinch it awake to hear it cry before she can be satisfied that all is well.

"I Will Forget I Have a Baby and Leave It Somewhere!"

I have had several very vivid dreams in which I put the baby in his car seat and sat it on the trunk of my car while I dug in the diaper bag for my keys, and then, after finding the keys, jumped into the car and sped off, leaving the baby sitting on the hood. Another one of my Girlfriends used to fret that she would take her baby shopping with her and then accidentally leave it in a dressing room, not realizing her mistake until she got home. There are several variations on this theme of failing to care for your baby in the most fundamental ways. My Girlfriend Chrissie used to have nightmares that she would drop her baby over a hotel balcony. It would happen in slow motion and she'd be powerless to stop the sequence, even though she knew how it would turn out. Let me hasten to reassure you that Chrissie's kids are nearly grown now, and obviously the products of truly great parenting, so the dreams were not the sign of a sick mind, but simply the sign of a mother who was afraid of how much she loved and wanted to protect her kids.

"I'll Sleep Through a Feeding and the Baby Will Starve to Death!"

A startling, at least to me, number of new mothers rely so completely on the feeding schedule that their pediatricians suggest to them that they feel obligated to wake a sleeping baby to make sure it doesn't miss a feeding, as if it will perish without those precious four ounces. Babies don't really exist perilously from feeding to feeding; they are meant to be slightly more durable than that. The only time I can think of to wake a sleeping baby to feed it is when you are breastfeeding and your breasts are threatening to explode if someone doesn't suck the milk out quickly.

Remember, the goal is for your baby to learn to sleep all through the night without needing to eat. Relax and be grateful if the baby has skipped the traditional 11:00 P.M. feeding; he or she will eat enough at the next feeding to make up for it. Wake it during the day if you must, but not at night. Babies usually get one decent stretch, so it is better for everyone concerned if that stretch comes at night, after all the good (or at least watchable) television shows are over.

"What If the Baby Doesn't Like Me?"

A lot of Girlfriends, particularly those who had a mother's helper or grandma to help them with the baby for the first few weeks, said that they worried that their babies liked their caretakers better than they liked their moms. They said that the babies cried more or were restless when they held them, but calm and sleepy when someone else held them.

I can't offer any guarantees for fifteen years from now, but at this age, your baby loves you with every ounce of its existence, because you are what stands between it and a difficult world. It may not love you for your wit and charitable deeds, but it will love you as part of itself. There is nothing you have to do to earn this love; it's far more fundamental than that. Your baby has to love you—it's the rules. He might just be reflecting your own nervousness when he fusses. Or, more commonly, he is simply expressing his excitement at the meal that awaits him, since you smell like a milk wagon to him. If your baby loves other people in addition to you, don't be selfish; there's plenty to go around.

"What If I Don't Like the Baby?"

You will always love your baby, but you may not always *like* it very much. A mother who has been walking the baby up and down the hall for five hours without being able to get it to sleep may be very close to wanting to sell the little one. If our friends, or even our spouses, were to be as demanding and selfish and oblivious to our personal happiness, we would drop them like hot potatoes. (Though you will be astounded at your capacity to tolerate a very high degree of bad manners in your own baby.) No, you haven't seen neediness until you have had a baby; this is the Grand Canyon of need. And what do they give you in return? A crooked smile now and then, perhaps a dirty diaper. When you feel a cloud of resentment sinking down around you, ask some benevolent soul, like your mother or husband or Girlfriend (don't you just love your Girlfriends?), to take the baby somewhere where you can't hear it or see it for an hour or two. The respite will work wonders.

"Why Is My Life Such a Mess?"

Even the most finicky and organized of us lose all control of our environment when a new baby comes home to live with us. You will wonder, as you step over piles of laundry on the living room floor, how one tiny baby can require so much time and work. Forget writing thank-you notes and returning phone calls; you are lucky if you get a shower in, and a miracle worker if you put on clothes that actually match and are clean. Generally, you look crummy, the baby needs something and you and your husband haven't eaten anything but Lean Cuisine in three weeks. Then your mother-in-law calls to say that Aunt Grace has asked her five times whether you got the *Pat the Bunny* book she sent you, since she *still* hasn't heard from you.

This is the real postpartum depression, not that wimpy little tearfest the books tell you you might experience in the hospital after the baby is born. All this, combined with about two solid months of sleep deprivation and sore nipples, can really get a Girlfriend bummed out, and possibly give her a nasty cold. I wish I could give you the secret cure to this condition, but there isn't one. The best advice we can give you is to accept your limitations and accept your friends' and family's offers of assistance. Sure, they may drive you crazy or be completely unable to find their way around your kitchen, but let them try, because they are still more capable than you are. Just know that we all have suffered what you are suffering, and we sympathize deeply. This, too, shall pass (just much more slowly than seems humane).

"I Hate Nursing!"

It is very politically correct these days to breast-feed our infants. The justifications are numerous, and reverently listed in every other book on pregnancy. The Girlfriends' position on breast-feeding is this: Try it. If you like it, keep doing it. If you don't like it, you have our permission to quit. The world is filled with women who rank failure to nurse right up there with child abuse, and they love telling you about how they nursed their own children until they were ready to start school. These stories, even to Girlfriends who nursed, are boring and judgmental and should not be allowed to make you feel guilty about your decision. Is breast-feeding better than bottle feeding? Sure, I guess so. But then, so is baking your own bread, making spaghetti sauce from fresh tomatoes and never drinking coffee.

The reality is, nursing can be painful at first. It also requires a mother to handle the baby feeding all by herself, unless she becomes proficient at pumping. As far as I am concerned, a nursing woman is still a little bit pregnant; her body is still working for someone else's benefit. Some Girlfriends have also mentioned that their husbands have a hard time feeling sexual about them while there is a baby sucking on their favorite playthings. No judgments here, just the facts.

So, if all these things are true, why do women ever choose to nurse? Well, it is home cooking at its finest for a little baby. It is also very simple, once you have mastered the technique, to open up your shirt, feed the baby and button back up. No dishes to wash, no ingredients to buy and it's a lot cheaper than formula. In the middle of the night ("middle" meaning any time of the day or night after you have had at least an hour and a half of sleep), when your hungry baby cries, one of the last things you will want to do is warm up a bottle of formula. It is much easier to just whip out the breast and doze while the baby suckles to its heart's content. Another great medical benefit for the mother is that nursing helps shrink your uterus back to its normal pear size after it has been stretched to the size of a duffel bag.

Now here is one thing you might not know about nursing, but we Girlfriends swear it is true. After the sore nipples are healed and you know what you are doing, nursing feels really, really good. I am talking about good like sex feels good. A hormone is released in you that has a sedative effect when you nurse. That slightly drunken feeling combined with the gentle contraction of your uterus (like after an orgasm) can lead to one deeply satisfied mother. That's why so many nursing women have goofy smiles on their faces. Another less glamorous chemical is released that will make you thirstier than if you had eaten ashes. When nursing or before you lie down to get some sleep, make sure that you have a large (about the size of a bucket) glass of water at your side. My girlfriend Dona used to take a huge glass of ice to bed, so by the next nursing period the water wouldn't be lukewarm.

For me, the best thing about nursing was that it forced me to prioritize my life properly to make room for the new baby. Nursing forced me to neglect the meaningless busyness of my life and pay attention to the baby and me. One of our greatest mistakes as mothers these days is to rush our recovery from pregnancy and childbirth. If it took us nine months to build up to this condition, we should give ourselves at least that long to get out of it. Maybe we are rushing things a bit by having babies and trying to be back to our former lives just six weeks later.

"What If I Have to Go to the Bathroom?"

This basic function of the human body will provide your first physical crisis since the baby was born. Just wait until you have delivered a baby, either vaginally or by C-section; the thought of moving your bowels and passing something of substance down that particular passage will make you shudder. As a matter of fact, this reminds me that there is one very compelling reason to have a vaginal birth rather than a C-section, if you have the choice: You can't leave the hospital after a C-section until you have earned your release by showing your nurse a bowel movement of your making. With a vaginal birth, they will release you with little more than a promise to poop sometime in the near future, in the privacy of your own home.

You will probably still be very sore down there, and certainly not eager to stretch out any of the healing tissues. But poop you must! Some doctors will recommend that you take a stool softener daily, beginning the day your baby is born, to mitigate the discomfort somewhat. What they should really prescribe, however, is a tranquilizer, because the anticipation is almost worse than the deed. A couple of days after the baby is born you will get that unmistakable feeling that your body is getting over its trauma and is ready to "move" again. If you are a chicken, like I am, you will try to ignore this sensation until you are on the verge of exploding, and then you will tearfully go to the bathroom like Anne Boleyn going to the chopping block. You will be certain that a bowel movement is going to rip your episiotomy stitches, and that it will not help your hemorrhoids one little bit. But just like during delivery, there comes a time when you have no option but to push, no matter how faint and sweaty you feel. It is over quickly, and you will survive without any tearing, even if you do bleed a little. Does it hurt? Yup, but I promise, it won't hurt like this again, at least not until you have your next baby. Your hemorroids may not be too happy, but that's what those little round medicated pads were invented for.

"What If My Husband Wants to Have Sex With Me?"

Let's make a pact among all the Girlfriends of the world right now: Even if your doctor tells you at your six-week checkup that it is all right to start having sex again, *you must not tell your husband.* All Girlfriends must agree to tell their husbands that they absolutely may not have intercourse for three months.

For heaven's sake, the doctor's exam itself will nearly have you hanging from the ceiling. Sexual pleasure at this point is an oxymoron.

Why, you may ask, wouldn't a healthy, sexy woman not want to make love after the baby is born? Well, here are a few reasons that come quickly to mind:

1 *Fear of pain.*

Two hemorrhoids and about five thousand episiotomy stitches can make your labia and vagina feel like ground beef. There is also a certain amount of bruising and swelling in your perineum, that area between your vagina and your anus.

2 *You may still be bleeding.*

For the longest time after the baby is born, you will experience something like having the never-ending period. At first it is copious and red and rather clotty (pardon me, but accuracy dictates a certain amount of vulgarity here). With time it changes to brownish and then yellowish. Depending on your personal sexual tastes, this may be off-putting to you or your husband.

3 *Dry as a bone.*

A new mother's vagina is so dry that it needs a humidifier. Your hormones will suspend the production of any lubrication whatsoever, especially if you are nursing. It seems obvious to me that the Grand Plan of Nature intended that mothers of little babies not get pregnant again until the first baby was able to survive in the world, so it made us unsexual. Feel free to try this anthropological explanation on your horny husband; maybe you will have more success with it than some of my other Girlfriends.

4 *Not in the mood.*

Becoming a mother is so physically and emotionally overwhelming that it is quite tempting in the beginning to make an entire universe out of just you and your baby. After a day of having a little person suck on you, burp on you and otherwise help itself to your body parts, at the end of the day, the last thing you may want is to have your amorous spouse do the same thing. You just don't feel like shaving your legs and putting on sexy lingerie; you want to lie in bed all by yourself, in sweats, watching sitcoms and with absolutely no one touching you.

Contributing to the lack of interest in sex is the small matter of what you look like for the first couple of months after the baby is born. It will probably be several more weeks before your stomach stops drooping when you roll onto your side and your nipples stop scabbing (if you are nursing), and you may be a bit frustrated by the fact that you still don't look like *you*. You know for certain that *you* wouldn't want to have sex with someone as out of shape as you, and you can't imagine why your husband would, either.

5 *You are so tired you could cry.*

Most of my Girlfriends agree that this is the single greatest impediment to resuming a normal sex life after the baby is born. If you have time for sex, then you have time for a nap, and the nap will sound far more enticing for the first few months. You will be tired because you are recovering from the ordeal of childbirth, you may be tired because your body is working hard to keep up the milk supply and mostly you will be tired because YOU ARE NOT SLEEPING! The fatigue that comes from existing on catnaps and never even having time to dream anymore can make you demented.

6 *Fear of drowning your husband.*

Let me be the first to share with you one of Mother Nature's practical jokes: Sexual stimulation and orgasm can trigger a nursing mother's letdown reflex. This means that, right when things are getting good during sex, you might start squirting milk all over the two of you. Perhaps you should try keeping your bra on (with extra nursing pads in place) while you ease your way back into the saddle again (yet another reason to postpone this act). Think of the sensation as something like having sex in a car wash.

There, now that the *Guide* has managed to reinforce your dread of having intercourse ever again, let us help you out of this mess. I promise you, you will want to have sex again sometime (and the sooner the better, as far as most husbands are concerned). I have put together a few of my Girlfriends' suggestions to break the ice.

1 Get away from the baby for at least an hour before you even think of having sex.

You really must break out of the "mommy cocoon" and get reacquainted with your husband. It may be impossible for both of you, but do try not to talk about the baby during this preparatory stage. First of all, you will miss the chance to really catch up with each other, and second, thinking of the baby may cause your milk to start leaking out.

Now is the time to express to your husband how fragile you are still feeling and how much you would appreciate it if he would take it nice and easy, in spite of his eagerness. Begging, bribes or threats are completely acceptable at a time like this.

2 Have a glass of wine.

I would have suggested this anyway, but now there is even a recent medical study indicating that wine is an aphrodisiac for women. I think most of my Girlfriends have known this about wine all along, but even if it weren't the case wine would be good, because it helps you forget what you were worried about in the first place. It still may hurt a little when you have sex, but if you are tipsy, you won't care as much.

3 Moisten things up down there.

It is not enough just to inebriate, you must also lubricate for your first sexual reunion. There are several jellies available over the counter for this very purpose, so go out and stock up in advance. Otherwise, you will find yourself rummaging through your medicine cabinet and making do with something icky like petroleum jelly or baby oil—or worse, using something from out of the kitchen pantry. A variation on this lubrication idea is to begin the reunion with a massage. I am sure you could use one at this point, and no husband is going to miss an opportunity like this. He is probably so eager that he would agree to do an oil change on your car first if you made it a condition of having sex. Don't just use regular old hand lotion; buy massage oils from a specialty store. My Girlfriend Sondra, sly thing, gave me *edible* massage oils. Think of them as dessert and let your imagination run wild.

4. Don't forget the birth control.

Let me join in the chorus of people who should be telling you, YOU CAN GET PREGNANT WHILE YOU ARE NURS-ING, AND YOU CAN GET PREGNANT EVEN IF YOU HAVEN'T HAD A PERIOD YET. Consider using a condom (especially if you are nursing and can't take the Pill), because the lubrication of the condom helps ease things along.

I don't think I have a Girlfriend who can honestly tell me that she had an orgasm during this first postpartum encounter. Well, maybe my Girlfriend Melanie did, but she also gave her husband oral sex in the hospital only a few hours after having a C-section, so she doesn't count. In fact, it's a mystery to me why I still like her so much. Anyway, the goal at this time is intimacy and affection, not sexual fireworks. I know it may be hard to imagine ever reclaiming your former sexual passion, but you will, I promise.

18

"The Old Gray Mare, She Ain't What She Used to Be"

The truth is simple: Having a baby fundamentally changes your body (and your mind, but that is a book unto itself). You can (and will) lose every pound you gained, you can do sit-ups until you have the control of a belly dancer and you can Kegel your insides until they are strong enough to crack walnuts. But you will never be exactly the same as you were before. I hear some women out there disagreeing with me, and soon they will be sending me pictures of themselves in string bikinis to make their point. Save the postage! I am not saying that you won't look as *good* as you did before. In fact, you may look *better*, but you will not look the *same*.

Girlfriends have told me stories about having curly hair until they had babies, then watching as their hair went straight as a board. Others have said their skin changed from dry to oily, or vice versa. Lots of them complain that their hipbones are never as narrow as before the baby was born. My own personal gripe is my belly button, which is no longer perfectly round and "inny" anymore. But more about the things we cannot change later. First, let's talk about the things we can.

Losing the Weight

You all know that the only way to lose weight is to stop eating so much and to start exercising like a fanatic. You are just wasting your valuable time trying to measure fat grams and live on SnackWell's. So eat well, but in small portions, and exercise every day. But let's not go any further into the details of a weight loss plan, because it will only bore and depress us both.

What *The Girlfriends' Guide* would like to add to the body of wisdom regarding losing weight after having a baby is this:

1   It will take longer than you think. Just to be safe, start thinking in terms of "Nine Months Up, Nine Months Down." The weight will come off, but since all pregnancy weight is not baby weight, it will come off more slowly than you might wish. The good news about giving birth is that most of your big belly goes away immediately. The bad news is that once it's gone you will notice all the other places where you got fat, like your arms, behind, thighs and face.

2   You will have forgotten what you used to look like. I swear that this is the reason why so many women just stay about seven pounds heavier after becoming mothers than they were before they got pregnant; they simply don't *remember* how slender they actually were, and they will settle for a reasonable facsimile of their former selves. The only foolproof test to see if you have truly lost every pound is to put on your oldest pair of jeans and wear them for a few hours. If they don't give you a "wedgie," then you have reclaimed your old figure.

3   You will not get your old figure back until you stop nursing. This flies right in the face of everything nursing advocates will tell you, but the Girlfriends and I stand by our statement. Yes, it is true that hundreds of calories are burned every day that you nurse, more than you would burn on any treadmill or stair-climber. So, in the beginning of your weight loss experience, nursing will be your friend.

When you are down to the last five or ten pounds, however, your old friend turns on you. Nature absolutely refuses to let go of the fat deposits in your upper arms, your thighs and, of course, your breasts until you stop nursing. That way there is little danger of the mother running out of the fuel she needs to keep the milk factory operating.

4 Even when you have lost the pounds, you will have to wait for nature to take her own sweet time about tightening your flabby skin back up and pulling your hips back together again. You know that cereal commercial where they ask you if you can "pinch an inch"? No matter how thin you get, you will be able to get a good *handful* around your middle for several months. Or, if you have four kids like I have, you can carry that extra skin with you to the grave.

5 Do not get pregnant again until you have lost all the weight from the first baby. There is no capital punishment connected to this law, so don't get panicky if you fail to obey it, but the basic rule is: Any extra weight you are carrying when you get pregnant again is *yours*, and you are no longer entitled to call it "baby fat." Of course, we think you can safely use that term for a good nine months without inaccuracy.

The Legacy of Pregnancy

Now it is time to talk about the physical changes which result from pregnancy that you cannot change, at least not without the help of a good surgeon.

1 *Bigger feet.*

This isn't a universal experience, but it has happened to enough of my Girlfriends to make it worth mentioning to you. I don't know if carrying the extra weight of pregnancy flattens your feet or stretches the ligaments in some way, but most of my Girlfriends have gone up at least half a shoe size after having a baby. Don't worry, this doesn't seem to happen with each successive pregnancy, so you won't have to change your entire shoe wardrobe every time you have another baby. I am embarrassed to tell you this for fear of sounding even more frivolous than I actually am, but it really may be advisable to weed out your too-tight shoes after the baby is born and *throw them all away* because your feet will not shrink. From now on, on your new, larger foot, comfort should prevail over vanity.

2 Smaller breasts.

Actually, it is probably more accurate to say "thinner" breasts, because the skin remains the same size, but a lot of the fat that used to fill it out is gone, gone, gone. There is a debate about whether this condition is made worse by nursing, but my observation is that it is the pregnancy more than the nursing that takes the toll.

If it is any consolation, when you get pregnant again, you will have another nine months of great tits, but the end of the story remains the same. I have only two words of comfort: Wonder Bra.

3 More skin.

This may hardly be noticeable to you if you are blessed with great skin tone. If you are a freckled, thin-skinned Irish lass like I am, however, the skin on your belly will fold down like a little accordion whenever you bend over at the waist. I suppose, on a dare, I could get away with wearing a two-piece bathing suit, but I would have to stay standing at attention to pull it off. I swear, you could throw a ten-carat diamond at my feet and I would not bend over to pick it up, because it would show the world my "pleats."

4 Darker nipples.

You will have noticed early on in your pregnancy that your nipples got larger and darker. After about a year postpartum, your nipples will probably have returned to their former circumference, but they will stay darker forever.

5 Relaxed vagina.

Perhaps you should go pour yourself a drink before proceeding with this discussion, because my Girlfriends hate this subject almost as much as they hate the subjects of infidelity and menopause. But not talking about it doesn't make it not exist, so here goes: Once you have vaginally delivered a baby, your vagina will not be as tight as it was ever again. All of your friends who have had babies (unless they are very confident and generous) will tell you that everything down there goes back to its former self, but they are just saying that because it worries them to think that their sexuality has been diminished in some way. The truth is, they are slightly looser—*and* they are probably even sexier than they were before. Experienced and fulfilled women are *always* sexier than novices.

If you have the nerve to ask your husband if he notices a difference, he will probably do some hedging or outright lying, because he can undoubtedly well imagine that this is an extremely sensitive topic for women. His future sex life may be completely nuked by too candid an answer. Now don't panic! You won't be left with a vagina stretched out like some old underwear elastic; you just won't be quite as firm. Your doctor knows this, even if he or she doesn't discuss it with you. That is why most of them are so willing to stitch you up nice and tight after an episiotomy; this is their idea of a consolation prize. Your husband will still want to have sex with you, and you will still enjoy it. As a matter of fact, you may enjoy it more, since your husband might now take a little longer to climax and that might give you time to catch up with him. If, however, you are not enjoying sex because your vagina feels too flaccid, or feels uncomfortable for any reason, see your doctor as soon as possible, because there are simple surgical procedures that can easily fix this condition.

6 *Lazy bladder.*

Another sensation which lots of Girlfriends describe that falls into this vaginal-looseness category is bladder weakness. There are degrees in this area. For example, thousands of women who have had vaginal births cannot sneeze without wetting their pants. Others say that trampoline jumping and jogging on hard surfaces present challenges their bladders can no longer meet. Then there's the situation where you just can't "hold it" like you used to; when you have to go to the bathroom, you have to go sooner rather than later. You may also be unable to sleep an entire night without getting up to go to the bathroom. Look at it this way: This little stroll provides a nice opportunity to check on your sleeping kids and make sure they haven't kicked off their blankets.

Before you go rushing off to schedule a C-section in hopes of saving your pelvic floor, let us put things into perspective for you. Many things in life exact a toll, but they are such great experiences that we are willing to pay the price. Take sunbathing; we all know it is skin poison, but who can resist a vacation in Hawaii?

Top  Greatest Concerns of
Pregnant Women

10
Will My Breasts Stay This Big Forever?
(Please, God!)

9
Will I Feel This Sick and Tired for the Entire
Nine Months?

8
Will My Husband Ever Really Understand What I
Am Going Through?

7
Will It Hurt to Deliver the Baby?

6
How Badly Will It Hurt to Deliver the Baby?

5
Will It Hurt More Than a Bikini Wax? Less Than
a Broken Leg?

4
Will I Get All Ugly and Fat?

3
Will Everything "Down There" Shrink Back to
Normal After the Baby Is Born?

2
Will I Be a Good Mother?

1
Will the Baby Be O.K.?

Postscript

I just realized that it has been nine months since I started putting all my ideas in writing. Get it? NINE MONTHS! (O.K., so it was really more like ten.) Talk about your coincidences! Like all my pregnancies, this has been interesting, tedious, enlightening and just a little too long for my attention span. But, just as with my babies, I know I am going to be forever grateful that I was willing to take the journey.

The things you have to look forward to! You will love your baby with such a fierce single-mindedness that being someone's mother is the only endeavor on earth that you will be certain nature fully intended for you.

Try to take it easy. Enjoy it while it lasts. Be grateful for this blessing. And don't stop laughing.

Index

C

D